Doc

Doc

The life and times of Aussie rock legend

DOC NEESON

JON BRADSHAW & ANNE SOUTER

ALLEN&UNWIN

SYDNEY · MELBOURNE · AUCKLAND · LONDON

First published in 2021

Allen & Unwin
83 Alexander Street
Crows Nest NSW 2065
Australia
Phone: (61 2) 8425 0100
Email: info@allenandunwin.com
Web: www.allenandunwin.com

A catalogue record for this book is available from the National Library of Australia

ISBN 978 1 76087 536 7

Set in 12/17.75 pt Adobe Garamond Pro by Midland Typesetters, Australia
Printed in Australia by McPherson's Printing Group

10 9 8 7 6 5 4 3 2 1

The paper in this book is FSC® certified. FSC® promotes environmentally responsible, socially beneficial and economically viable management of the world's forests.

CONTENTS

Part II   **THE MAN BEHIND THE MASK**

Anne Souter

Prologue

New Year's Eve in hell

Anne Souter

It was a wild New Year's Eve in 1978 when I first set eyes on Doc Neeson. I had been out for dinner with a few friends in Coolangatta, and we'd then headed down to Greenmount Beach, where Jeff St John and the Copperwine were playing. A fierce electrical storm was rolling down the coast, and a spiderweb of lightning streaked across the smoky night sky. With deafening cracks of thunder directly overhead, the threat of an imminent downpour made us worry that Jeff and his band might be electrocuted.

'I can't stand it!' shouted Spin over the top of the thunder. Her real name was Lyndal, but she didn't like to use it at night. By day Lyndal was the perfect embodiment of Cool and Style, with a very impressive job, but she also liked to rock. Although normally very laid-back, tonight she was seriously alarmed. 'I don't want to see them get fried,' she yelled. There was a strange yellow haze above the stage and then the sky burst open and heavy rain sent everyone scrambling for cover.

'Let's go somewhere else,' said her boyfriend Phil, turning to my then fiancé, Peter, who everyone called 'Rab' after Rabbit. In two seconds flat, Rab suggested The Patch.

When we arrived, The Patch was packed with hyped-up drunks, but Spin's face immediately lit up. 'Angels! Now we're talking!' she said as she looked approvingly at a sign that announced the headline band that night.

The streaming river of nightclubbers at the entrance carried me towards the bar and away from Spin and the others. One girl was so gone that she stubbed her cigarette out on my arm as if it were an ashtray. I was furious, because the guy she was with had tried to grab one of my breasts as I stood trying to get served; she shrieked 'Stay away from my guy!' into my ear, like it was *MY* fault her guy was so revolting.

I scanned the crowd for Rab, but he was nowhere to be seen. Everyone in the room seemed to be roaring drunk, so I fled to the Ladies to escape the madness. There I found myself walking on broken glass; a barefooted girl was washing her gashed foot in a basin spattered with bloody water. Another girl had her friend bailed up in a corner, where she was slamming her head against the wall. Wild eyed, screeching and makeup-smeared, they were fighting like animals. The place was bedlam.

I had to get out! I fought my way back through the seething mass looking for Security, but I couldn't find anyone. Finally, I found my friends and told them we had to go, because this place was insane.

When Rab turned towards me and asked why I wanted to leave, Spin looked horrified. She told me that we couldn't go, because The Angels hadn't even come on yet. When I asked innocently who The Angels were, Spin shouted '*Doc Neeson!*' and punched the air. I told Spin I didn't care who was on, I just wanted to get out of there, but she told me 'NO!' we weren't going anyway because it was *Doc Neeson*. She'd been looking at me like a snake before, but now her eyes were huge.

'Who's Doc Neeson?' I asked.

'He's like God,' she snapped, giving me that withering look again.

Suddenly the lights went down, and everything seemed to come to a standstill, and people started yelling 'Angels! Angels! Angels!' Shadows were moving on the darkened stage. The music started softly ... slowly ... then increased in volume and the shadows were obliterated by blinding light. In that light the band members appeared like monoliths in the fog.

Then I saw the frontman. Fast as a flash, this very tall character in a suit hurled himself sideways, out of the dark, across the stage, with his legs slicing through the air, bringing the spotlight with him.

Spin shouted 'Doc!' as the band's cool intro immediately exploded into a deafening attack. Simultaneously the stage lights came up ... spotlights framing the three motionless guitarists. The combined assault and impact on the senses hit us like a shockwave.

I glanced across at Spin and saw that she had flung her head back as if to absorb every sound wave into every pore of her body. She was smiling and had her eyes closed tight. I tried to say something, but Spin put a finger to her mouth saying 'Shhhhh!' and then turned back to face the band. All she wanted to do was soak this up. As far as she was concerned, I wasn't there anymore, and Rab, who was a guitarist, was similarly absorbed by the guitar work.

We'd been pushed against the front of the stage by a very drunk and stoned crowd, and I now found myself looking straight up into the wild piercing eyes of this obviously delirious maniac. Was he looking at me? ... Yes he was, and he wasn't looking happy.

It was as if this leering, shadowy stranger knew what I'd been saying, as if he could read my mind. I felt like he was looking right into my soul. I had never seen a look like that. It was a probing look of terrifying intensity.

It wasn't the song he was singing, it was a psychodrama he had dragged us all into. He was terrorising the crowd, sometimes seen, sometimes not, but constantly prowling, always with his eyes fixed on someone as if that person were his prey.

The songs and the lights were in perfect sync, like nothing I had seen in any live performance of any band ever before. It was a constantly moving, hard-driving musical kaleidoscope.

Doc had the entire audience in the palm of his hand. He had sung them into a trance—holding the gaze of people in the audience one by one, as if he were trying to get inside their heads.

Strutting across the stage towards band members, he started to examine them in the way an alien might look at a human. He grabbed the mic stand, whirled it around like a yo-yo, landed it carefully, and glided forward to transfix his next subject with his eyes before climbing over a speaker box and leaping into the jam-packed solid mass of fans. They let him move through, leaving the last subject stunned in his wake, to ask a friend 'Did you see *THAT*?'

Eventually returning to the stage, riding on a sea of writhing humanity as the pounding music gradually dissolved into a brilliant harmonica solo, Doc carefully extracted every last bit of emotion from the last song and fed it to his audience.

I had never seen a performer like Doc—not even at the Albert Hall in London, where I had seen Robert Plant in Led Zeppelin live and many other super-bands. And this, as I was to learn, was not Doc at his best.

Doc was a chameleon who hid behind masks and wove a story through songs, always interpreting them in his own special way . . . whether it was the maniacal madman in 'Devil's Gate', champion of the under-dog, paranoid lunatic, grieving or angry lover, distraught sufferer, relentless interrogator, or circus ringmaster of later days.

I was soon to discover there was often something about Doc's performances that was almost religious. Many believed that listening to his music meant getting to know him, getting access to his inner soul and feelings, making it possible for the audience to believe that they had come to know him. And this night was no different.

As the show at The Patch went on, the audience became a connected entity, joining in on choruses and refrains, surging forward like a tidal wave in the near dark, a wild sea of up-stretched arms. Spin was right. This was no ordinary man. There was no way we could leave.

I'll never forget that night. After the gig, hundreds of people spilled out into the streets, like a drunken, seething human maelstrom, still drinking, and getting more out of control by the minute. Later, 52 people were arrested and locked up after hundreds either fell down or decided to sit down on the main road and party on.

It was frightening. There were all-out brawls and fistfights going on; men rolling in the gutters, empty cans and bottles everywhere, blood on the pavement. But it was also very exciting to remember— once we were out of the crowd.

Unknown to me at the time, The Angels' line-up that night had been the classic five—'Doc' Neeson, Rick and John Brewster, 'Buzz' Bidstrup and Chris Bailey. Rick, who was then on good terms with Doc, had photographed him posing next to a magnificent Buick on a back street somewhere near The Patch before the band had hit the stage.

Sadly, Doc and the Brewster brothers were eventually to become strongly opposed and estranged. Buzz and Chris, despite battles in between, were to remain friends with Doc for more than three decades after this.

What I could not have imagined, even in my wildest dreams, was that Rab and Spin would know Doc well in later years, and I would become his partner. And 35 years on, a copy of that photo of Doc standing next to the Buick near The Patch was sent to Doc, probably as a peace offering from Rick, after a very bitter band-war that lasted for many years.

Part I

FROM BERNARD NEESON TO DOC AND THE ANGELS

Jon Bradshaw

Chapter 1

Lured . . .

The Angels were inducted into the ARIA Hall of Fame at Sydney's iconic State Theatre on Tuesday 20 October 1998.

The big night drew an audience of 2500 of Australia's entertainment luminaries while a million or so more around the country watched the Channel 10 broadcast.

Later, band principals Doc Neeson and John and Rick Brewster were gathered in a hospitality room to meet the music press. One of the journalists asked: 'You started out in Adelaide, so tell us a bit about growing up there?'

Doc replied: 'It was a great place to leave.'

His words hung in the air like a hand grenade with the pin pulled. He hesitated, forming in his mind the further substance of his reply.

Rick and John quickly jumped in: 'Adelaide was a great place to grow up . . . the music scene was unbelievable . . . that's why so many bands came from Adelaide . . . there was music in the air.'

Doc's comments somewhat defused, the interview moved on.

If only the others had known what thoughts were going through his mind.

————

With other disembarking passengers the Neeson family stood at the rails on the upper-tiered decks of the big white SS *Strathnaver*, the 30-year-old P&O ocean liner and converted troopship that had brought them to South Australia, watching with growing anxiety and trepidation out over the coastal mangrove swamps bordering the channel approaches in the direction of their new home.

Compared to other Australian maritime gateways in April 1960, Port Adelaide was certainly the least attractive or welcoming. In fact, back in the previous century, such was its general unpleasantness, plagued with flies and mosquitoes, a lack of fresh water and located on frequently flooded foul-smelling tidal mudflats and mangrove swamps, it had acquired the name of Port Misery.

Their first impressions were not encouraging either, and like most new arrivals the Neesons had mistaken the approaching wharves and towering cranes at the end of the Port River channel as their final destination. Adelaide city is in fact some 16 kilometres further inland and was then the centre of a resident population of around half a million people.

Greeting them from their elevated perspective as the ship finally came to a stop on that late autumn afternoon was an entire previous century dockside panorama of rusty, rundown and dilapidated corrugated iron roofs; the stained brickwork and flaking paint of neglected dockyard buildings, grimy sheds and silos, a large, well-faded rooftop billboard for ice cream and the acrid smoking chimneys of nearby smelting and acid works.

All the appearances and trappings of a third world shanty town!

New arrivals buoyed high with expectations, hopes and dreams for their new life were devastated at the sight. Many migrants, emotionally charged in anticipation, burst into tears.

Disembarking from the good ship *Strathnaver* there was a remarkable lack of any incoming immigration process. A folding table placed at the top of the gangway down to the quay and a casual glance over each family's documents of identity by dour-faced immigration staff. Certainly an almost complete absence of attention. No waving expectant relatives, no friends or even the unlikely thought of an official welcome to the families that were leaving the ship before they were shepherded from the bottom of the gangway into a large rusty corrugated iron shed that faced an adjacent rail siding.

Waiting was their transport into Adelaide. A small black steam locomotive sat smoking and hissing expectantly; attached were four little carriages and a baggage car that together looked like something from the American Wild West. The obviously ancient carriages were complete with covered boarding platforms at each end, inside were varnished wooden slat seats and trim, wrought-iron luggage racks, frosted patterns around the perimeter of the window glass and, overhead, ornate electric chandeliers. Passengers were amazed and increasingly disconcerted about what they had come to.

Eventually, after a lot of delays as the final luggage from the ship's hold were stowed away in the baggage car, the little train started on its way. At first shuffling backwards and forwards as it negotiated all the spur lines on the docks, it eventually reached a long stretch of partially elevated track over a series of muddy oil-streaked lagoons along which they trundled and puffed slowly towards Adelaide city.

Adelaide Railway Station was much more reassuring. A very ornate stone pile patterned on New York's Central Station set back

into a low hill next to the River Torrens; ten platforms, a cavern-
ous waiting hall with expansive dining and waiting rooms, a large
newsagency fronted with cascading magazines and newspapers.
Nearby a colourful stall sold seasonal fruit in a display of red, green
and gold.

Their immediate destination, the Elder Park Migrant Hostel,
was only a short walk from the station. It provided very short-term
accommodation, mostly just one or two weeks, for migrants who
had already signed contracts with the South Australian Housing
Trust to purchase homes in the new town of Elizabeth. Each family
was allocated a hostel room, painted out in drab olive about 12 feet
square, with matching polished lino floor, odd ceiling-level hopper
windows, steel bunk beds, a small table and a couple of kitchen
chairs. A single light bulb in a rust-spotted tin shade hung from
the ceiling. Paper-thin walls between adjoining rooms meant that
there was little privacy and conversations were largely conducted in
lowered voices and whispers.

Toilet blocks and showers were on each floor and a communal
'Mess' hall on the ground floor provided meals served to two lines
of family-sized tables. Adjacent was a 'Rec' room with a few old
sofas, lounge chairs and a side table with the daily papers. This was
the best level of hostel accommodation for migrants arriving in
Adelaide, but it was certainly not, as was claimed in the local media
at the time, a 'luxury hostel'.

The day after their arrival, the Neeson family went out exploring
and, a few days later, they were advised that trips had been arranged
for them to visit and select their house at Elizabeth, the new town
that was to be their final destination. A representative of the South
Australian Housing Trust would drive the family the twenty miles
(approximately 30 kilometres) out there.

The journey took them out from the city, up the gentle slope of Montifore Hill, through exclusive largely residential North Adelaide and past the city's glamorous new international standard hotel: the elegantly rose-tinted glasshouse facades of Hotel Australia, which from its elevated position boasted the best panoramic views over the central city area.

Then through a strip of parklands and onto the Main North Road, the city's major north–south arterial route, past refined inner suburbs of red-roofed brick and stone bungalows and along an undulating main road shopping strip past car yards, churches and hotels. Residential development then tapered off as the road slowly descended through more car yards, car repairers and petrol stations to the sprawling five ways Gepps Cross intersection with Grand Junction Road, which offered a compass card of possible onward route directions.

Nine miles (14 kilometres) from the Adelaide GPO, Grand Junction Road is the longest east–west thoroughfare in the Adelaide metropolitan area. When the Neeson family arrived in April 1960 it was also the black asphalt line in the dry red dust that indicated for many Adelaide people where the known world ended. The northern end of civilisation. A metaphoric Styx, a demarcation, an economic and certainly a cultural divide.

To the left the road ran west to Port Adelaide; to the right it climbed steadily towards pleasant green foothills. But looking north could be seen the regimented rows of shabby tunnel-shaped corrugated-iron Nissen huts and washing lines of the main Gepps Cross migrant hostel. Immediately ahead were two single-lane roads running through the aptly named Dry Creek area. This contained the bulk of Adelaide's noxious and offensive industries: the city's abattoirs, the putrid-smelling, suburb-enveloping odours of rendering, hide and tallow works, fertiliser factories, salt pans, scrap yards and smoking heaps of household garbage.

Another ten miles up the road was their destination, the emerging new town of Elizabeth. A further ten miles beyond that was the small country township of Gawler, with the increasingly pot-holed and narrow road continuing north some 400 miles in a straight line past isolated dusty pub and church hamlets towards the Flinders Ranges, then on to the small outpost of Maree, which serviced the remote northern sheep and cattle stations at the junction of the legendary Oodnadatta and Birdsville tracks, the desolate dirt stock routes to Outback Australia. The road to nowhere.

They continued along the Main North Road past the livestock saleyards and abattoirs, set back from the road with unloading ramps, pens and saleyards shrouded in a grove of pine trees, its reality obvious by the truckloads of sad-eyed animals lined up weekly at the roadside. Then through the roadside strip of small single-storey terraces that housed the workers for the abattoirs, over a low bridge, and an almost endless rural outlook beckoned. Some vacant pastures, low-lying scrubby salt marsh and on past Parafield aerodrome with its two large green hangars and concrete control tower. The highway became narrower and the roadside paddocks progressively drier.

Thin gaunt-looking sheep, cattle and even a few camels dotted the increasingly barren-looking brown landscape, grazing on remnant patches of parched grey wheat stubble.

From inside the rep's car, the Neeson family could see a large box-shaped dilapidated tin shed—a Neptune truck stop called 'The Rolling Wheel'—with a couple of pumps, where they stopped for petrol before driving on further. The road, now bordered by wire fences with tall dry grass and giant grey scotch thistles, eventually reached a small traditional Aussie pub with shady verandahs and some unusually lush willow trees nestled into the right-hand bank besides the Little Para creek crossing. 'The Old Spot Hotel' was to be the last cool green oasis on the parched road northwards.

As their car climbed up over the rise from the creek, the roadside fences ended and laid out before them was an endless flat dusty plain, hardly a tree or a building virtually as far as the eye could see. An uncertain low haze heralded something shimmering in the distance, the single strip of bitumen spearing straight as an arrow towards it. Little willy-willies, small dust whirlwinds, pirouetted across the plain in front of them, spiralling swirls of red dust skyward. It seemed that figuratively and physically they had come to a desert. The sense of isolation and estrangement was complete.

The rep from the housing trust pulled the car to a stop off the road and turned towards them in his seat as they viewed the bleak panorama. 'Welcome to Elizabeth . . .' he said with a grin and a flourish of his hand towards the distant horizon, 'Home of the Brave.'

They all tumbled out of the car and stood around dumbfounded. 'This is the southern boundary of the new town,' the rep announced. 'Three thousand acres of it. In ten years' time there will be houses from here as far as the eye can see. Trees too,' he added. 'There are going to be lots of trees. Elizabeth is going to be a planned city, a city of the future—electricity, water, sewerage and provision for future telephones will be underground.

'This is a huge undertaking,' he went on. 'We're aiming to settle a thousand families a year. That's twenty houses a week, built, finished, sold or rented. For jobs, General Motors are completing their car plant, over there in the distance. A bit further out is the Weapons Research Establishment, where UK Defence contractors have set up . . . and over this way a sewing machine factory.'

'Well, *that* sounds a useful thing,' mused Bernard's mum, Kitty, in a low voice to nobody in particular.

'What about public transport?' Bernard's father, Barney, asked. 'Well,' said the rep, 'there's the train . . .' his voice trailed off, '. . . and pushbikes are a good idea for short distances.'

They all looked at the vast dusty plain before them and the deeply rutted dirt tracks leading off to the industrial area, immediately thinking that, when it did eventually rain, a bicycle was hardly going to be the transport of choice. Then they all got back in the car and drove on in silence.

'What about schools?' asked Kitty suddenly. 'And where are the shops?'

'There's a small shopping centre in the south,' said the rep. 'A dozen shops or so and a smaller strip of five shops at the north. Enough for the basics. For the rest, you will need to go into town.'

'Schools?' He hesitated. 'Well, we have got small primary schools at both the north and south. As far as secondary schools are concerned,' he continued, 'we are not planning to build one for another couple of years.' He paused. 'Students will have to be bussed . . .' his voice lowered to a barely audible, '. . . to the city.'

As they continued along the road, a large rectangle of bright green grass, several hundred metres square in size immediately adjacent to the road, commanded attention. 'That's your footy field,' said the rep. 'Aussie Rules,' he added, to explain the four tall posts at each end of the pitch. South Australians were very keen to convert all new arrivals to 'league football' to the absolute exclusion of any other code.

The drive on the road north then reverted to the red earth plain for another few miles before they arrived at a dirt service road, where several new houses in the final stages of completion faced the main road.

One of these homes stood out straightaway. An attractive long cream brick bungalow with white trim. A paved verandah shaded the entry with a row of windows facing the street over a low timber-framed chain link fence. The rep pulled the car to a halt and the Neeson family followed the rep across the front yard and stood smiling at each other as he sorted through his collection of house keys and let them into the house.

The paved verandah led into an entry porch, L-shaped lounge and dining area through a door to the kitchen. Another door from the lounge into a passage with doors to the bedrooms at the front and end of the house with the kitchen, laundry, WC and bathrooms facing the back. The rep flushed the toilet and turned the bath taps on and off a couple of times with emphatic enthusiasm. 'There you go,' he grinned. 'All mod cons.' The Neesons didn't recognise the significance of this at the time but were to learn that much of Adelaide still had outside loos and laundries. Unlikely to have hot water on tap. Nearby farms on the Gawler plains, highly unlikely even to have electricity . . .

They walked around the outside of the house and gathered back in the front yard. Bernard's parents looked at each other and nodded. His father turned to Bernard with a smile.

'What do think then, Bernard . . . our own little house on the prairie?' Bernard was, his father knew, much taken with all things Wild West, and in games he used to play as a child had named himself Doc Holliday after the famous Wild West gunslinger.

And so it was that 631 Main North Road, Elizabeth North, became the home of the Neesons for over forty years.

Chapter 2

Skewered, beaten and beguiled . . .

The Neesons' new house at Elizabeth provided welcome space for their growing family. A large end room for the four eldest boys; sister Maureen, baby Kevin and parents Barney and Kathleen in the other two. Like all new arrivals with limited funds, they struggled to provide initial furnishings. Ex-army steel bunk beds and straw-filled mattresses for the four eldest boys, basic furniture, rugs on polished floors and a few religious prints to decorate the walls.

But the view for the Neeson family from their house was nothing like the coloured brochure on Elizabeth that had been given to them by Australia House in London to support their purchase commitment on the property. The enticing illustrations included one that was supposed to be the local Elizabeth hospital, but it was actually a photograph of a new hospital in Adelaide itself. The promised 'local beach' was a picture of Victor Harbor, which was 70 miles away on the Fleurieu Peninsula!

Fifty years later, when Bernard addressed a celebration gathering of the greatly expanded forty-member extended Neeson family in Australia, he looked back on their thoughts at that time.

'When Mum and Dad bought their house at the now famous 631 Main North Road, there was only one block of houses north of us and that was the [northern] end of Adelaide. Around us were barren sheep paddocks marked by the whitened bones and skulls of long dead sheep. A stark wilderness.'

———

The town of Elizabeth in the late 1950s and throughout the early 1960s had a very different image to what it has today. Rather than being perceived as a collection of struggle streets hosting the disadvantaged, high unemployment, drugs, desperation and crime, in those early years it was promoted heavily as South Australia's exciting, planned city of the future.

The original post-war concept was for a planned 'satellite' community north of Adelaide inspired by the emerging UK post-war 'New Towns'. Residents would either work locally or commute to Adelaide's inner-city industrial suburbs. It would also support the transformation to peace-time manufacturing of the war-time armament and munitions industries, together with various UK aerospace companies.

An influx of migrants was not in the original plan. The key impetus initially was to meet the needs of the rising population in Adelaide and to respond to the post-war housing shortage. But it gradually morphed over the years into the Playford state government's visionary solution to South Australia's fundamental economic problem—its lack of a critical mass of population.

In retrospect, it was a very bold, wildly ambitious—perhaps even grandiose—proposal to transform what was up until that time South Australia's comparatively small, largely rural economy into an automotive, aerospace, defence industry and whitegoods manufacturing powerhouse. The town of Elizabeth was to house the engineers and scientists, skilled technicians and tradespeople, blue-collar workers and experienced service businesspeople who, encouraged by an attractively subsidised passage, would arrive from a recently war-ravaged UK and Europe to create a modern industrial economy, start new service businesses and build a new life in South Australia.

South Australia had been keen to stimulate industrial development during the war years and afterwards. But given that the current residents of Adelaide, especially those from the leafy green eastern and suburban beach suburbs, had absolutely no interest whatsoever in relocating to the dusty treeless paddocks and denuded wheat fields of the Gawler Plains, it became inevitable that the new town of Elizabeth would become populated almost entirely by migrants who had no other choice: either because they had contracted to purchase homes there so as to prioritise their migration applications or were being accommodated in hostels until rental homes there became available.

And so, to most Adelaideans, Elizabeth quickly became known as 'Little Pommy Land'. More than one million Britons were to migrate to Australia in the peak years of 1945–71, for many different reasons. Around 150,000 initially migrated to South Australia.

For most migrants arriving at this time, the reality and the enormity of their decision quickly sank in. Apart from Australia House in London and what remained of pre-war library books, there was virtually no source of information available to them about their prospective new home. Furthermore, there was little chance at that early stage of being able to contact anyone who had actually been through the process and could provide feedback. Most were seduced by the technicolour promotional films and brightly coloured brochures produced by Australia's federal and state governments, promising a warmer and better life to war-weary Britons.

For newly arrived British migrants like the Neesons, life in South Australia started out as a good-natured adventure; their community was not as it was soon to be popularly portrayed, a seething hotbed of 'Whingeing Poms'. People accepted the fact that the new town was a work in progress, but the constant reminder of the slow progress in establishing the essentials of modern life in a rapidly expanding population of 25,000 soon brought the situation to a head.

———

It was immediately obvious that the extravagantly promoted new town development in SA was totally under-resourced and lacked virtually everything promised, anticipated or expected in jobs, wages, support infrastructure and services.

Apart from a basic single-route infrequent rail system, there was no public transport. No feeder buses even to connect people to their new suburbs miles from the rail stations. A reliable motor vehicle was therefore for most new arrivals the second most essential acquisition after a place to live. A popular conjecture, in fact, supported by the obviously car-centred town planning, was that the South Australian government had done a deal with GMH not to improve Elizabeth's public transport to make it essential for new arrivals to buy cars!

There were a couple of small groups of shops, but there were no supermarkets, no department stores, no electrical or furniture retailers, no car yards, hardware shops, cinemas or theatres, no proper library, home phones and certainly no corner delis or fish-and-chip shops!

Even the recently arrived Anglican 'Priest-in-Charge' of the Elizabeth Mission District, the personable, rugby-playing Welshman the Reverend Howell Witt, was to describe his parish as a 'new town outside Adelaide set in a treeless, dusty plain with one telephone box and no cemetery'.

For socialising with new friends there was just one pub, the Elizabeth Hotel, and it shut at 6 p.m. Migrants quickly discovered the bleak reality of South Australian liquor licensing laws: there were no convivial local pubs or clubs where men and women could socialise over a pork pie and a pint or two of ale or cider, no football pools to provide a weekly wager. Women could only drink in the Lounge Bar or have their drinks taken out to them in the car.

Little wonder that a significant proportion—some say at least 50 per cent—of those who were originally settled on the dry, dusty Gawler Plains at Elizabeth were to eventually return to the UK or move interstate to Melbourne, Sydney and Brisbane in search of better job prospects, lifestyle, opportunities and the greener and considerably better serviced and much more attractive vistas promised by the original films and promotions to prospective settlers.

This figure would have been considerably higher if the migrants who had invested their lifesavings in house deposits with the South Australian Housing Trust had been able to sell their homes and return to the UK or move elsewhere.

———

Returned Second World War service veterans were actively targeted through British military and returned service club promotions to migrate to Australia so there was certainly a common home-life dynamic in many of the families that settled in Elizabeth.

Bernard's father Barney had been recruited in Northern Ireland in 1938 and had slowly worked his way up to Sergeant Major rank in the British Army. By 1960 he had completed twenty-two years of war and post war service, including the momentous retreat off the beaches at Dunkirk in 1940, recruiting and training the cross-channel invasion forces and returning to France a few days after D-Day in 1944. Involved in the advance across Europe until the end of the war, he was to remain in a shattered Germany and Singapore with the occupying forces. He and his wife Kathleen ('Kitty') had then decided to come to Australia with their children because they felt that returning to the poor economy of an increasingly unsettled Northern Ireland was not a good or safe place to bring up a young family.

Between the half dozen British Army postings to military bases across Europe and in the Far East that the Neeson family had lived in while the children were growing up and the ten or so different schools they attended, they had ended up being the 'new kids' quite often. This experience can often isolate a child growing up, and certainly for them it seemed to be a wearisome challenge to continually have to make new friends and settle in again and again. As the eldest child, Bernard was expected to be able to tackle the challenges of living in a new town in a new country on the other side of the globe almost as an adult would.

The six Neeson children had received lessons in acceptable behaviour early and frequently, with arguably as much if not more discipline than their father did back in his early days in army boot camp. Some of the lessons were questionable.

Bernard later recalled a particular weekend shopping expedition as a five-year-old that was indelibly branded into his memory. His behaviour so displeased his father that he was told he did not deserve to continue as a member of the family. 'Got no use for a bad child,' his father had exclaimed as he hoisted his son into a large empty steel dumpster, where the boy was left to contemplate his situation while the rest of the family walked on down the road.

Virtually every child growing up in those times suffered strict and heavy-handed discipline in both the home and at school and it was certainly difficult to see much family affection on display in those immediate post-war years. Returned soldiers like Barney had been exposed to unspeakable horror-filled experiences and battlefield conditions during the years of war and invariably returned to civilian life as emotionally hardened, detached and embittered strangers to their wives and families. Irrational anger, violent outbursts and mood swings dominated the home dynamic. Today we'd consider them mentally damaged by the experience and suffering post-traumatic stress disorder, but back then there was no counselling or treatment available. Keeping busy, working hard, socialising, drinking and smoking was the accepted and universal panacea.

Barney had little in the way of transferable skills or qualifications to help him find peace-time employment as there were few jobs that suited the skills and experience of ex-servicemen. He was dependent on employment with organisations that offered retraining to semi-skilled work. But such entry-level jobs were transient and best suited those who were young, fit and agile. Barney walked straight off the boat into a job at General Motors-Holden assembling cars, but this did not last long.

———

Out in the new town the seasonal changes brought additional issues. In summer, before the days of home insulation or air-conditioning, Elizabeth baked oven-hot with a furnace-like blast whenever you opened the front door. There were frequent choking dust storms that reduced visibility to a few yards. In winter, if it rained, what remained of the topsoil became a sea of red-brown mud. Adelaide's tap water was undrinkable: so hard that soap wouldn't lather. It smelled of earth and had a constant chocolate colour that stained the clothes and left rings around the bath.

Flies were an absolute pestilence in summer. Dense black swarming clouds of them originated from the nearby farmlands, from the Bolivar sewage farm, from the open rubbish tips and from the much-touted 'local beach', eight miles away at St Kilda, which was in fact a foul-smelling mangrove swamp that was inaccessible to the sea. Flies were such a problem that, immediately before the Queen's first visit to the town in 1963, municipal spray trucks drenched Elizabeth's suburbs in DDT daily so she would not be bothered by them.

There were thousands of carefully nurtured, freshly planted seedlings, trees and shrubs that struggled valiantly in the long-denuded red soils on the roadsides and in the future parklands. There was a drive-in theatre on the town's southern fringe, if you were lucky enough to own a car. A large Besser Block, tin-roofed shed did double duty as a roller-skating rink and occasional community centre.

The reality of Bernard's early life at Elizabeth was also far different to the formative years of his considerably better off and elite private-schooled band mates in The Angels. Adelaide's refined eastern suburbs had paved streets and footpaths shaded with leafy green European trees, numerous shops and regular connected public transport, state and private schools, libraries, art galleries, cinemas, theatres and dance halls. Their family villas were set in park-like gardens surrounded by privet hedges and thatched brush fencing. And the Adelaide establishment also always enjoyed unrestricted round the clock drinking privileges at the Adelaide Club, as did members of other similarly long-established institutions.

Even established working-class suburbs offered employment close by with significant industries. Some had their own well-established licensed social clubs and sporting facilities. There were comparatively well-equipped primary and secondary schools, shopping strips, numerous hotels, sporting clubs, churches, corner delis, parks and a network of regular bus services as well as rail.

———

The start of the collapse of the dream that was Elizabeth arrived in the aftermath of the Australian federal government's November 1960 credit squeeze—the 'Holt Jolt', as it was called in the media of the day. The ensuing stop–go economic policies continued until 1983, when the Australian dollar was floated. As part of the economic measures of the time, bank overdraft rates were increased and banks were instructed by the Reserve Bank to cut lending. These measures stopped a booming and supposedly runaway national economy stone-dead, and quickly re-introduced Australians to mass unemployment.

South Australia was disproportionately affected, both by the tighter lending restrictions and by the imposition of a crushing sales tax on the emerging Australian automotive industry. There were fewer and fewer jobs available in Adelaide. And where union membership had previously been an encouraged and positive attribute for migrant selection, it now became a distinct dis-advantage in securing or keeping a job. The recently opened new GM-Holden plant at Elizabeth was forced to lay off many recently engaged staff. Barney Neeson, as one of the most recent and oldest hires, was among the first to be let go, less than six months after he'd started.

Bernard's father was to have twenty-two jobs between his arrival in Elizabeth in 1960 and his early retirement following long periods of enforced unemployment twenty years later when he was in his early sixties. Too many employers took advantage of a dysfunc-tional labour market, lax regulations and a vulnerable migrant demographic, offering them underpaid jobs involving hazardous conditions and dangerous work practices.

Despite being told by Australian immigration officials before leaving the UK that ex-servicemen were highly sought after for well-paid positions, Barney's sad experience, and that of countless other new arrivals, was otherwise. His longest employment, for six years, was as a warder at the Yatala Prison, where his army experience provided elements of qualification. This was over an hour's bus and train journey around shiftwork rosters until the family could afford a car. It was a physically demanding and dangerous job, which he eventually had to leave as recurring injuries and advancing age took their toll.

To make ends meet, Bernard's mother Kitty, despite the recent arrival of baby Kevin, was forced to return to her pre-marriage career as a nursing sister. Woodville hospital was a 90-minute train, bus and walk from Elizabeth at each end of her three-shift roster. It was fortunate that she was able to organise Kevin's care at the hospital's crèche, but this meant the added burden of dressing and bringing the baby with her on the long journeys to and from work. The long days of hard manual work and lengthy daily commutes returned both parents home grey with exhaustion. This was a common situation for many new arrivals and often led to arguments and family breakdown. Elizabeth was also the 'town without grandparents' or extended family, so there was seldom available childcare before and after school, or respite care for stressed or fractured relationships.

Bernard, like many other children and teenagers in Elizabeth, listened nightly to his parents wrangling and fighting, often violently against a soundtrack of slamming doors and the crashing of smashed china over issues linked to the financially disastrous and untenable positions that they found themselves in.

———

My family arrived in Adelaide in January 1958 on the PO *Iberia*, a couple of years before the Neesons. We too had signed up to buy a house at Elizabeth as a condition of our speedy approval as migrants. Bernard's family home and mine had identical layouts. Initially we struggled hard. As with Barney, until Dad secured work with a defence contractor at Edinburgh some of the jobs he took on in desperation to put bread on the table were absolute shockers. Fortunately, my mother had trained as an infant teacher prior to her marriage. She successfully applied to attend teachers' college in Adelaide and requalified. Her financial contribution definitely saved us as a family.

By the early 1960s, when I first met Bernard, we had mostly recovered from the experience of migration and my folks had created a comfortable home for themselves. But for the Neesons, the early 1960s were desperate, hand-to-mouth times. Making the mortgage payment each month meant all financial resources were stretched almost to breaking point. One way Kitty saved money was to make the mattresses for all the Neeson children herself. She had bought a few yards of blue-striped cotton ticking and made simple mattress-sized bags on her old sewing machine for each of the children. Barney had ordered a couple of bales of straw delivered and, hey presto, job done. The mattresses always felt lumpy and were most uncomfortable, even to sit on.

Bernard also needed to look after his clothes because, as he outgrew them, they were handed down to Seamus and then on to Terry. Bernard would often cut up layers of cardboard to slip inside his shoes, because holes in the leather soles meant that he was walking on his socks. A regular job for his father was repairing the family footwear. Sitting on a stool on the small back verandah, he would nail Blakey's—little metal shoe protectors—onto the soles to make the shoes last another few weeks.

Barney and Kitty Neeson, like other early migrants to Elizabeth, felt they had been conned by the South Australian government. As a condition of migration, they had been coerced into buying a house in an appallingly serviced area that was miles from any jobs. Within a few short years they would find themselves in their mid-fifties with little prospect of employment until they retired. They were trapped in Elizabeth as owners of almost valueless properties that were demonstrably cheaply built and structurally substandard, located in an area where selling was virtually impossible because the town had gained a bad reputation from its escalating social problems.

Chapter 3

Immigrant boy

The realities of life in the new town for its recently arrived teenage inhabitants were daunting. Just when they had been finding their way through their adolescent years in almost normalised post-war UK cities, their parents had torn them up by the roots and resettled them half a world away, where they were expected to find new friends, feel secure and re-establish themselves in what was a less-than-friendly environment.

Boys and girls were often pressured to leave school to find any sort of job in Adelaide, in order to contribute to the family finances. Girls might also have had to leave school to look after young family members so that mothers could work. Boys sought apprenticeships in the manufacturing industry or in the motor trade. Teachers' college was a wise choice. Part-time jobs as waiters or waitresses in Adelaide hotels and restaurants were eagerly sought after.

Thirteen-year-old Bernard was learning the new dynamic of life in Elizabeth. Migrant children were generally completely subservient and obedient to their parents. At school they were expected to work hard and to take every opportunity to do so. As money was tight, they learned how to make their own toys and devise their own games. They kept their rooms tidy, helped around the house, assisted in the raising of siblings and, in their parents' absence, took responsibility from a very early age.

Bernard's daily life became established in this new routine. With his parents on shiftwork, it was up to him to keep the family going in their absence. His father's previous army career and his mother's nursing background meant that his life and those of his five younger siblings were well organised. On his return home from school, an hour-plus journey, there were meals to be prepared and dishes to do, rooms to be kept clean, clothes to be washed and ironed, cupboards to be provisioned. Bernard's sister Maureen seemed saddled with most of the care of baby Kevin on her mother's afternoon and night shifts, a responsibility way beyond her ten years, but Bernard was accountable. Once he had cooked the family's evening meal and ensured that each of his siblings had completed their rostered duties, so that the house was tidy and clean for his parents' return from work, he could make a start on his homework.

Bernard was expected to also assume responsibility for the behaviour of his siblings during their parents' absence. When his parents returned home each day, he was immediately reprimanded for any faults they could find. Inevitably he became resentful that his parents promoted him to be the 'head of the house' in their absence but reverted to treating him as a child immediately they returned.

He had an almost overwhelming level of responsibility for someone in his early teens. It was relentless and unavoidable. He had few opportunities to pursue his own interests. When he did so, they became clandestine, stolen moments about which he felt both guilty and resentful.

————

The Irish Catholic community in Elizabeth made the Neeson family very welcome and quickly involved them in the local activities of their faith. Bernard and the younger children were enrolled in Adelaide's Catholic school system with the older Neeson boys attending St Paul's College for Boys at Gilles Plains run by the adjacent Christian Brothers seminary.

Disturbingly, children enrolled at Adelaide's Catholic secondary schools suffered the worst excesses of the strict disciplinary policies that were encouraged throughout South Australia's church and state school systems at the time. Classes of often over 40 students, of diverse age groups and capabilities, were jammed into small classrooms that baked in summer and froze in winter. Students wrote tediously, often cramped into tiny desks, with nib pens dipped endlessly in inkwells.

Corporal punishment, in the form of savagely humiliating canings and strappings, were carried out daily for the most trivial of real, imagined or perceived misdemeanours. Students were not only disciplined for disobeying rules or for disorderly behaviour, but simply for not understanding a lesson or for answering a question incorrectly. Sometimes the whole class would be lined up and caned or beaten for no specific reason other than that the teacher felt like it.

St Paul's College on Grand Junction Road was a 25-kilometre rail and bus journey from Elizabeth. Its catchment area covered Adelaide's industrial inner suburbs. It was a tough working-class area and discipline was very strict.

Peter Collaton, a school friend of Bernard's, recalls: 'It was a pretty tough area and teenage boys could be a bit of a handful. The older brothers at St Paul's, who were more experienced and worldly, could usually manage the discipline in class without resorting to getting the strap out. The younger brothers, however, had no patience and would turn into sadistic fiends in the blink of an eye.

'There was, however, an older brother who every month or so would line the class up and strap everyone, just in case we thought we had got away with anything.'

Bullying in Adelaide schools was endemic and almost a natural consequence of the violence meted out by those in authority. Migrant students who spoke, dressed or acted differently were particular targets. Teachers rarely intervened and seldom ventured into the schoolyard during recess periods.

Secondary-school students living in Elizabeth had to travel up to two hours every day; they bussed daily to Adelaide in overcrowded army surplus buses or caught trains to Gawler. These journeys provided captive targets for violence and this often forced children to hitchhike.

St Paul's specifically prohibited hitchhiking under any circumstances. It was considered dangerous and reflected badly on the school; for anyone caught, there were no excuses. One morning Bernard was caught hitchhiking by one of the senior brothers after he had missed his bus and train connections from Elizabeth. The penalty was a searing six strokes of the tawse.

Like a cruel mediaeval instrument of torture, this was a long thick leather strap split lengthwise to pinch the flesh as each blow connected. Three horrifically painful overlapping red weals on each hand were savagely administered by the Master of Discipline as a humiliating example in front of the entire school. It counted not one jot that Bernard was an otherwise exemplary student: his academic record was in the highest percentile, he excelled at sports and was to be a future class captain and school prefect. The rules were applied equally without favour.

———

Probably the most redeeming feature of the South Australian secondary education system was its almost overwhelming commitment to sport. If you could show any talent or skill in any sport you were accepted. It did not matter where you came from or who you were.

Bernard shone at sport. He was naturally talented and had the build and height that suited athletics and Australian Rules football. He was a state schoolboy high-jump champion and in the First XVIII at St Paul's and, later, at Elizabeth High School. At university, and even during his national service in the Australian Army, he received encouragement to pursue a sporting career.

Peter Collaton recalls an amusing moment that resulted from a friendship Bernard made on the football field.

'Brother O'Doherty organised a school singing competition and Bernard entered a duet with fellow football team member Bohdan Jaworski. There were about twenty teams in the sing-off. I think they chose a pop song by the Everly Brothers.

'Brother O'Doherty led the panel that made the assessment of each entry and, when the auditions were finished, Bernard and Bohdan were placed stony-broke last. Song choice was probably a factor, particularly if the brothers were expecting a rendition of "Ave Maria" or similar.

'Brother O'Doherty announced their placing with the advice: "Well, Bernard and Bohdan, I don't think it would be wise for you lads to be choosing a musical career."'

Peter caught up with Bernard many years later at an Angels' concert and they enjoyed a good laugh recalling Brother O'Doherty's prediction!

————

Bernard made friends at St Paul's who were important to him and who would remain in contact with him all his life. Peter Williams was a country lad whose family had moved from Millicent in the south-east of the state up to Adelaide and had settled in Elizabeth. Peter, as the eldest in another large Catholic family, had similar home responsibilities to Bernard.

Peter's father also had good carpentry and mechanical skills and, assisted by his son, had built a small wooden cabin fishing boat with an inboard motor that soon allowed regular fishing trips with several of Peter's friends into the coastal reaches of the Port River and Spencer Gulf. The mangroves were a rich fish and crab nursery; there was an abundance of great table fish in the coastal waters and every trip provided a bounty of bream, yellowfin whiting, mullet, salmon, trout and blue swimmer crabs that fed tasty meals to several families. Rod fishing, crabbing and netting were skills quickly learned, and friends had fun fishing together at night with a light for garfish, with sweet black tea boiled over an alcohol stove in the boat's small cosy cabin taking the chill from the wind that often whistled up Spencer Gulf.

Another friend was Dave Ratcliffe, whose father was a senior engineer at the Weapons Research Establishment at Salisbury. Their family had been one of the first from the UK to settle in Elizabeth and they had even purchased a block of seafront land at Port Elliott's Boomer Beach on the Fleurieu Peninsula. A war-surplus cabin home was purchased and relocated to this block to become a shack that could be used by their children and friends. Dave was one of those people who others were always at ease with. He never appeared to get rattled or let people worry him. He seemed to be grateful that his family had the shack and was happy to share it.

When Bernard could escape, he spent many holiday weekends with Dave, Pete and me at the Boomer Beach shack in the mid-60s trying to body surf its monster waves. We would live on a diet of buns, fresh from the nearby bakery, and cook up meals of spaghetti cheese, waking to the sound of the booming rollers only metres away and chilling out from hassles at home.

The surf at Boomer was consistently large; the occasional monster, rolling in off the Southern Ocean to dump noisily on the beach, needed to be avoided. When the beach was used for surf carnivals, races between the wooden surfboats of the era often resulted in boats reduced to splintered driftwood if they broached broadside under a huge breaking wave. Body surfing in the mostly marginal conditions was . . . interesting!

Bernard arrived one day with a bright-red Li-lo, an inflatable rubber mattress that he had borrowed from a friend. He informed us he was going to surf with it.

We rolled our eyes. Yeah, right.

We entered the water and swam out through the surf, riding the building waves and diving through those that were about to break, Bernard paddling his Li-lo in front of him until we arrived at the calm water a hundred metres or so from the beach. We trod water there, getting our breath back from the swim out, chatting and sizing up the lines of rising swells that indicated the approaching waves.

Dave, who had the best knowledge of the local surf, would offer advice on the best wave to catch. 'Not this one . . . nah, not this . . . let this one go.' We were waiting for one that looked good, so we could match speed as it approached and then angle down the face of it for the run in to the beach.

An approaching swell could be seen building a hundred yards further out. Definitely one to be avoided. Noticing Bernard's interest, Dave cautioned, 'Not this one, Bern, it's going to dump. You'll get killed.'

Undeterred, Bernard launched the Li-lo into the building crest of what was going to be a huge wave.

'Bern, no!' Dave shouted in vain as Bernard disappeared from view, except for occasional glimpses through the rolling swell of a gangly stick figure pulling himself up to his knees on the Li-lo.

From the beach Bernard could be seen perched right on the crest of the largest wave of the day, kneeling on the Li-lo and riding the massive shining vertical wall of green water as it crashed down and exploded into a mountainous maelstrom of seething foam.

Incredibly though, as the foam subsided, there was Bernard, hanging desperately on to the Li-lo as it careened towards the beach. He pulled himself upright from the surf. There was a red splash of blood at the corner of his mouth.

'Wow, Bern,' Dave said. 'You were *so* lucky to get through that. What did you do to yourself?'

Bernard just grinned. 'What a ride. But I don't think I will do that again. I bit my tongue as the Li-lo crashed down through the wave and I hit the sandbar.'

Chapter 4

The new musical firmament

British teenage migrants arriving in Australia during the late 1950s and early 1960s were to lose virtually all connection with the UK's burgeoning music scene. In those years rock-and-roll only filtered very slowly into Australia, and local youth culture generally had become gradually aligned with American trends and influences rather than British.

In Sydney, Channel Nine had been keeping an eye on what was happening locally and, after testing a couple of teen music show pilots, started *Bandstand* in November 1958. Four months later *Six O'Clock Rock* debuted on the ABC. But it wasn't until late 1959 that TV arrived in Adelaide, when NSW9 and ADS7 commenced broadcasting.

The Australian TV shows were based on overseas formats—*Bandstand* on the American show of the same name and *Six O'Clock Rock* on a British show called *6.05 Special*. Both shows were initially centred around US music-industry offerings, supporting touring

American acts and promoting emerging local artists who could replicate the American sound.

Many of the young migrants that came to Elizabeth at this time from the UK were enthusiastic followers of the scene they had left, where Tommy Steele had been launched in 1956, and Cliff Richard was by then in the pop vanguard of an evolving fusion of rock-and-roll, skiffle and rhythm and blues. Before leaving the UK, these migrants had attended the concerts of these and later inspirational artists, and their encyclopaedic knowledge and detailed appreciation of these musical influences were to contribute significantly to Australian youth culture. British and European trends in music and fashion, from London and other regional cities, arrived with each boatload of young people, and were to quickly provide role models for the wider group of Australian-born Adelaide youth to follow.

———

To their credit, the various church organisations in Adelaide had from the very beginning lost little time in responding to the obvious communal needs at Elizabeth. Infrastructure such as community halls for recreation, cultural and social pursuits would have stimulated a sense of identity, inclusion and kinship, but the woefully benighted South Australian government considered this completely unnecessary. Premier Playford himself labelled such amenities as 'frills not fundamentals'.

When St Theodore's Anglican church at Elizabeth South opened in 1958, there had ensued much discussion about ways of making religion relevant to young adults. The newly appointed Reverend Howell Witt, suggested that teenagers in his parish youth group might hold small weekly gatherings, dancing to records on

Sunday evenings. South Australia's antiquated ordinances of that time outlawed the use of churches for anything other than church services, so 'The Rev' somewhat euphemistically described these gatherings as 'church services' in order to navigate his way around the regulations. He did not wish to deliberately flout the law; this was simply his practical solution to the need for a hall to provide activities for local teens.

US artist Bill Haley's song 'Rock Around the Clock' had at this time featured in the controversial film *Blackboard Jungle*, which, after being banned in several US states, had lit a box-office bonfire. While local radio stations were still reluctant to play the song, many new arrivals were keen to find somewhere to meet new friends, play their records and show off their newly learned jive moves. Howell Witt's suggestion definitely struck the right note and the first Sunday evening youth group event at St Theo's drew around sixty local teens, where previously he had been hard pressed to get a dozen.

There was an immediate reaction to this from Adelaide official-dom after a positive front-page article in the Adelaide *Advertiser* on Monday, 8 December 1958 was accompanied by a picture showing Elizabeth teenagers happily jiving around inside the new church with the ecclesiastically robed Reverend Witt.

Blackboard Jungle had shocked and surprised adult audiences with its fictional tale of unruly youths in a New York high school and its rock-and-roll soundtrack. The film's purpose, described in a scrolling sensationalist newsreel-type prologue, was to express concern over the causes and effects of juvenile delinquency, especially 'when this delinquency boils over into our schools'. Therefore any subversive attempt by the Reverend Howell Witt to contribute to Adelaide's perceived escalating juvenile delinquency was sure to create a moral panic. The bastions of this highly conservative city foresaw imported American youth culture creating an imminent crisis and a breakdown of adult authority in their state's schools. This demanded immediate and firm action.

On the next Sunday evening, the St Theo's youth group gathering was raided by the full resources of the Vice Squad from Adelaide Police Headquarters. They arrived with flashing lights, sirens blaring, two squad cars and a paddy wagon. A couple of burly uniformed police and a black-suited detective stormed past the teenagers milling around the door and into the church, cornered the stunned and amazed Howell Witt and demanded to see the deeds and the occupancy certificate covering the use of the new building. Given that these were obviously not immediately available, they satisfied themselves by lining up all those attending and taking their names and whatever identification they might have.

In a scene reminiscent of the Keystone Cops, those teenagers who had arrived on motorcycles or in cars were subjected to the police checking their vehicles for roadworthiness and the licences and sobriety of the riders or drivers. The Reverend Witt was sternly chastised and cautioned over his less-than-truthful description of the youth group's illegal and anti-social activities. He was firmly instructed to discontinue the dances and go back to studying the Bible on Sunday evenings!

Fortunately this setback did not stop the local teens from finding other places to meet up, play records and create music away from the parental restrictions of life at home. Even the equipment shed at the council waste tip was to become a rehearsal room for local musicians.

By 1961 the Presbyterian Church had completed building St Stephen's church hall at Elizabeth North and were keen to commence evangelising among the local youth by also launching a youth group that met after church evensong on Sunday evenings. It quickly filtered through the teenage grapevine that this group regularly had two or three dozen attendees, who would bring and play records to an unheard of 10.30 p.m. The new church hall had somehow got around the restrictive legislation the Anglicans had endured a year or so earlier.

The Reverend Witt's Anglican Church had also learned from their previous brush with the law and around this time charted a more appropriate course as they established St Peter's Mission. This was a well-designed centrally located hall and pastoral outreach hub in tune with the practical needs of the community. It quickly found a steady stream of local activities, clubs and associations keen to take advantage of its multipurpose facilities.

The new building sat isolated and remote on the edge of Elizabeth Way, a new strip of bitumen that linked Elizabeth South and Elizabeth North. The Mission, as it was known, was an attractive barrel-roofed building about twice the size of St Stephen's hall with large side windows that could be seen by anyone walking up or down the main road some 200 metres away. In the evenings, the lighted windows helped attract interest in whatever activities were taking place inside.

Anything that involved teenagers interacting with each other proved an instant hit; if you added the faint strains of popular music, they came in like moths to a lamp. This was one of the very few places in Elizabeth for teenagers to meet and have fun; it provided a welcome distraction from the dramas of moving into a new house and taking the next big steps forward: schools, jobs, settling in, learning more of the day-to-day details of life in a strange land.

On Tuesday and Thursday evenings in the early 1960s, St Peter's Mission hosted fellow migrants Bob and Margot Horsburgh's

'Elizabeth Ballroom Dancing School'. With very little for teenagers to do, this quickly became very popular; for girls particularly, it was a venue that most parents approved of. The boys quickly followed!

The Horsburghs were extremely capable and experienced teachers. On Tuesdays they taught the formal steps for the modern waltz, quick step, foxtrot and, easily the most popular, modern or American jive. Latin American Thursdays were also popular with the rumba, samba, tango and cha-cha.

Most of those attending were regulars: fifty or so teens, and a few older couples seeking to refresh earlier interests and skills. With the chairs pushed to the sides, the big overhead lights reflecting off the polished timber floor and the music playing, the Mission assumed an ambience that always seemed to make everyone happier and brighter.

Music was provided by a radiogram, one of the latest 'stereophonics', a grand polished wood affair with two eight-inch speakers and a professional turntable. These new stereo players, with separate bass and treble controls, were much louder than the old mono machines and didn't distort at high volume. A couple of boxes of records sat on chairs to one side. If you owned a particular record that was judged to be the 'correct tempo' you could bring it along to be played in the practice session. This was a very popular opportunity to share, dance to and enjoy the latest music—sent by extended family members or brought by new arrivals from the UK—without the persistent chorus from parents at home to 'turn that bloody music down'.

———

Bernard stood out immediately as a new arrival at the dance classes. He was straight and tall, in a brown corduroy jacket and slacks, as he walked away from the reception table at the Mission hall entrance, a few yards from where I was chatting with mate Brenton Spry waiting for the classes to start.

Unusually for Elizabeth, Brenton was an Australian lad who had recently moved to the area with his parents from the mid-north of South Australia. His father was a wool merchant for Elders who had been promoted to their Adelaide office. Brenton bussed daily from Elizabeth to attend Roseworthy Agricultural College, way up on the edge of the Barossa Valley.

A reserved and polite fellow, Brenton was a stand-out character who could not only ride and balance unaided on a unicycle but could also play virtually any musical instrument put in front of him. With the laconic dry humour of a typical Australian country lad, Brenton looked the lanky newcomer up and down and put out his hand in greeting with a friendly grin.

'Howyergoin Stalk,' he said, referring to Bernard's height.

We all shook hands. 'Hi, fellas. It's Bernard,' he replied in a soft Irish brogue. 'I wonder if you can tell me how things happen around here.'

We gave him the rundown for the evening. Bernard noticed some records in the shopping bags that a number of teenagers had brought along and expressed immediate interest. A local alternative underground music scene was already becoming established and hip Elizabeth teenagers were well ahead in recognising that the mostly mind-numbingly boring rubbish churned out by the local offices of mainstream US record companies, which dominated the playlists of the Adelaide radio stations, was completely ignoring the seismic musical rumblings from their UK homelands.

We showed Bernard the 45s we'd brought along. They were recent releases and included a Cliff Richard live concert EP sent over from the UK; these studio-audience recordings were incredible, spine-tingling, with an impact and engagement that canned music up till then had failed to capture. One of the tracks by Cliff and his early backing band the Drifters was a jive number, the 1959 rocker 'Move It'. These records had not been available in Australia at the time of their UK release and took many months, if ever, to arrive in Adelaide's record shops.

Bernard—his name quickly shortened to 'Bernie'—immediately wanted to hear the Cliff 45.

'Don't reckon ol' Horsburgh will go for it,' I cautioned, 'but I brought it anyway!' The records needed to be played loudly for their full effect and, being live recordings, there was a lot of screaming from the girls in the audience all the way through the track.

Bernard smiled encouragingly. 'Well, bring them up to my place then. My four kid brothers and a sister are always crying and yelling about something. With my olds at work, we can play it as loud as we like and a bit of extra screaming will never be noticed.'

Well, as expected, Bob Horsburgh listened to the first few seconds of the first track and shook his head, lifting the needle off the record.

'Mmm,' he said, 'not really suitable as a dance record. What else have you got?'

But the teenagers standing round the radiogram and listening to the opening riff from 'Move It' were immediately galvanised. Hearing it through some decent-sized speakers at volume, rather than from a tiny transistor or played 'quietly' from a portable gramophone in their bedrooms at home, they demanded to hear the track right through.

Bob Horsburgh smiled and said, 'Well, OK, it's coffee break for a few more minutes anyway.'

The volume was turned up to the top and we stood around grinning at each other, some listening for the first time to the now famous staccato intro played by Ernie Shear on his Hofner President guitar. The hair rose on the back of our necks, the visceral impact and excitement of Ian Samwell's tune coursing through our veins.

'Move It' is not a love song of the common sort; it does not even contain the word *love*. Its lyrics are a review of the popular music trends of that time: it argued for musical superiority—and demanded its own identity and your participation. With strong riffs and driving back beat, the song became almost a siren call to the millions of younger people who by then had delightedly accepted that style of music as almost personally their very own.

Consisting of just three chords, the song was originally dismissed as 'rubbish' by EMI head honcho Norrie Paramour, and initially released as a B side. But ultimately it was widely acknowledged to be the first true all-British rock-and-roll record and a seminal influence on every Brit rock-and-roll band from The Beatles and Rolling Stones down.

Compared to the other music being played at this time, it sounded as if it came from another planet. Wow. Yes, this was it! Life in Elizabeth—and music itself—was never, ever going to be the same again.

In a small way these early musical interactions encouraged Elizabeth's teenagers to work out, at a very subtle level, what was really going to be important and different in their new lives, and the means to achieve it. Music would set the mood, materialise emotions and act as a powerful expression of identity in their new country. Individual taste would influence the success of romantic relationships, express the inexpressible, form bonds between strangers and reflect the values of their new community. Music became a common denominator, no matter whether you listened, played or taught, sang, danced or crafted musical instruments or were involved in related clubs or venues.

For those involved at the time, this period in our lives would remain an overwhelmingly affectionate memory. It was to be absolutely the best fun of our teenage years; it distracted from the unending drama of everyday issues that life in Elizabeth represented. Our music was infectiously spectacular and became a common enabler; all the various involvements developed as both separate and combined entities. It was social, it was creative, and it had a sustainable eco-system that grew organically.

New UK releases arrived daily by post from friends and relatives. Arriving teenagers brought with them from the UK their treasured collections of 45s and LPs from their favourite artists. Youthful migrant musicians, who had brought with them travel-worn and even homemade instruments, played and replayed these records, forensically dissecting and learning each and every note and word—even the breathing and phrasing of the vocalists—to arrive at a faithfully replicated and authentic performance.

There was certainly an early realisation among Elizabeth teens that Adelaide, if not the whole of Australia, was way behind in appreciating that the new wave of popular music from the UK was about to open a whole new rock-and-roll era, to become the catalyst for the musical firestorm that would change forever the world as they knew it. We had moved on from Bill Haley, and from skiffle, country and rockabilly music. Even Elvis's star had waned during his two years in the US Army. We were tuned in to the new sounds from the UK that represented a significant shift and progression from what had gone before.

And it's certainly not a stretch to say that Elizabeth was to become something of a cultural melting pot, like Florence during the Renaissance. Here teenagers began to realise that they could enjoy themselves in their new country, relearn from their previous lives and emerge energised from this cradle and foundry forge of Australia's next-generation music scene.

There were other musical epicentres in 1960s British and European migrant settlements in New South Wales and Victoria, but they did not have the concentrated critical mass of youthful enthusiasm and responsiveness that marked out Elizabeth. It was a remote bright star in the new musical firmament, but we would have to go it alone for a while in our part of the universe until the unenlightened rest of the country caught up.

Back at the ballroom dancing classes, it was suggested it might be a bit of fun to take records along to the next gathering of the Sunday evening youth group at St Stephen's in Elizabeth North. Bernard, Brenton and I also learned that evening that we all lived within a few hundred yards of each other and shared an interest in music of similar genre. Brenton was a couple of years older, and he actually taught guitar, so it was arranged that we would all meet at his house on the next available weekend.

Chapter 5

Early days

From their arrival in 1960 through until 1962, everything north and west of the Neesons' new home was a building site. Their recently occupied home, with a handful of others, was marooned in a small residential strip that had been roughly completed for Housing Trust media events and photo opportunities alongside the Main North Road. There were no roads or footpaths. A pair of gumboots was essential for a winter walk to the railway station. A mud scraper and shoe rack were by the front door, with lines of newspaper spread on the floors. Like most of the other houses in Elizabeth, their home smelled of sawn timber and fresh paint.

One positive was the opening in late 1961 of a set of about a dozen shops on Woodford Road. The largest shop in this new block became Elizabeth's, and arguably Adelaide's, first proper American-style serve-yourself grocers. The store owner, Lynn Gilcrist, had visited the US and brought back their innovative ideas for grocery-store operation, including shopping trolleys. Bernard, living a few hundred yards from the new shops, was soon able to secure a part-time job on Friday evenings and Saturday mornings at Gilcrist's, packing shopping bags for customers at one of these amazing new ideas—*the checkout.*

As well, at the rear of the haberdashery cum dry-cleaning cum parcel delivery outlet in the small cluster of new shops was a small sublet area with a desk, rug and a couple of music stools. A sandwich board that could be put outside the shop announced: 'Musical Instruments, Guitar and Drum Lessons'.

The youthful proprietor of the sublet was a newly arrived enterprising cockney named Mike Taylor. His day job was driving the van to deliver and pick up local dry-cleaning, exposed rolls of film from the chemist for printing and other consignments from or to Adelaide-based businesses. His after-hours venture was music lessons and the sale of musical instruments, for which he was an agent for an Adelaide music shop.

On Friday evenings Taylor would stand busking next to the sandwich board outside the shop and run through a repertoire of tunes, mostly by UK chart-topping skiffle king Lonnie Donegan. There were a couple of acoustic guitars on stands and a snare drum set-up conveniently close by in his 'showroom'. Bernard, packing shopping bags barely thirty yards away, heard and caught glimpses of these performances every week as he worked; they quickly firmed up his musical aspirations.

Bernard desperately wanted a proper acoustic guitar to replace the ukulele he had owned from childhood, but at first that was impossible. After Barney lost his job at Holden and before Kitty found out that Woodville hospital would allow her to use the hospital crèche for baby Kevin, so she could return to her nursing career, the family's financial situation was dire. To begin with,

Bernard pledged his entire part-time earnings to the cause, but when Kitty's wage relieved the situation she allowed him to retain his earnings from Gilcrist's for a while and he became the proud owner of a burgundy-coloured Maton cutaway acoustic guitar.

The purchase included three introductory guitar lessons, but Taylor was better at selling musical instruments than teaching. Bernard's progress beyond a couple of basic chords being slow, Taylor was keen to enrol him in a longer, relatively expensive tuition course run by a colleague in Gawler ten miles away. From Bernard's perspective, with little money and limited transport options, this might as well have been on the moon.

But his attendance at Horsburgh's dance school and meeting Brenton had been fortunate. Brenton, an only child, shared musical interests with his parents. His mother, a capable pianist, and his father often sang together around the piano at home. When Brenton showed an early enthusiasm to learn the guitar they had arranged private lessons in Adelaide with Roy Wooding, one of the stars of the 5DN 'Radio Canteen' showband and leader of the Roy Wooding Trio. Brenton soon proved himself a quick learner and diligent pupil; by sixteen he had been able to make some pocket money by giving guitar lessons himself to budding local teenage musicians.

Brenton's mother, however, had frequently seen an exhausted Kitty Neeson passing her house on her long daily trek home from the railway station after a long day at the hospital, often with baby Kevin in a pusher and laden down with shopping bags, and cautioned her son, 'I don't want to hear that you have been taking money off that lovely polite Bernard lad. His poor mother, with all those kids, them being Catholics and all that, an absolute saint having to work all the hours there are too.'

The Sprys had purchased one of the first two-storey houses built by the Housing Trust, only a few hundred yards north of the Neesons' home and also on Main North Road. It boasted the very latest architectural feature—a large rumpus room, which took up two-thirds of the upper level and provided the ideal venue for musical recreations. Brenton's parents were an older-than-average couple, and they seemed genuinely pleased to welcome his friends into their home. They weren't too fussed whether we played music loudly either, and there are many fond memories of weekend jams, band practices, cups of coffee and Mrs Spry's CWA cakes at their home as our musical interests developed.

————

As secondary-school students we certainly didn't have enough of the necessary to progress our musical interests to electric guitars and amplifiers from the small allowances our parents provided or our meagre earnings from part-time jobs. A new electric guitar and amplifier from Allans or Cawthorne's in Adelaide was hugely expensive. The massive import duty and sales tax inflated prices so they cost as much as a good second-hand car. Given the absence of public transport in Elizabeth, the latter got a much higher priority in the greater scheme of things once we eventually began to work.

However, Roseworthy Agricultural College and Nailsworth Boys Technical High had provided Brenton and me with a couple of years of comprehensive vocational skills training in wood- and metalwork. The solution therefore was blindingly obvious: we would make our own musical instruments. Our recently acquired skills could be deployed into infinitely more useful challenges than making the galvanised-steel laundry buckets, pencil boxes and coffee tables that comprised school projects.

How hard could it really be?

The idea rapidly progressed over a few weeks to a shared aspiration to build from scratch an electric guitar each. I wanted to tackle a four-string electric bass and Brenton a copy of a Fender Telecaster. We both made trips down to the city to suss out the matter.

Adelaide city's retail music stores in the early 60s were still very much establishment places, with dark-suited staff, shiny pianos, piano rolls, sheet music and violins. Some cellos and shiny trumpets were displayed, with a few acoustic guitars and pictures of Andrés Segovia on a little stand in the corner. Electric guitars were expensive items; although displayed in the shop window during the day, they were removed to safer storage at night.

The wood- and metalwork we thought we could certainly do. The pickups, fret board and hardware could probably be sourced or imported. The electrical connection, tuners and switches did not appear to constitute any real problem. After all, through our parents and friends we knew people who worked at the nearby Weapons Research Establishment where they built state-of-the-art electronic systems for guided missiles, rockets and even atom bombs!

Amplifiers would be a separate issue, but the father of a friend built public-address systems at a very reasonable price for local clubs. Beyond that, speaker boxes and a cabinet were doable too.

I had also seen a small advert in a very tattered edition of the *New Musical Express* magazine about the German Hofner 'violin body electric bass guitars'. These looked very different and interesting compared to the ubiquitous Fenders and lookalikes that every band had or aspired to have. This was at least a couple of years before Paul McCartney made the Hofner 'Beatle Bass' world famous.

Several weeks later, a brochure on the *Violinkörper E-Bass-Gitarren* came back from Hofner. All in German, but the illustrations were pretty good, so I scaled the dimensions off the pictures and went to work to build the body of the guitar from some pieces of furniture-quality plywood salvaged by my dad from the packing case for an English Electric Thunderbird ground-to-air missile en route to its testing at Woomera.

After a bit more research we also managed to find out that we could obtain the machine-head string fittings, a neck blank, pickups and fret board relatively cheaply from a specialist musical instrument repair supply shop in Melbourne, but all the rest I made up in the small tool shed at home. This was a very, very slow process and I ended up with lots of cuts, bruised fingers, blackened fingernails and blisters as testament to my developing skills.

———

A week or so after meeting at Horsburgh's to play a few records, we got together at Brenton's house to play the Cliff and the Drifters EP through a couple of times, and tunes from Eddie Cochran, Chuck Berry and Little Richard.

Bernard wanted to know if Brenton might be able to teach him an entire song.

Brenton was at heart a country and western fan, but Roy Wooding had him playing everything from the Ventures and Duane Eddy to Buddy Holly.

'How about the chords for "Apache" by the Shads?' Brenton suggested.

'Really?' said Bernard.

'Sure,' said Brenton. 'I'll show you the chords. It'll be a good exercise and provide chords that you can also use in lots more songs. We'll learn those now. You can practise them at home, and then next week we will put the song together.'

And so our first group came to be. Assemblies of budding musicians were always called 'groups' at that time, never a 'band', which was very uncool—there were just too many brass bands, pipe bands and marching bands in the 50s communities.

Our group was a three-piece combo called The Joneetons, an amalgam of our three names—Jo + Nee + Ton. Bernard and Brenton were on acoustic guitars and, as an interim measure until my bass was completed, we added a snare drum, a foot-pedal high hat and a further cymbal. This produced a better sound—more like the Everly Brothers, Buddy Holly, Eddie Cochran, Chuck Berry and The Shadows/Ventures than traditional UK skiffle.

All in all, my homemade bass came out pretty well, certainly good enough for those early musical forays. It worked fine and looked stunning—like a 'bought one'. Brenton had embarked on his own scratch-built project and created an iridescent blue Fender Telecaster-style solid body, complete with tremolo, and Bernard had his Maton acoustic cut down to a more stylish semi-acoustic by a luthier in Adelaide and fitted with some electric pickups.

Bernard and I teamed together and bought a second-hand two-channel Goldentone amp and by that time we had also recruited a drummer who had a complete drum kit.

We now had a proper electric band, loud enough to finally get ousted from the Spry rumpus room and the Bradshaws' garage, to migrate to an isolated football-club hall at the back of the Elizabeth garbage tip.

We had also decided that, with the re-formed line-up, we needed a name change.

We became The Innocents. Yes, Bernard's pick—it was biblical!

Chapter 6

Getting ahead
of the game

As 1962 progressed, our musical interests began to assume a significant part of any free time we had. We were regularly attending Bob Horsburgh's dance school on Tuesday and Thursday evenings, which was always a good spot to meet new people, and the Sunday evening youth group at St Stephen's in Elizabeth North sounded like it might be just the place to liven up the quietest night of the week.

The deal at St Stephen's Presbyterian church was that youth group members had to attend the Sunday evening service that finished at 7.30 p.m. Then the curtains would be drawn closed in front of the altar, the chairs pushed back to the sides and a couple of small tables would be set up—one for the electric urn, tea, coffee and biscuits and the other for the gramophone. Everyone would bring the records they wanted to play.

This went on for twelve months or so with word slowly getting around that there was an opportunity to meet up with local friends for a few hours on a Sunday evening, play the latest UK releases fairly loudly, practise the latest dance moves, drink coffee and be relatively unsupervised. Strict parents usually had no problem with their teenagers attending a church youth group on a Sunday evening.

The insistence on church attendance beforehand, over time, was informally softened. And with increasing numbers, no real problems and a door charge for 'late arrivals' proving to be a nice little earner for the local Presbyterians, and seemingly outweighing any religious sensibilities.

———

The Innocents worked hard on learning an initial set list of about twenty songs. The most competent musician, Brenton was the leader of the group. Nevertheless, he was always quite fair in the selection of songs for our playlist and their musical arrangement.

We had developed musically to be a slightly out-there R&B ensemble that played The Animals, Fats Domino and The Pretty Things covers along with our Chuck Berry and Eddie Cochran favourites, finishing with the Big Bopper showstopper 'Chantilly Lace', which was topped off with the tinkling bell of a wind-up telephone that Bernard scrounged during his later stint with the PMG.

Brenton had learned pretty early from Roy Wooding that the guitar, not the saxophone, was rock-and-roll's essential lead instrument. One of his heroes, Duane Eddy, had settled any argument with his country twang and rippling tremolo, which would be heard soon from legendary guitarists such as Jeff Beck and George Harrison. Watching Bernard play guitar throughout his life often gave cause for reflection on Brenton's very capable tuition and generosity of spirit.

The eventual set list for The Innocents reflected many songs and artists that are now recognised as the classics of the era. Songs learned painstakingly over a number of years, played often with the easy familiarity of revisiting an old friend. Songs that Bernard would later use to catalyse and characterise the first iterations of the band that would define his life.

———

Of course, we weren't the only teenagers in Elizabeth with aspirations to start a band. Soon there were literally dozens of nascent groups in the area looking for an audience. Sunday evenings at St Stephen's provided the ideal low-key launching pad and a couple of the growing number of small local skiffle and musical groups were encouraged to contribute their limited playlists in live spots between the records.

Almost immediately attendances ballooned. Where at first there had been just a few teens each week, this grew to a steady stream, a flow and then a flood. What had once been the quietest night of the week suddenly became the most fun. Where previously we had perhaps two or three dozen teenagers dancing to records each Sunday evening, we now had a hundred.

One of the early bands to play at our youth group was The Tornados. Playing lead on a red Guild guitar almost as big as himself was a slight and earnest young man from Manchester, Terry Britten. Terry would later become a hometown hero with local supergroup The Twilights, before eventually becoming an international songwriting superstar, composing songs for people like Tina Turner and Cliff Richard and winning a Grammy in 1985 for 'What's Love Got to Do with It'.

At the time, it was actually The Tornados' drummer's supersized metallic-green flake drum kit that got the attention. With two large kettle drums on either side of the bass drum, a full set of tom toms and a couple of the largest Zildjian cymbals anybody had ever seen, his enthusiastic percussion had the lads talking for a week.

These sorts of acts obviously completely overshadowed any previous perception of what St Stephen's thought a church youth group should be. The moment the chairs were cleared away and the music started, the church elders were powerless to prevent the entry of a horde of exuberant young people who had timed their arrival to the minute the church service finished. The surrounding streets were soon alive with music from the hall, leaving the locals astonished at all the excitement.

It only took a few months for the Presbyterians to realise this worrying popular-music thing was apparently not going to go away any time soon. Attendances had now increased to over two hundred each week and, from their perspective, things were becoming rather uncontrollable. They felt they had to move quickly to decouple from such exceedingly popular entertainment and return their beloved church hall to the restraint and sombreness of a traditional Adelaide Sunday evening.

However, a few of us quickly realised that there was an opportunity to hire the St Stephen's church hall quite independently and run our own musical evenings. So, with Sunday evenings now returning to something quieter, and Saturdays often taken up with trips to the cinema in Adelaide, we settled on Friday night.

The Presbyterians were very pleased to receive the income from a regular weekly booking for their hall, and everyone appeared to be quite happy with the result.

———

By this time Bernard and I had become members of the management committee that ran the dance, which we called 'The Hydaway Club'. We met as a group every month in somebody's house to discuss the club's progress and plan other activities, such as bus outings for beach parties and barbeques. The small profits we made from the dances were invested in a proper PA system, a turntable and two large speaker towers that could be arranged to provide a stereo sound system, a spotlight and a couple of portable light stands with dimmers providing adjustable 'mood lighting'.

It was evident very quickly that what everybody really wanted was a regular live band. With local record releases running months behind the UK scene, there was ample time for enthusiastic local bands to obtain the UK chart favourites from relatives 'back home' and be playing note-perfect renditions well ahead of local release.

There were also other pressing issues to be resolved. The Hydaway Club was running out of room and concerns about security and behaviour were starting to surface. Parishioners and nearby residents had been patient and understanding, but some of our patrons were becoming hard to handle. The committee enjoyed very good relations with the local police—the daughter of the local station chief, Jack Cooke, was even a club member—but we had to be extremely careful. Legally, alcohol was not allowed within 300 yards of a 'dance hall' in mid-1960s South Australia. If the police came checking with closer scrutiny of the car park as well as their regular friendly walk-through of the hall, undoubtedly we'd be in serious strife!

———

Local young people were becoming increasingly demanding as musical consumers. While records played though a good PA system might have cut it in the early days of our dance club, live spots from emerging groups had whetted their appetite for something more.

By early 1964 it was clear that we needed a resident band that was completely on-message and in the vibe. I'd just started an engineering apprenticeship with leading Adelaide employer and BHP subsidiary British Tube Mills. Among its two thousand employees there was a solid representation of part-time musicians from Elizabeth and other northern suburbs. Frank Tarney, an enterprising young draftsman and former apprentice, had formed The Vectormen, an ensemble in the style of Cliff Richard and The Shadows. They were the stand-out Elizabeth group and the resident band at a weekly dance called the Matelot Club in Elizabeth South. Brenton, Bernard and I would make the trek down to the dance on Saturday evening with other friends, catching a taxi or cadging a ride with someone's parent. But it was difficult for Bernard. His domestic responsibilities seemed to be unrelenting.

To travel the four miles to the dance, Brenton and I would often meet at Bernard's house first. Both his parents often worked on Saturdays, but even when his father didn't Bernard was still required to make a meal if his mother was still at work. On one occasion we were waiting on the verandah of the house for the taxi to arrive when Barney opened the front door. 'Bernard,' he said, 'I'd like you to make my evening meal and supper before you leave to go out.'

The embarrassed and crestfallen Bernard turned to us and said, 'I'm sorry, fellas, you will have to go on ahead, I won't be able to make it tonight.' Brenton and I looked at each other and shrugged our shoulders. 'Nah, it's cool . . . We'll tell the taxi something's come up and see if he can come back in half an hour.'

———

From a low stage at the end of a postage-stamp hall, scarcely bigger than a couple of suburban lounge rooms, the musically polished Vectormen—with their red Fender guitars, identical grey suits and black-pencil ties—played to a crowd of a couple of hundred, packed solid to overflowing. The hall was pitch black, lit solely by a white spotlight and the glowing red-light switches on the Fender amps. There was certainly little room for any fancy jive moves.

But while The Vectormen's renditions of The Shadows, Cliff Richard and standards by Elvis, Buddy Holly, Chuck Berry and Little Richard were note perfect, a massive new popular musical maelstrom was approaching from the UK and about to engulf the teenagers of the time.

The Hydaway committee wanted to make the jump to music more forward-looking and relevant. It was a chance to create an identity and a soundtrack to their new lives. Recently arrived homesick young people already identified strongly with the new British sounds that would soon come to dominate the airwaves. These were the sounds we wanted for the Hydaway Club.

I had become friendly with another fellow Tubies apprentice, Colin Byford, who was the frontman with a new group, The Vikings, led by a recent arrival from Scandinavia, guitarist John Wahlstrom. When we learned about their set list, we decided to book them without delay.

The Vikings had got hold of The Hollies' Parlophone debut album *Stay with The Hollies,* which had been just released in the UK and had gone immediately to the top of the UK charts. Months ahead of the album's Australian release, The Vikings had already learned these songs and were aiming to position themselves as a five-piece group using the musical harmonies of The Hollies, as well as new exploding stand-out tunes from other similar UK bands.

The Vikings' first gig at the Hydaway Club was jaw-dropping. The word on the new group had spread like wildfire and the hall was packed in anticipation that this local band would be playing live music that wasn't yet available in Australia.

The group was musically perfect, launching into 'Just One Look', all kitted out exactly as the original artists! Initially nobody danced—they just watched, stunned. Colin Byford—using the stage name 'Col Ford' and with a new spiky haircut gelled up like The Hollies themselves—was well-rehearsed and professional. Their set list included the most recent releases from The Beatles, The Stones and The Who. The Hydaway Club was definitely ahead of the game. Migrant teenagers let loose in a space they had created for themselves with live music played loud—pure fun, zero dramas!

————

As Bernard was to say many years later, 'It's not all hugs and kisses in a band, y'know!' When a group of people are put together in a creative dynamic like a band, superficial differences and even minor exchanges soon surface and quickly become serious.

It was band practice on a Saturday afternoon in 1964. Brenton, Bernard and I were in the rumpus room of the Spry's two-storey home. As the most accomplished musician in the group, Brenton had been helping on bass lines for a new addition to The Innocents playlist. Bernard had been practising the chords for the rhythm component of the song when he disappeared. Nothing had been heard from him for quite a while.

'Where's the Stalk gone?' inquired Brenton, mildly irritated.

'Dunno,' I replied. 'Gone for a leak perhaps.'

'Hardly, he's taken his guitar with him,' said Brenton as he walked out of the room. There was a brief pause. 'Jeez, Bern, you are the vainest person.'

Bernard was standing on the first-floor landing in front of a full-length mirror. The strap on his Maton guitar had been shortened so that the instrument sat very high on his chest.

'I was checking how it looked, and how I could play it,' he exclaimed defensively.

In the 1960s pop heyday, when it became de rigueur to wear guitars as bowties, there was plenty of conjecture and spirited discussion as to the way to go. Bernard was looking for his musical identity. As was our group, The Innocents. Playing music is after all a very personal form of communication, unique to each individual musician, and guitarists particularly reveal themselves not only in how they wear their instruments but also their note choices, the tones they choose and their playing styles.

There were conflicting visions as to what sort of musical identity The Innocents should have. Should we follow the crowd and just play the popular songs of the day? Or should we try to do something different? It was obvious that the quickest route to commercial success was to replicate the current chart hits, but there were already local bands that could do that better than we ever could.

We talked about developing a rock and blues act where direct comparisons would be more difficult and went looking at the formative influences of the new British sounds: Chuck Berry (probably the most influential rock musician ever), Buddy Holly (who with The Crickets had really invented the rock band) and solo guitarist Eddie Cochran (the most under-rated artist of his generation), whose heavy chugging, driving sound was unlike anything heard before. The origins of hard rock, punk and even The Angels' distinctive driving back beat began right there. Cochran and Holly, two of the most enduring artists from the Big Bang of Rock, were certainly for Bernard two of his principal musical influences.

Most of our contemporaries were realistic in their musical aspirations. They had career directions in 'real jobs' mapped out. Playing in a band was fun but becoming outstandingly proficient as a musician and an entertainer was an entirely different proposition. Even harder was getting more than one paying gig a week. The Innocents' appearances were limited to the occasional guest spot at the Hydaway Club and sharing the bill at the Elizabeth West Workingman's Club, where we knew a couple of people on the management committee.

Bernard and I felt in our hearts that even with significant effort it was unlikely we'd ever be outstandingly musical enough, but a different kind of involvement in the popular music industry looked possible. We needed to work from what we knew and leverage that experience. We had the experience of what worked and had a nucleus of connections. How hard could it be?

———

The Hydaway Club desperately needed a larger venue than the St Stephen's hall, and it needed be more centrally located. We would need security, parking and guaranteed tenure, without too many of the commercial conditions and pages of regulations that would come to characterise any booking of the two larger council halls that were finally being constructed.

St Peter's Anglican Mission was the obvious choice of venue, but how would that fit with the Reverend Howell Witt? He had been way ahead of the game when local teenagers emerged as an identifiable social entity, and right at the forefront with progressive ideas, but in the conservative Adelaide Anglican Church hierarchy there were some vocal and persistent critics of his larger-than-life personality and his unconventional views on church matters.

My family were members of the Elizabeth Anglican community and by then I knew Howell very well. When I turned up on the doorstep at the rectory in Elizabeth South with a tall, softly spoken Irish Catholic in tow, he welcomed us in.

Over rectory tea and cupcakes, it was soon resolved that the Mission was available for a permanent booking on Friday evenings, except Easter. Howell agreed that we could use the kitchen and install the drink vending machines we had hired from Coke. We would pay for extra electrical outlets for the band amplifiers and for our special lights.

Most encouraging was that Howell was very pleased to see the new hall used for something that he had tried unsuccessfully to achieve a few years earlier. He was delighted at the multi-denominational 'extended family' that had been created, with members of the local Anglican, Presbyterian and—beaming at Bernard—*Roman Catholic* churches and that we were running the club as a not-for-profit activity in response to community need. On the basis of all this, he was happy to extend a 50 per cent discount on the normal commercial hall-hire charges.

We walked out of the rectory grinning, each clutching one last cupcake. We were well pleased with our 'negotiations' and the real progress for the club.

———

Looking back to 1963 and 1964, it's hard to believe that the whole Beatles musical phenomenon actually happened. When 'Please

Please Me' was released by EMI Parlophone Records as a single in the UK in January 1963, by mid-February it had topped the UK charts. But when the record company was keen to replicate this success in the US, their distributor, Capitol Records, initially resisted releasing Beatles records, supposedly due to pressure from their signed local artists. For example, Murry Wilson, the manager of the Beach Boys (and father of three-fifths of the group), is said to have made personal representations to discourage the marketing of Beatles records in the US. Presumably, similar pressure to protect American artists was applied in Australia, where, astonishingly, the first Beatles records were not available for ten months after their UK release.

That's probably the reason Australian radio DJs initially showed no interest in the latest UK music. When Bernard and I together with recently arrived friend Alan Hale went to see leading Adelaide DJ Bob Francis with a copy of 'Please, Please Me' in June 1963, he listened but immediately dismissed the song. The record was not in any way suitable for the station's audience, he said. 'We cannot play songs like that. It's way too suggestive,' predicting that it would never be a local hit.

Capitol, of course, eventually exercised their US distribution option in November 1963 and the floodgates opened in the US, Canada and Australia. All spare record production capacity world-wide was cranked into action and the first locally released Beatles record, 'I Want to Hold Your Hand', went straight to the top of the Australian charts.

Within six months the Australian music industry was to be turned upside down: the British invasion would dominate the charts and DJs would have to play what their listeners wanted to hear. Even the opinions of Big Bob Francis turned full circle as he led a chorus of prominent locals and Big End of Town businesspeople, including the iconic John Martins department store, pushing for Adelaide to be included in The Beatles' upcoming tour.

Ultimately Adelaide was triumphant, and The Beatles came to town. The build-up to the arrival of the band was electrifying. Tickets went on sale on Monday, 20 April 1964. We arrived straight from school or work on the Friday prior and started queuing in shifts, organised to ensure that we got the best seats to see the hottest music act in the world. After next to no sleep for three nights, we had ours and just a few rows from the front. We were jubilant. All tickets had sold out in a few hours.

The frenzy that had been building in Adelaide for six months hit its peak the day The Beatles arrived, drawing crowds into the streets in numbers not experienced since the Royal Tour of 1954. Almost half the population of the state lined the route from Adelaide Airport to the city on a bright cold winter's day, perhaps more than 300,000 people.

Keen to gain a good vantage point for The Beatles' arrival, Bernard had taken up a possie, perched precariously on a ledge outside the second-floor balcony of the Ambassadors Hotel, almost opposite the official Adelaide Town Hall welcome. His tall lanky figure braced against a nearby awning with his waving arms outstretched, he teetered over a forty-foot drop to the street below. This drew the attention not only of two members of The Beatles but also of the publican, who came rushing to the window demanding that he return immediately inside to the hotel function room.

The concerts that evening and the following day were far different to the elaborately themed, costumed and magically lit sound-filled extravaganzas we expect from international artists today; truly memorable in their own way even though they presented no differently from what was being put on every week at the Hydaway and

Matelot clubs at Elizabeth. Four guys with their musical instruments and amplifiers on a stage.

We were hushed for the band we had all been waiting for. Ladies and Gentlemen . . . the biggest performing act in the world . . . The Beatles! The hall exploded into a euphoric tumult of ear-splitting screams—six months of pent-up excitement released in an instant!

The Beatles performed the same ten songs at all their Australian shows, and within half an hour it was over. When the lights came up, the audience looked at one another as if they'd been through some sort of religious transformation.

The concert of the century? Yeah, maybe. Unforgettable? Certainly!

———

By mid-1964 Bernard's father Barney had finally managed to secure a stable job as a warder at the Yatala Prison, which allowed the family to rethink what was plainly an unsatisfactory situation for their eldest son.

At the beginning of 1964, having completed Fourth Form, Bernard was pressured to leave St Paul's so he could contribute financially to the family. He took up a PMG linesman cadetship. This career choice was strongly endorsed by his school after a PMG careers adviser made a convincing presentation, promoting the cadetships as a pathway to an interesting and rewarding career in the exciting new electronics sector.

To Bernard, given that he was keen to know more about electronics, amplifiers and recording technologies, it certainly had sounded interesting, but the reality was quite different. He enjoyed climbing telephone poles and working at heights, but most of this job seemed to involve cleaning years of dirt and grime from an antiquated communication network. Within months it was recognised that he was totally unsuited to such work.

Bernard was intelligent and certainly capable of taking on more than just any job to help support his family, so it was decided he would go back and finish high school, hopefully to matriculate so he could then consider better-paid career options.

Resigning from the PMG, he commenced a home study program to help him transition back to school the following year. But he still felt pressured to contribute financially to his family.

At this time I had a part-time position in Elizabeth West, serving petrol at the Mobil West Service Station on Peachy Road, a now infamous drag through the neediest suburbs in Adelaide, and managed to get Bernard a job working with me for a few months.

In 1964 Elizabeth West was still under construction and an epic muddy quagmire for months on end. An enterprising local farmer kept a tractor behind the servo so it could be used to extract bogged cars, axle deep in mud, from local streets and driveways. The housing mix in Elizabeth was changing, too. Instead of predominately homes for purchase, over 75 per cent of houses in these later built suburbs were Housing Trust build to rents. Deliberately hidden back behind attractive houses for purchase on the main road were the future ghettos of conspicuous inequality; street upon street of identical semi-detached basic rental accommodation for the desperate last gasps of what had become by then a cynical immigration program offering vain and nebulous hope to some of the UK's poorest and most socially disadvantaged people. It was also a dumping ground for Adelaide's welfare recipients and desperate broken families. Just a couple of hundred yards away from where Bernard and I were serving petrol, checking tyres and cleaning windscreens, seven-year-old Jimmy Barnes was living in Heytesbury Road.

The proprietor of the servo, Bert Wood, had something of a selfless streak and was helpfully responsive to customers he knew were genuinely doing it hard. He never made a fuss but would quietly come up to me while I was filling oil bottles or making cups of tea and say, 'I've got that battler with the tribe of kids and the noisy old banger that guzzles oil coming in tomorrow. They are doing it tough, but that muffler will get him booked. Can you put it on the hoist when he comes in and see if you can put a patch on it? I've told him it will be alright!' Elizabeth people were like that. Migrant teachers at the Elizabeth West Primary School ran after-school literacy and numeracy classes in their own time, to help young mums who had fallen through the cracks of South Australia's archaic under-resourced education system.

Bernard eventually matriculated and became a teacher after two years at teachers' college. He later attended Flinders University after returning from national service. But this only reinforced his awareness of the significant differences between the real struggle and demands of his formative life in Elizabeth and that of his mates, who came from Adelaide's 'better' suburbs. Little wonder that he frequently had to bite his tongue!

It was not surprising that, like tens of thousands of others, Bernard welcomed the opportunity to leave the economically backward state to escape a systemically flawed labour market with no jobs and few opportunities. In later years he was to rail against the uncompromising attitudes that were so evident in a number of the principal relationships within the band as typical of the 'Adelaide landed gentry', a divide and mindset exemplified by what he saw as an outdated and ridiculous sense of superiority and lifetime entitlement.

However, to his neighbourhood mates from the early Elizabeth days, especially his close cadre of old school friends, fellow rock-and-roll soldiers, local heroes, fans and followers he remained a friend for life. For those who had also managed to 'escape' from South Australia, he was always the animated fellow-conspirator.

By 1998, 'A great place to leave' was for Bernard certainly something of a reflective understatement.

Chapter 7

Apprentice impresarios

The Hydaway Club's move to St Peter's Mission provided the opportunity to improve the format for Friday evenings. The resident band, The Vikings, would do the opening and closing sets, and then either three new groups would be showcased, doing a couple of songs each during an extended intermission, or a more experienced outfit would fill the break.

During the five years that the Hydaway Club was at St Stephen's hall and at the Mission, the committee booked just about every local band and vocalist that was to emerge in this period—well over fifty. Every band and artist was paid, even those in the showcase who performed two or three songs. For many it was their first gig, and a number would go on to be significant on the national scene. Some of the individual musicians and vocalists that appeared on the Mission's stage went on to become local and international stars: Terry Britten, Jim Keays, John Perry, Darryl Cotton, Trevor Spencer, Beeb Birtles, Kevin Peek and Alan Tarney.

It was a formula that seemed to work; attendance numbers continued to grow. So it wasn't long before Adelaide's radio DJs were making regular trips north to see what all the noise was about. They were friendly and personable, and it wasn't long before a deal was worked out whereby the club would drop a couple of the DJs a few dollars to introduce the bands appearing in the showcase guest spot and the DJs would then say a few words on air during the following week about the club and the bands.

Although this resulted in more of Adelaide's with-it teens making the trip out to Elizabeth, we were well aware that it was only the absence of suitable venues and connection to local bands that kept the city's established promoters and booking agents from muscling in on the action.

Everything was going along famously until the Octagon, the first council-owned theatre, opened in Elizabeth Way in August 1965, barely a few hundred yards from St Peter's Mission. The Octagon was a spacious venue, with a proper curtained stage and a large dance floor.

We were not surprised to hear speculation that the club was moving to the recently completed venue, but we were absolutely astounded to open the local paper in late 1965 and read: 'Hydaway Club to Move to new Octagon Theatre'.

We charged over to the local newspaper office to be shocked by the news that, yes, a group of DJs from an Adelaide radio station had 'taken over' the Hydaway Club and would be moving it to the new venue. The council quickly confirmed the Hydaway Club had booked the Octagon for a regular booking, commencing in a couple of weeks.

The penny dropped. We had never registered the Hydaway Club as a business name. We were in our early teens when we started it; we had never expected it to be more than a regular not-for-profit event that ploughed everything back into better shows for the members with an occasional donation to the Salvos. The radio personalities we had welcomed into the club had smiled to our faces and been paid for their night of deejaying but had then gone out and hijacked our name. Welcome to the business ethics of the Adelaide Establishment, fellas!

Angry and fired up, we returned to the newspaper office. The reporter who had written the original story was sympathetic and a story was put together headlined: 'Adelaide Radio DJs Involved in Hydaway Club Name Scam'.

'It's not a good look for the radio station,' the editor said. 'Whether the DJs think they can do it or not is immaterial. I'll ring the station for a comment.'

Twenty minutes later he was back. 'Well, the shit has hit the fan down there in Adelaide radioland. They've asked me to hold the story until they come back with a solution.'

Later that evening we received an apology for the 'misunderstanding', and we were asked to contact a firm of local solicitors who would help us, at no cost, through the process of nominating public officers to allow the return of our now registered club name.

However, we did realise that things would change with the opening of Octagon and the inevitable arrival of more experienced promoters.

———

From the moment Bernard enrolled at Elizabeth High School in early February 1965, he knew that returning to school to complete his secondary education was the right move. The difference between his previous school, St Paul's, and Elizabeth High was like night and day.

For a start the 600-student Elizabeth High was a friendly place; it was also co-educational and Bernard immediately made a mental note of the name of the attractive young girl in the maroon gingham uniform who was given the job of showing him and other newbies around. Elizabeth High drew its students mainly from the earliest established suburbs of Elizabeth, whose parents had been among the first to purchase homes and to settle in the town. Generally, these were middle-class people with aspirations for themselves and for their children. IQ testing by the South Australian Education Department for streaming purposes was to confirm these children as the brightest in the state. Invariably they had commenced their secondary schooling at Salisbury, Gawler or in city schools, but the eventual opening of Elizabeth High finally brought them together in their very own school, even if poor planning meant that large classes were the norm and that the large shelter shed did double duty every day as an impromptu classroom.

The large grassy sports fields were kept green by constant watering and helped break down barriers and establish friendships. Bernard's sporting prowess immediately placed him in the top Aussie Rules football team; he also became the state schoolboy high-jump champion. Most of the school's teachers, like their pupils, were migrants. They were well educated and trained, meaning that there were few issues with discipline.

Bernard's home life also became much easier without his two-hour return commute each day to the PMG in the city. He could concentrate on his school assignments and keep an eye on his siblings. Both Barney and Kitty had settled into a regular employment routine and Barney had even managed to buy a reliable small Volkswagen.

———

The Australia-wide excitement generated by The Beatles' visit in 1964 was quickly followed by a globetrotting cavalcade of UK musical artists. The Rolling Stones, Kinks, The Who, The Hollies, The Searchers and The Animals were among a flood of headline acts who toured every Australian state capital over the next couple of years to rapturous receptions from thousands of fans. That enthusiasm was to generate the same sort of 'I can do that too' response among local teens as had the barnstorming concert tours by US artists such as the Everly Brothers, Chuck Berry and Buddy Holly in Britain during the 1950s and early 1960s.

Adelaide at this time had a critical mass of keen, largely migrant musicians, but working in Adelaide alone was unsustainable. There was simply insufficient work to support anything more than a few good bands, which could hope to get one or two evenings and maybe a Saturday afternoon gig a week. Any income was further diminished by the cost of managers, booking agents, equipment transport, set-up and, if travel to country towns was involved, accommodation costs.

Melbourne, on the other hand, offered real opportunities. It had three times Adelaide's population and an established vibrant and sophisticated cultural scene that was eventually to support around a hundred regular venues, with the half dozen or so largest offering a rotation of several bands across an evening's entertainment. A group that had a solid following could work almost every night of the week.

No sooner had The Beatles left Australia than the idea of a 'National Battle of the Sounds' competition took hold. Originally launched by the Sydney mass-market magazine *Everybody's*, the competition was ultimately sponsored by the chocolate confectioner Hoadley's and became known as 'Hoadley's Battle of the Sounds', with Melbourne-based *Go-Set* involved on the magazine

side. Radio stations all over Australia organised heats in capital
cities and country towns; the semi-finals and the grand final were
held in either Melbourne or Sydney. The valuable first prize for the
winning band was return passage by boat to England on the Sitmar
Line, plus two booked concerts in London and prize money.

Preparation for the competition was intense. During the run-up
to the heats, every available garage, church hall and shed in the
country became a rehearsal venue. It was like preparing for a rock
Olympics.

———

Bernard and I had by then teamed with Alan Hale in a fledgling
band management enterprise called Wedgewood Blues and we
were very keen for our bands to enter the comp. We had been
involved in the development of many bands through auditioning
and booking them for the Hydaway Club and associated promotions.
Through visits to other local clubs and attending the concerts of
visiting overseas artists, we had become experienced in evaluating,
rating and comparing acts. We were avid readers of the UK music
magazines and had developed an encyclopaedic knowledge of bands,
individual musicians, their musical influences and careers.

We took it in turns to write a weekly music column on the
Elizabeth scene for the local paper. Alan had also negotiated the use
of North Adelaide's Gamba recording studio. The studio's owner,
Derek Jolly, an ex-grand prix racing driver for Lotus and colourful
Adelaide bon vivant, allowed local hopefuls to book directly with us
to record demo discs. These would be used to support live appearances on an Adelaide TV teen show that went to air on Saturday
mornings.

Then a breakthrough: one of our bands, The Chosen Few from nearby Tanunda in the Barossa Valley, who had performed at the Hydaway Club, convincingly won the 1966 South Australian finals of the Battle of the Sounds, pitted against very capable competition including the up-and-coming Masters Apprentices.

Unusually for the time, they were also capable songwriters. As Bernard was later to observe, 'Playing covers of the Top 40 music of the time, although a key to some sort of success, was an admission that you couldn't do any better.'

Bernard, Alan and I drove to Melbourne for the weekend of the national finals. All the bands that performed in the final round of the competition deserved their place on the stage. They were the distilled winners from over five hundred bands across Australia.

That the former Adelaide band The Twilights, which had moved to Melbourne the previous year and had won the Victorian final, would win the national competition was pretty much an accepted certainty. They were the leading Melbourne band, and their very enthusiastic and vocal following would cheer them on to be popular winners. Band members Terry Britten and Glenn Shorrock would each go on in later years to achieve international success.

We had also scored invites to a ritzy cocktail party held in the basement reception room of a city hotel. We chatted to the other bands, their management and music industry people as well as the owners of Melbourne's top teen venues, all of them keen to offer us hospitality. Later that evening we managed to visit two of these, The Thumpin' Tum and Berties. Behind the Tum's two-storey backstreet bluestone exterior were red velvet curtains, tiffany lampshades and a ceiling of floating upside-down umbrellas. Berties offered a top-hatted doorman in a velvet-and-lace suit and an opulent Edwardian-styled interior. Here was Melbourne bohemia at its extravagant best, but due to the archaic licensing regulations of the time none of Melbourne's dance clubs were allowed to sell alcohol. It was all about live music, the bands and the vibe, and people came in droves. Oh, but there was plenty of Mary Jane!

These clubs set the gold standard. Nothing Adelaide offered came remotely near what Melbourne nightlife had.

————

Six months or so later, the Anglican Church called time on the Hydaway Club's long-term Friday night booking at St Peter's Mission. With the Reverend Howell Witt's elevation to Bishop of Western Australia, there was to be a new direction for their community outreach services and the hall was required for a regular Friday night 'Bargain Market'.

In a way this development wasn't too awkward. There was a feeling among those who remained from the small group of friends who had kicked off what was to become the Hydaway Club in 1961 that the venture had run its course and it was time to be involved with other things. The Elizabeth of 1966 was a very different place to what it had been five years earlier, and we were different people too—we were close to twenty and those lads whose numbers were drawn in the upcoming 'birthday ballot' would have to endure two years of conscription in the Australian Army.

There had also been increased competition since the opening of the Saturday evening 'Dance Scene 66' at the Octagon Theatre and another popular dance at the Salisbury Youth Centre. The promoters of the dance at the Octagon were aligned with an Adelaide radio station, which meant saturation advertising support that we obviously couldn't match.

Additionally, we were becoming worn down by the argy-bargy with a number of dance promoters, particularly those involved with Adelaide's traditional venues, and from the demands of a fast-emerging network of newly minted booking agents all anxious to secure the largest share of what had quickly become a lucrative new market. As well, our ex-UK Paras security guy, Colin Burt, wanted more money to engage some additional muscle. He was emphatic that someone was behind an orchestrated move for rough elements from Adelaide to cause problems for us, with the objective of making local youngsters wary of attending our dances. The larger dance clubs had become major cash businesses and, later in 1967, at least three popular venues—the 123 Club, Sergeant Peppers Disco and the Beat Basement—all suffered mysterious after-hours fires that forced them to close.

The consensus was that we should wind things up rather than try to move the club to another venue. The club had been a big part of our lives growing up and we were sad that its long involvement in the local musical entertainment and social scene had come to an end.

———

Bernard and I had not lost interest altogether in running dances or clubs, but we knew we would need to organise the offering in a different way so it would be difficult for competitors to copy us.

We had been avid followers of the second wave of UK music, which had gradually morphed into a unique British blues sound from regional cities: The Animals from Newcastle, Them from Belfast and the Spencer Davis Group and the Moody Blues from Birmingham. There was also the influence of the Mods, who took elements of R&B, soul and jazz. Their poster boys were undoubtedly The Who, with their slogan of 'Maximum R&B' and their RAF roundel logo that had come to symbolise the Mod revival that brought together garage rock, classic R&B and contemporary rock music.

Essential reading in those days were the UK music magazines. Editions of *New Musical Express* (*NME*) and *Melody Maker*, which were sent by UK friends and relations, becoming progressively more tattered and torn as they were passed around.

One of the *NME* reviews described a specialist English R&B club called The Magnet, an illustrious and iconic place in Liverpool's musical history. It consisted of two venues under the same roof: a street-level bar called the Rumblin' Tum and the basement Sink Club. This was one of that city's first dedicated R&B music venues and entry to it was made by hanging a sink plug around your neck on a short length of chain that carried your membership number. We thought that was cool!

Was Elizabeth—or even Adelaide—ready for something like that? How could we do it? What would it cost to start off? The more we thought about the idea of an R&B/Mod-themed club the more we liked it. But could we attract sufficient people on a regular basis to make it pay?

Maybe we didn't even need a permanent location or a regular event, but we thought we needed something more than a shed. We knew our patrons had become more discerning. The more we provided the more they wanted: bands, go-go girls, atmosphere, ambience, a sound-and-light show, coffee and toasted sandwiches.

R&B bands we could certainly do, but how could we create a temporary, architecturally interesting atmosphere? Something that could be put up and taken down in a few hours, that could be lit with stage and black lights to create shadows, fluorescent effects and contrast for spotlights that followed the onstage artists.

We looked at a council hall in Elizabeth East. It was a cheaply built, soulless, narrow space as long as a train, with exposed steel trusses supporting the roof and hopper windows up high along each side. It had poor acoustics and an echo that would bounce endlessly around the walls. Mainly because of this, it was available at a relatively low cost. A couple of hundred teens would improve the acoustics, but the place needed atmosphere.

'Maybe we could hang something from the ceiling, like at the Tum,' suggested Bernard. We looked at using some old parachutes from an army surplus shop in Adelaide but that was too expensive and would be a fire hazard. They'd also be time-consuming to hang every week.

What about some lightweight hanging panels? We decided we needed forty of them, painted in iridescent blue, purple, yellow and silver, with flashes of white and illuminated by black lights that would highlight white objects and fluorescent materials to achieve a vibrant glow-in-the-dark effect. They would hang around the stage at varying heights to create a cave-like effect.

Another idea was to have a couple of round plinths and on them net-covered enclosures for go-go dancers; they would be lit from the inside, like exotic lanterns. It was all coming together. The new venue would be named The Sink. We liked the idea of small sink plugs on chains as the membership token; we would stamp out cards with membership details that could be pressed inside the bottom of the plug.

To get the word around we would need high-impact posters to put up around Elizabeth and nearby Salisbury. A printer said he could replicate a stunning black-and-white poster for London's legendary Marquee Club featuring Pete Townsend from The Who with his windmilling arm and the slogan 'Maximum R&B'. Yes, Maximum rhythm and blues! But we would need to find someone tall with a guitar to be photographed in the pose.

'Me!' said Bernard emphatically. He was a big fan of Townsend, not only as a flamboyant guitarist and prolific songwriter but for his stage presence, which combined theatre and opera. A contradictory personality, articulate and literate, Townsend was definitely the original Punk.

For the shoot, Bernard ducked up the street to an art supply shop and returned with a pack of plasticine. Mixing the pink and white sticks, he fashioned a flesh-coloured addition to his own nose as a salute to Pete's rather prominent proboscis.

We had pretty well decided that we were going to have a go. How hard could it be? We would need enough money to fund the set-up and to see us through for at least a couple of weeks. Alan had recently been retrenched from his job and was working part-time at a booking agency. He obviously didn't have any cash, so Bernard and I agreed to accept his IOU.

Council was only prepared to offer a week-to-week arrangement, and we were required to book and pay two weeks in advance. We agreed to launch the club on Saturday, 11 June 1966 as a 'preview' and then revert to what we hoped would be a regular Friday evening arrangement.

Bernard and I took a half day off from the servo for the first night, borrowed an old FJ ute and hired a trailer. We picked up Alan and loaded the forty hanging ceiling screens we'd built, lights, a couple of step ladders, the stage modules and stands for the go-go girls. Rather surprisingly, the ceiling screens went up pretty easily. The stage modules and stands for the dancers were pushed into position. The PA and lights were hooked up. The bands set up. Posters were tacked onto sandwich boards by the door, and a small table and chair were positioned by the entrance for us to collect money. We also had boxes of the sink-plug membership tokens on their lengths of chain. The caterers even had a real espresso machine.

Within an hour, as dusk settled, the audience started to arrive. Peeking through the open door, they were astonished by what they could see of our makeover to the dreary council hall. We were no longer anxious about getting a good roll-up.

Last to arrive were the go-go dancers, giggling with excitement. Dolly birds with big hair and mini skirts. We were good to go.

Showtime!

Chapter 8

The wings of change

The Saturday night preview for The Sink had gone off pretty well—a good crowd of around 350, mostly faces from the Hydaway Club, but a few who had made the trip over from further afield. The fit-out had drawn a lot of attention; it definitely had atmosphere. A couple of known troublemakers had been turned away at the door and there had been no incidents inside the hall. The bands had been great, the go-go girls a hit. Everybody had fun, and the coffee and toasted sandwiches had gone down a treat. We had gone home quite pleased with the outcome and very optimistic for the future of our new venture.

When we arrived early on the Sunday morning to clean the hall, we were very surprised to see a police car and two council vehicles outside. There had been a spate of incidents in the surrounding area overnight. The nearest public telephone had been vandalised. A brick had been thrown through the glass front door of the hall. Thieves had broken into shops across the road through the roof, apparently under cover of the music, and stolen cigarettes. Beer bottles had been strewn nearby. And shock horror . . . a pair of female knickers and a car rug had been found under some bushes!

Complaints about excessive noise and rowdy behaviour had also been received from two residents living over 200 yards from the hall. And the council hadn't approved of the hanging screens; despite each being suspended on four separate wires, they claimed they might fall down and injure someone. The black lights could catch fire.

We had walked into a shitstorm despite police logs of their drive-bys and walk-throughs during the night indicating that there were no issues—the club was 'well run by experienced operators'. The council officers boarded up the front door and left us to clean up. We were asked to drop by the council office the following Monday 'to discuss further bookings'.

It did not end well. The Sink Club was not an appropriate regular booking for their hall, explained a rather snooty booking clerk. We would be allowed one further booking, because it had already been paid for and promoted. The screens around the stage and the go-go girls could stay, but they weren't allowed to hang over the large dance area.

It was a valuable experience: all our focus had been on setting up the club and not enough thought given to how we'd manage events away from the supportive environment of the nearby police station that we had enjoyed at the Mission.

———

Bernard matriculated from Elizabeth High at the end of 1965 and enrolled in a two-year teaching diploma course at Wattle Park Teachers College. This provided a small weekly allowance, which he supplemented by busking around Adelaide, at coffee lounges for coffee and cakes and outside early opening bakeries for fresh rolls and buns. He even passed a hat around at the legendary Cowley's Pie Cart outside Adelaide's Post Office as customers lined up for a 'pie floater'—a meat pie in a bowl surrounded by a generous serving of thick green pea soup.

With his guitar and by now polished repertoire of songs he quickly became popular, enjoying an almost instantaneous entrée to parties, impromptu jams and events across the college campus.

As we neared the end of 1966, Bernard and I would spend evenings at Alan Hale's house discussing ways that we might take forward our interest in band management. Alan was still chasing permanent work, but with his car off the road he was finding it hard. Late in November he asked me if I could help him with his part-time job at the booking agency by picking up an artist and taking her to and from a couple of gigs.

That artist turned out to be Denise Drysdale who, at eighteen years of age, was already a popular TV star and seasoned variety enter-tainer with a couple of songs on the hit parade. She was a bubbly, friendly personality and a very talented young woman. Her backing group at one of the gigs was Down the Line, four enthusiastic young musicians from Christies Beach south of Adelaide.

We were always interested in new bands, and Bernard and I would frequently hop in the car and check out venues around town. We decided to check out the Down the Line guys at a dance they were playing at Noarlunga. We listened for a while and left a note asking them to give us a call. A few days later Darryl Cotton rang me at home. We agreed to meet the following Saturday.

On the drive down that day, Bernard and I talked. We wanted to discover a Mod-themed band that would cover songs by artists like The Who, The Kinks and The Small Faces. Such songs were strongly represented in Down the Line's set list, but the band's name hardly provided enough connection and affirmation to fans of this fast-growing rock sub-culture. We discussed the fact that The Who had briefly changed their name to The High Numbers before becoming famous. Among the songs they recorded under this name was 'Zoot Suit', a nod to the fashionable retro clothing favoured by Mods. While to most teens the word 'zoot' would be unlikely to mean anything, for a Mod fashionista, the word was a dog whistle, a secret sign to other diehard followers.

Darryl's folks lived on a headland overlooking the sea. As we sat out on their wooden deck drinking Cokes on that warm summer afternoon, we told the guys about our success with Y4 and The Chosen Few and made the case that, given the future of these bands would be increasingly centred on the Melbourne scene, there would be greater opportunities for newer bands to fill their places in Adelaide. We were therefore prepared to offer them a management contract, but we would encourage them to change their name.

'Y'know, you should change your name to something short and punchy, like Zoot,' Bernard suggested.

The Down the Line guys seemed rather underwhelmed that we wanted to change their name, and only showed polite interested in the idea.

'You mean Zoot as in zoot suit?' Darryl asked.

'That's right,' said Bernard.

'Ahh,' replied Darryl.

We left them to consider our proposal, but in the end outside events intervened and took us all off in different directions. Bernard and I were, however, somewhat amused to learn sometime later that the band had subsequently changed their name to Zoot and, of course, went on to make a significant Mod-style impact on the national scene.

––––

Late on Friday evenings, and on Saturday afternoons, Bernard, Alan and I would frequently record bands at the Gamba Studio, which, with a wine shop and Decca's restaurant, sat on Melbourne Street in North Adelaide. This cosmopolitan locale was ahead of its time: nearby were several other restaurants, art galleries, upmarket shops and Derek Jolly's Lotus showroom. His sporty white Lotus Elite or black Ferrari sedan almost always sat parked in the driveway. Just being there was an exhilarating and often entertaining experience.

Decca's restaurant was one of Adelaide's top eateries and employed a somewhat excitable chef of Hungarian extraction. He had gained notoriety for a late-night penchant of chasing the waitresses around the adjacent car park and all the while firing a large ancient pistol into the air. There is at least one early recording of an Adelaide band where, over Bernard's attempts to sing back-up, plaintive shrieks and pistol shots can be heard.

But despite the seeming glamour and perennial shenanigans, we were learning from our increased exposure to Adelaide's promoters and booking agents that everything to do with the city's musical entertainment scene was anything but ethical. Con men, DJ wannabes, thugs and wide boys all looking to turn a dollar, with many of the scams and shady deals attached to these new entertainment opportunities concocted in the leafy green suburbs favoured by Adelaide's elite. Trying to collect overdue money from venue owners and promoters became hazardous and dangerous.

Slowly Bernard and I moved on from our involvement in the Adelaide music scene. We spent a few months supporting our bands in their attempts to break into the Melbourne market, but on a part-time basis it was arduous and invariably conflicted with Bernard's obligations at college and at home and my regular employment. And Alan had been sussing out opportunities in Adelaide's club scene and would shortly start the Beat Basement at the bottom end of Rundle Street.

Bernard also knew by then that he had been called up for National Service and was increasingly making the most of the Adelaide social scene with his friends from teachers' college in the limited time before he had to leave. And it was on a Saturday night trawl through Adelaide's club scene that he was to meet his future wife, Dzintra Karklins, whom he proudly described as 'the luscious, beautiful, dark-haired, green-eyed Latvian girl' of his dreams.

We had both reached an important way point in our careers. The previous years had been a lot of fun; we had learned a lot and had undergone some remarkable character-building experiences. We were heading in new directions, but we would stay in touch and remain friends for the rest of our lives.

———

For young men growing up in the 1960s, the decision by the Menzies government to introduce conscription through a limited ballot of twenty-year-old males prompted an immediate uprising of dissent, protest and civil unrest that was to polarise a generation. With birthdates just a month apart, Bernard and I registered for the same conscription birthday lottery. If the marble with your birthday on it was drawn, the prize was a two-year stint in the Australian Army and the almost certainty of a tour of duty in Vietnam.

Bernard was pretty sure 'his marble had come up' when he arrived home from teachers' college to find his mother about to leave for her night shift at the hospital. Unable to contain herself and fearfully anxious to learn the contents of the official-looking letter addressed to her son, she had torn open the envelope and burst into tears at the news. Bernard put his arms around his mother, reassuring her that, while he would have to go into the army, his moral convictions would not allow him to kill anybody. He fully intended to seek a transfer to a non-combatant role.

Bernard was allowed to defer entry to the army until the completion of his teaching course. So it was just a couple of weeks after his 21st birthday in 1968 that saw him at the gates of Adelaide's Keswick Barracks joining the army bus to the airport and a flight to Melbourne, where another bus would take the conscripts north to Puckapunyal and the Recruit Training Battalion.

It was quite a pleasant journey and he enjoyed meeting his fellow recruits, who were all as anxious as him about what would happen in the next few hours and coming weeks.

However, the moment the bus passed the guard house at the camp perimeter and came to a halt at the edge of the parade ground their worst fears were realised. The abrasive and abusive process of 'resocialisation'—where regular army staff were charged with making soldiers out of the new arrivals—began.

Bernard had his hair cut short in readiness, but it was not short enough to avoid the all-over 'induction buzz cut' from a stern-faced army barber. His father had advised him, from his own long experience as a sergeant major, that the one thing you didn't want to do on your first day in the army was to stand out. Unfortunately, Bernard's towering height made this virtually impossible. He had the sinking feeling that he had returned to his early school days at St Paul's and the tender mercies of the Christian Brothers.

Bernard knew from having grown up as an army 'brat' that recruit training was going to be tough as the army set out to sever the connections and behaviours of his previous life, but he was not really prepared for the physical and psychological intensity of the following few weeks. Most of the non-commissioned officers training the new recruits employed the mantra 'You are in the army now, Recruit' to justify mindless bastardry that was even worse than the Christian Brothers had inflicted at school. It looked like it was going to be a very long two years.

Recruits were taught to be aggressive, to respond automatically, to be neat and tidy, to march and drill endlessly and to clean and polish their kit till it gleamed and shone like the sun. They learned how to fire rifles and machine guns, use rocket launchers, throw grenades, conduct ambush formations, undertake contact drills, use hand signals and devise assault tactics. They were brought to peak fitness through physical training and conditioning, through running and route marches carrying full packs and through clambering over obstacle courses.

Unfortunately, Bernard on occasion hardly helped himself. He infuriated his trainers by too frequently demonstrating the same accident-prone, daffy clumsiness around things mechanical that was to plague his whole life.

On one training exercise the safety catch on his semi-automatic rifle jammed. He called out to his platoon leader, 'Sir! My catch has jammed!' while pointing his rifle directly at him. 'Point the gun down, Neeson, towards the ground,' the officer calmly explained before screaming in his ear, 'You idiot! Never ever point a gun at any of us if the catch is jammed!'

It soon happened again with the same platoon leader. After the training session was over and it was time to get on the truck for the 30-kilometre drive back to camp, the officer in charge said, 'Not you, Neeson. You can walk.' He was left to find his own way back to camp on foot—returning just before dawn the following day.

Initially Bernard showed skill at target shooting on the rifle range, but he quickly realised if he kept that up he would end up being selected for special training as a sniper—hardly the best move for someone who didn't want to have to kill anybody. He stopped trying so hard to hit the targets.

When asked what the hell was wrong with him, why was he slacking off and what had happened to his aim, 'Don't know, Sir,' he would reply.

Following basic training, recruits were assessed, promoted to the rank of private and assigned to a variety of corps, but mostly to the rifle companies in infantry battalions. Bernard had made it as clear as he could to the army that he did not mind where his placement was as long as it was in a non-combatant role. He provided letters from his Catholic Monsignor and the Coadjutor Archbishop of Adelaide attesting to his religious beliefs and moral convictions. None of this appeared to aid his cause, and he was assigned to a rifle company in 3TB, the 3rd Training Battalion at Singleton, New South Wales and scheduled for service in Vietnam. This was another 90 days of training to equip Bernard with the specialist skills he would need for deployment to the war zone. After that he would be assigned to the battalion he'd serve with in Vietnam.

Fortunately for Bernard, while he was learning to rappel out of helicopters hovering 10 metres off the ground—carrying a full pack, his rifle, a heavy field radio and bandoliers of ammunition for his squad's M60 machine gun—a top-secret project was being put together in Canberra.

The Australian Army was very quietly beginning the planning to send another taskforce overseas. This time it was to Papua New Guinea and for a very different purpose, using as its principal weapons blackboards, chalk and the professional services of over three hundred Australian schoolteachers who had been called up for national service. The plan was to raise the educational level of the troops of the 2500-strong Pacific Islands Regiment (PIR), in what turned out to be critical years leading to Papua New Guinea's independence. Army Education Director at the time Brigadier Ernest Gould declared that the intensive education program was 'without parallel in military history'.

For Bernard, this development came like a bolt out of the blue. One day, about halfway through his training at Singleton, his commanding officer called him into his office. Bernard initially feared he was facing exposure for his forbidden acquisition of a spare pair of highly polished boots, an immaculate hat and a full set of shining badges. He kept these on standby to avoid any penalties, including loss of leave and privileges, that might arise if he had to unexpectedly face an impromptu parade or kit inspection.

Bernard's commanding officer was sitting behind his desk. 'At ease, soldier!' he said, looking up from some papers. 'You are going to Sydney for an interview. I do not know what it's about, but here are your orders and tickets. You are on the bus in the morning. All clear? Dismissed!'

The orders contained a sealed letter that he was to deliver to the Army Education Centre, Chowder Bay, Mosman in Sydney. It wasn't until he got to the picturesque harbourside address that he learned what the interview was about.

In August 1968 Bernard was posted to Sydney to undergo pre-embarkation training and medical checks at the Army Education Centre. He would be going to Papua New Guinea with the Royal Australian Army Educational Corps with 25 other conscripted teachers from around Australia. A couple of month later, with the new rank of sergeant, 'Chalkie' Neeson was in front of a class of

PIR soldiers at the Goldie River Training Depot, teaching English, social studies, mathematics, science and civics.

He later recalled, 'How can one forget the class chants, learned by rote! "Democracy is government *of* the people, *for* the people and *by* the people."' Chalkies in Papua New Guinea also joined armed patrols to the Highlands, supporting investigations into tribal punishment spearings and pay-back killings.

It wasn't all work, though. The army participated vigorously in the Port Moresby sporting community and the super-fit Bernard's prowess in the high jump quickly earned him a place in the regimental team that entered the 1969 South Pacific Games. Bernard received the acclaim of his regiment by winning the gold medal in the event.

But the twelve-month posting went slowly at times. Accommodation at the base was very basic and the huts, constructed from asbestos sheeting, were frequently overrun by plagues of enormous hair-covered bird-eating tree spiders, some as large as dinner plates. He would amuse himself by encouraging the spiders to jump to catch small pieces of meat suspended from a long stick. Bernard lamented his forced separation from girlfriend Dzintra, the girl he had met at Adelaide's Twenty Plus Club. She was off backpacking around Europe, and her letters made him envious of the freedom being enjoyed by most of his friends.

With a shortage of single female company in the close-knit army base community, he began thinking about his partner options for the upcoming regimental dance. The base commander had a very pretty daughter, but the word was that any social contact with her was completely off limits for soldiers on the base. Bernard's athletic efforts, however, brought much favourable attention to his regiment; he had even met and chatted to the girl briefly when she had visited the games with her father. Now the army wanted photos of him and the base commander for the defence forces' magazine.

Not one to be the slightest bit intimidated, Bernard was encouraged by the commander's favourable disposition towards him at the photo shoot. He took the opportunity to enquire if he might invite the officer's daughter to the upcoming dance.

The commander stared at Bernard for a long time and then said: 'Well, soldier, that's a matter for discussion at a level way above my pay grade. I'm going to have to get back to you.'

Several days later Bernard received a message to attend a meeting with the commander at base HQ. It was all very formal. He was marched in by the aide-de-camp. Salute. Hats off! Stand easy!

'Well, Sergeant Neeson, I have looked into your proposition regarding the person concerned and I'm pleased to advise that we would like to extend an invitation to you to join our table at the regimental dance. Any further engagements will be entirely at the discretion of the person concerned. Do you understand that? We would also be pleased to have you visit the house for tea next Sunday, Bernard, if you'd like that. I do need to warn you, though,' the commander continued, 'that if your intentions are anything less than completely honourable or if you hurt the person concerned in any way, I will have you immediately transferred to our hill station up in the Highlands, where you will spend the rest of your tour. I'm not sure what help our educational program might be to the tribesmen up there, but we'd really like to encourage them away from aspirations around souveniring and shrinking the heads and various other body parts belonging to our station officers for use as decorator items around their huts . . . I'm absolutely sure that you get my drift.'

The commander paused. 'We'll be pleased to see you about 3 p.m. on Sunday, Bernard,' he smiled.

Chapter 9

The evolution
of The Angels

By the time Bernard finished his national service, I'd accepted a career progression with my employer and moved to Melbourne. Bernard had also been successful in obtaining a career-changing study grant and scholarship, courtesy of his national service, that enabled him to undertake a two-year post-graduate degree course in Drama and Film Making at Flinders University.

We were soon in regular contact again, catching up on my occasional trips back to Adelaide and talking on the phone. Our exchange of postcards became a habit over the years as we each moved around Australia and later overseas. He told me about his involvement in a new band, an alternative music outfit, the Moonshine Jug and String Band, which played 1930s-inspired jug-band blues enlivened by university revue vaudeville. He took great pleasure at being a member of Adelaide's equivalent of Melbourne's Daddy Cool and The Captain Matchbox Whoopee Band. The local potheads crowded into the band's smoky pub gigs to listen to acoustic guitars, banjo, washboard and blowing across the top of an earthenware jug to make a sound that was a bit of a cross between a trombone and a didgeridoo. Supported by an amusingly eccentric stage show, there was certainly something of an 'only in Adelaide' factor about the band and its enthusiastic and often slightly weird fans.

'But, Bern, you hate that sort of music,' I reminded him. 'All those arguments with Brenton about learning The Rooftop Singers' song "Walk Right In".'

'It's surprisingly popular, though. I can't knock it,' he said. 'For a few broke uni students, it's money for jam and pot for free. But I'm working on them. I've taught them all our old Chuck Berry and Eddie Cochran songs, and we slip a few of those in the set list. And the Big Boppa's "Chantilly Lace". I wish I'd kept that ancient wind-up telephone from my PMG days that we had in The Innocents.'

Bernard's new life on campus meant he was caught up in the vitality and relative naivety of freshman students. Most were at least five years younger than he was, which was decidedly strange and unreal. University was a completely new experience and dynamic and it definitely rattled him. The difficult years at Elizabeth, then teachers' college and two years' national service, had provided him with life experiences his friends were unlikely to be able to relate to or even comprehend.

But by early 1971 he had emerged from that long dark tunnel into a much more enjoyable life. He was living close to uni with friend and future manager John Woodruff in a home-share in the gentle green foothills at Glenunga. He needed to enjoy the experience of being a student again—to recover the joys of observing and discovering new things, which would shape the direction of his future.

With his soon-to-be fiancée, the elegant Dzintra, on his arm and clutching the handle of the well-worn black case containing his battered and much repaired Maton guitar, he was eager to embrace whatever of life's opportunities presented themselves. But he seemed loath—embarrassed perhaps—to acknowledge to his new, mostly private school-educated friends from Adelaide's affluent suburbs that the faithful instrument he carted around dated back to his early teenage years.

It was as if having to explain its origins would somehow require telling a part of his history that he wanted to move on from and forget. If asked, he would just say that it was an old guitar he had found or been given. The truth was that he had continued to send money to his family during his national service, and what was left in his pocket he had saved to buy a small car. Until he secured a part-time job, there was certainly no money for a replacement guitar.

————

The chance for Bernard to join a few of his new uni friends in February 1971 in the recently formed acoustic Moonshine Jug and String Band was remarkably good fortune. They had a weekly gig at the city fringe Sussex Hotel, generating a small but regular income.

The band had a uni-student low-budget quirkiness about it; it offered a fresh take on the American hillbilly tradition and its entertaining routines quickly built up a small crowd of regulars. The group was an eclectic mix. Its principals, the Brewster brothers, John and Rick, were polar opposites musically. 'Rick was a classical pianist,' Bernard later recalled. 'John was the rebel. He was a total Bob Dylan fan and an advanced blues harmonica player.'

Bernard's key qualification and unique contribution to the rather unwieldy six-piece ensemble was that he could sing and also play the rhythm guitar accompaniment for fifty or so 1950s and

1960s rock-and-roll, rockabilly and country blues standards. These songs had been tediously learned during his early days with The Innocents. Since then they had been polished into a confident and personable solo act, through busking and joining impromptu jams at parties and social events. This was sufficient to impress the band members and gain entry to the zany and infectious jug band groove.

Bernard had few illusions about his musical talent. He knew that with his practical experience as a performer and the new skills he was developing in his drama and filmmaking degree course he was more of a budding entertainer than an aspiring guitar virtuoso.

Joining the jug band also provided him with the opportunity to indulge his partiality for the clandestine. Undoubtedly this was a result of the most enjoyable parts of his teenage years needing to be kept away from critical parental judgement. In another age, he knew he would have thrived as a secret agent or a mysterious and elusive scarlet pimpernel, a daring hero who cultivated a separate identity or even several of them.

Continually irritated that his first name was shortened to 'Bernie' and wanting to ensure the cash he earned from gigs did not attract too much official oversight, he settled on 'Doc Holliday'—and later 'Doc Talbot'—as his *nom de guerre*. 'Holliday' was a nod to the famous American gunfighter and the cowboy games Bernard had played as a child; 'Talbot' a nod to Crazy Horse guitarist Billy Talbot. Both names soon fell by the wayside and so, to his growing number of fans, he simply became 'Doc'.

As the years went by, it all got complicated as 'Doc' became a developed persona and his identity was increasingly compartmentalised, but in those early years it was a bit of useful fun and another one of the small things that enabled Bernard to move forward with his new life.

The band worked the small-room environments at the Sussex and Modbury hotels and at the Adelaide Rowers Club to develop a nucleus of several hundred fans who could be relied upon to turn up to gigs and encourage pubs and promoters to book them. This meant careful selection, and not a little luck, identifying venues in areas that might suit what the band was offering.

Their initial set list lacked mass appeal, however. The crowds only started to build as Bernard bulldozed the band towards broadening the format to include the rhythm and blues and rock standards that had made up the repertoire of The Innocents—the songs that he knew from experience would draw a crowd wanting to dance. Packed solid into small venues, their audiences were enthusiastic; good bar sales for the promoter meant regular, comparatively well-paid gigs on Tuesday and Thursday nights.

In some ways these early gigs proved a little too successful. Their audiences became increasingly hard to control, were crazy even. And there was a concerning three-way divide between their fans.

Adelaide's flower children of the late 60s were the laid-back pot-smoking acoustic jug band followers of the city's foothills and beaches. But fans from Adelaide's northern and western suburbs, an increasingly disaffected, industrial heartland, found encouragement in raw punchy lyrics framed by louder and harder-edged iterations of 1950s and 1960s rock music. They split between the increasingly violent rocker and Mod factions. Combining all three in a crowded room was like mixing gunpowder. If you added alcohol, the result could be explosive.

The band had also acquired John Woodruff, Bernard's house mate, as manager. Woodruff had previously managed Adelaide rock group Buffalo Drive to local prominence and had started the Sphere Organisation, which teamed with the Central Booking Agency to book Adelaide bands and exchange bookings for reciprocal tours by interstate and local bands.

Woodruff was initially anxious about moving the band too far from the formula that was obviously working, but he was finally convinced that to be sustainable they needed to broaden their appeal beyond their enthusiastic core audience of ageing hippy jug band supporters and embrace the new-generation rock fans, who would support their future entertainment aspirations.

The jug band members were also moving on. By 1973, their university studies completed, some of them were taking up the careers they had trained for. Bernard had even applied for a film-making role with the ABC, but when he discussed the future with John and Rick Brewster the talk inevitably got around to the idea of taking the band to the next level: progressing from an acoustic to an electrified rock band.

They looked at the emerging top bands of the time, Skyhooks and Sherbert. They respected Skyhooks—musically very capable, zany onstage performers and strong songwriters—but Sherbert they thought they could match in a year. So the decision was made: they would electrify and start working to establish themselves in Melbourne and Sydney.

———

By early 1974 it was decided that the jug band needed a change of name and a refreshed identity that better reflected the fact that it had moved on from being a jug band to being a fair-dinkum electrified rock covers group. And so the Keystone Angels was born, with a four-piece line-up of Bernard (bass guitar), Rick Brewster (lead guitar), John Brewster (rhythm guitar) and Charlie King (Peter Christopolous) on drums.

This decision did not go down well with the large group of die-hard jug band fans at the Modbury Hotel, particularly when Woodruff recommended the band's relocation to a Thursday residency at the Finsbury, whose patrons represented a more appropriate industrial working-class demographic.

The band's personal lives were moving forward too: John and Rick Brewster had now married, and Bernard and Dzintra were engaged.

Woodruff's Sphere Organisation was also growing. Through the swaps he organised with interstate booking agencies he was able to place the Keystone Angels into Melbourne and Sydney venues, and by September 1974 the band had started what was to be a regular road convoy interstate, with gigs in Melbourne and then up the Hume Highway to Sydney.

The increasing popularity of the Keystone Angels and their recording aspirations meant there was a demand for the band to accelerate both their musicianship and their songwriting skills. The Brewster brothers came from a musical family: their father and grandfather had been prominent in the Adelaide Symphony Orchestra. Both brothers were keen, classically trained musicians and were certainly talented enough to become guitarists who could replicate the growing progression by US and UK bands towards harmonised twin leads and duelling solos. It was to be a steep learning curve, but they were committed and threw themselves into the task.

Rick Brewster's piano skills were invaluable, allowing him to identify each individual note when he heard a new recorded song and then to replicate that melody. Bernard was now sharing lead vocals and had taken over bass guitar responsibilities from John Brewster and was the proud owner of a stunning new red-and-white Rickenbacker bass. But the challenge to his musical skills was daunting.

As a child, he had participated in his family's frequent Irish sing-alongs and had even sung in the church choir at St Anne's in Elizabeth East, strengthening his voice from an early age. But bass playing had moved on a lot during the 1960s. Playing simple accompaniments and walking bass lines were not sufficient anymore. As Bernard lacked the Brewsters' formal musical training, his attempts at self-improvement in a band that was always on the move were always going to be fraught.

By 1975 I'd caught up with Bernard a few times since he got back from national service, and we met up during one of the band's early Melbourne visits. He was obviously enjoying his life but confided that he felt he was struggling with progressing his musicianship on bass.

I mentioned our friend Alan Tarney, Frank's brother and Vectormen bassist who had taught me the chops I needed for The Innocents. Alan had returned to the UK in 1969, becoming a session musician and songwriter, recording and writing for many top UK acts. When John Rostill, bass player with The Shadows, passed away tragically in 1973 Alan had become bassist for the legendary band.

I also mentioned session bassist Trevor Bolder, who had been on David Bowie's *Spiders from Mars* album. I particularly liked his gritty performance and driving backbeat—reminiscent of Eddie Cochran's 'Summertime Blues' and 'Somethin' Else'—in the Bowie song 'Hang on to Yourself' and the fact that his playing was so clear in the mix.

Bernard listened intently, writing in one of the notebooks that had become a habit dating back to high school. Stuffed with poems, rhyming couplets, drawings and doodles, they became a rich source of lyrics to complement John and Rick's fast-developing riffs and driving melodies. The fulfilment of Bernard's long-time aspiration to create an Australian songwriting partnership—similar to Motown legends Holland–Dozier–Holland—seems to have been almost serendipitous. 'Brewster–Neeson–Brewster, Songwriters' certainly had the right ring about it!

———

The Keystone Angels were starting to generate favourable exposure from their visits to Melbourne and Sydney. During 1975 they had performed at Sunbury and supported Ike and Tina Turner's Adelaide show and Chuck Berry's Australian tour. In October 1975 John Woodruff's Sphere Organisation secured three mid-week gigs at Port Pirie, Whyalla and Port Augusta, supporting the local leg of a national tour by the new Sydney outfit AC/DC.

The Keystone Angels had already played these three grimy South Australian 'Iron Triangle' cities on a number of occasions and their brand of 60s revivalist rock was popular with the locals. They were right in the vanguard, with a clear point of difference over the colourful affected cheekiness of the popular Melbourne-centric glam rock bands that had brought the punters back to Australian written and performed songs.

Australian music at this time was undergoing a fundamental creative shift towards writing catchy new songs; local artists were moving forward en masse from playing the music of overseas artists to writing their own music and the ten or so lyric lines in a composition that was becoming the key for a band's success.

AC/DC had in fact started out in the glam pack with its first single, recorded with vocalist Dave Evans. But the instant hard-living bad boy Bon Scott entered the scene everything came together for them. Bon was the real deal—a cheeky larrikin and capable songwriter who personified exactly what a rock-star frontman of that time needed to be. With the Keystone Angels leading the charge AC/DC literally exploded onto the stage at each of the South Australian venues with their incendiary take-no-prisoners performances fronted by Bon and flamboyant guitarist Angus Young.

'We played covers, AC/DC didn't,' Bernard said later. 'The familiarity of the songs we played got crowds moving. AC/DC's performances sold their unfamiliar songs to the crowds. It was a real eye-opener for us.'

AC/DC gave as good as anything they got. Neither Bon nor Angus were at all hesitant about gathering up Pat Pickett, their fearsome tattooed soundman/roadie, and wading, with fists flying and boots flailing, into a drunken crowd. While they aggressively sorted out any miscreant smartarse who might want to cause trouble by starting fights or throwing things, the rest of the band just kept up a blistering beat until they returned to the stage.

To the rugged blue-collar mining and shipbuilding towns' teenage inhabitants, these performances were the absolute best definition of an Australian good time! To the Keystone Angels, AC/DC immediately became the light on the hill. But how were they to top that?

The two bands immediately hit it off, jamming and sharing a few drinks together after their shows. Whether you accept John and Rick Brewster's story—that it was some sort of mutual meeting of the minds—or manager John Woodruff's account—that he had sent the Keystone Angels' two roadies, who were very mean and muscular looking, to extract AC/DC's share of the tour takings from a rather foolish Adelaide DJ who had run off with them—or a bit of both accounts, the end result was that AC/DC made a generous offer to their support act. They undertook to recommend the Keystone Angels to George Young and Harry Vanda—the former Easybeats who were now the house record producers for Albert Music—for a recording contract audition when the band was next visiting Sydney.

———

Today, if you look across Sydney's busy Goulburn Street to where the Chequers nightclub used to be beneath the now dwarfed three-storey block of time-worn art-deco apartments and the awnings of the retail strip, it still looks much the same. Chequers night-club might now be the 'Chequers Chinese Massage Centre', but there is still enough there to remind you that the stairs down into the now-redeveloped basement once led to Sydney's most successful nightclub of the 1950s and 1960s.

Chequers had played host to many of the biggest acts to visit Australia, but by November 1975 it had reached a seedy low point. Its flashy nightclub days hosting Shirley Bassey, Louis Armstrong and Frank Sinatra were long gone. It was tired and tawdry and smelled of stale beer and takeaway food, but it still had two bands and three shows six nights a week. It was close to Central Station, open till 3 a.m. and offered good-value entertainment for young people streaming into the city from the suburbs for a late-night live-music fix. The Keystone Angels had become popular here and a regular booking had them doing five sets a night from 9 p.m. to 2 a.m., for $120. It was hard graft, which the band would relate years later as their equivalent of The Beatles' Hamburg period.

The guys from AC/DC were as good as their word. So a couple of weeks after the South Australian tour, just as the Keystone Angels were rounding out one of their late-evening sessions at Chequers, they were not entirely surprised to see Bon, Malcolm and Angus, plus George Young and Harry Vanda, come down the stairs towards them.

After finishing their set, they all piled into the night manager's small office for a chat. Reflecting on that meeting years later, and the subsequent audition the following day at Alberts studio in King Street, Doc was to say, 'What George and Harry wanted to find out was what made us tick. AC/DC had told them we were committed and had certainly put in the hard yards as a rock band, but they wanted to understand what our processes were, what bands had influenced us and why, how we learned and performed songs and how we wrote and recorded songs.'

It was already obvious to Doc that, as prospective new members of Ted Albert's growing stable of artists, they were going to have to take the band forward musically in a much more structured way, developing their stage show and presentation and fast-tracking all the tricks and technologies of George and Harry's vast performance and recording experience.

The Easybeats' hit 'Friday on my Mind' had been produced in London by legendary US record producer Shel Talmy, who had recorded multiple mega-hits including 'You Really Got Me' for The Kinks and 'My Generation' for The Who. When the Easybeats folded, George and Harry had hung around London writing songs and recording with numerous artists before returning to Australia eight years later.

They'd brought back with them a bag full of recording experience and smarts, including their development of micing techniques invented by Talmy, which used carpet-covered booths, platforms and baffles to isolate drums, guitars and vocals and make them sound better. The Angels would be the first Australian band to employ these new recording ideas.

The contract between the Keystone Angels and Albert Productions was inked in the last week of November 1975. With George and Harry keen to make an immediate start on recording before Christmas, all the band's gigs in Adelaide were cancelled and they headed back to Sydney and Alberts' Studio One. They took a few brief days off for a couple of whirlwind tours up and down the New South Wales coast supporting Alberts' hottest properties, solo artist John Paul Young and the Ted Mulry Gang, feverishly pushing its number-one hit of the summer 'Jump in My Car'. Then it was back to Adelaide for a final round of concerts and to collect their possessions for their permanent relocation to Sydney and their work in earnest with Albert Music. It was an exciting time.

———

When the band assembled just prior to Christmas 1975 in the dark-walled surrounds of Alberts' Studio One, there was little indication that the recording process for their first couple of albums would severely stress-test the musical and songwriting abilities of each of the band members. It would prompt the most significant line-up changes to the band since its formation and would open fault lines in both current and future relationships that would be linked to some of the most tumultuous events in the band's long history.

An early but very significant indication of the pace of change that was about to commence was the almost immediate suggestion from George Young to think about dropping the 'Keystone' and just become 'The Angels'. The band members looked at each other and immediately agreed; after all, this was what most of their fans were already calling them.

But The Angels' new Sydney-based life, apparently so exciting and so full of promise, soon proved to be a financial disaster. While their relationship with Ted Albert, George Young and Harry Vanda was progressing well under the terms of their recording contract with Albert Music the company was not required to advance the band any money until the release of a successful record.

This might have been OK if they had had a consistent level of Sydney bookings, as that would have provided interim support, but there was no plan in place that would help them generate a regular income and so sustain them financially until a record was released.

To add to their woes, manager John Woodruff had all but deserted them. Immediately after the contract had been signed with Alberts, he left Adelaide for an eighteen-month working holiday in the UK. Before leaving he had made hurried arrangements with Peter Rix, who managed Sydney glam rockers Hush, to fill the gap while he was away. Unfortunately Hush, anxious over a perceived conflict of interest, scuppered these plans immediately. 'Sorry, guys,' said a stony-faced Peter Rix, 'it isn't going to happen.'

So now the band had no manager with influence and no local knowledge of booking agents and promoters. They were literally between the devil and the deep blue sea—stuck in Sydney while their profile and most of their fanbase were a thousand-plus kilometres away, in Adelaide and Melbourne, where they had just waved an emphatic goodbye. They had just purchased a truck and hired a roadie/soundman. Their living costs in Sydney were three times more expensive than in Adelaide. The three wives and Bernard's fiancée Dzintra had all given up good jobs in order to join them.

But Sydney was Australia's biggest city. It had fostered the icons of Australian rock-and-roll—Johnny O'Keefe, Col Joye and Billy Thorpe—and there was a comprehensive club and pub entertainment scene. They just had to find a way to break through. For that they needed the right product, opportunity, contacts and lots of work with booking agents and promoters. It was a case of all hands to the wheel. A new chapter was about to commence, much of it exciting and new. Success, glamour, media attention and adulation awaited them.

But other seeds were also being sown—of resentment, marital trouble, danger, temptation, trauma and strife, as the band members struggled to keep all the elements of their increasingly high-pressure lives together.

Chapter 10

The new centurions
of rock-and-roll

The first few months of 1976 were bleak, a tough hand-to-mouth slog as the band tried to secure even the barest toehold in the competitive Sydney entertainment scene. At this time there were probably 250 rock bands chasing work in 150 venues across Greater Sydney; the top echelon was performing an average of eight shows per week and these popular bands dominated the market. Without a manager with entrée to the principal booking agencies, it was becoming a virtually impossible task for The Angels to secure regular work.

They turned to the Cordon Bleu agency, owned by Jim Towers. Jim booked bands into a number of venues, including the iconic Bondi Lifesavers, and provided bands to country and regional centres; he was a hard-working and enthusiastic operator. He had also carved out a specialised niche, marketing music to fashion shows. Initially he did not want to take on another band, but he was sufficiently impressed by The Angels' contract and imminent record release with Alberts that he agreed to bring them on board.

Despite Jim's best efforts, the band was walking the knife edge of survival as they worked what clubs they could between practising, composing songs and recording. Life for John, Rick, Doc and Charlie at this time was only possible because their partners were earning incomes to keep the home fires burning. Country and interstate gigs imposed additional costs in travel, accommodation and wages. Vehicle repairs and maintenance blew carefully managed budgets apart.

Their approaches to Alberts for a $10,000 advance against future royalties, and to the Brewsters' parents to act as guarantors on a bank loan to support the band's investment in songwriting and recording, were all politely rebuffed. Declining the request from his two sons, Arthur Brewster told John, 'I think you've both made a big mistake.' Unless there was an upturn in their finances, the band expected to go broke.

Looking back, 'Am I Ever Gonna See Your Face Again' (or 'Face', as it was usually called) was an odd sort of song to launch The Angels recording career with Albert Music. Initially performed with country leanings, it evolved over time and had been tested on audiences to an indifferent reception. The band had even recorded a demo of the song a year or so previously, in the hope of landing a contract with EMI in Adelaide, but it had been passed over.

Its origins have become mired in history. A couple of its lyric lines trace back to Doc's teenage notebook jottings regarding a girl he met on a bus. Like a number of later Angels' songs, it also defied categorisation. In the beginning there was not even the remotest expectation that the song would eventually become one of Australia's most-loved music anthems. Following its first release, on 5 April 1976, it was shunned by disc jockeys, who judged it to be inconsistent with their curated selections.

Alberts' ebullient artist and repertoire man, Chris Gilbey, had even driven the band to 2UE to wish top Sydney DJ Bob Rogers happy birthday in the hope that he might support the new single. In an almost exact re-run of the experience with Adelaide DJ Big Bob Francis in 1963, when he spurned The Beatles' future mega-hit 'Please Please Me', Rogers put 'Face' on the turntable, listened for all of three seconds, sniffed disdainfully, pulled the needle off and declared that he would never play that type of music on *his* radio show!

With almost immediate signs that 'Face' would generate neither record sales nor bookings, things were getting desperate for the band members. But at the end of April 1976, Doc's parents signed as co-guarantors on a $4000 loan application. This was a significant amount of money—the equivalent of about $25,000 in 2021. Included in the possessions and household effects provided as security were both Barney and Doc's cars, Doc's Rickenbacker and Dobro guitars, his Eminar bass amp, and all the furniture and white goods in the Neeson family home at Elizabeth, including the fridge, the iron and the ironing board. The Neeson family stuck together fiercely and supported each other whenever help was needed.

With this loan the band could survive for a few more months, until hopefully their investment in songwriting and recording bore fruit with record sales and an increased gig income. But obviously things needed to change, and George Young was weighing his options on whether to persevere with the band or drop them. George in particular was not satisfied with Charlie's playing on the recording of 'No Lies', the second song they had recorded in their first session. George suggested getting in a session musician to re-record this track.

Looking back, the decision to sack Charlie appears to have been quite sudden, precipitated perhaps by a desire to be seen to be 'doing something'. After all, 'No Lies' was never released as a record and, despite subsequent versions by different musicians, nobody has ever managed to improve on Charlie's drumming on 'Face'. And there hadn't been any apparent concern about his drumming performance previously.

Undoubtedly the essential connection between the bass and drums needed strengthening; without a strong syncopated rhythm their music simply did not rock. It would seem that the decision to recruit a new drummer was more about shaking up the recording ability of the band's rhythm section, rather than any weakness by Charlie in his gig performances. George Young, as a very capable drummer and guitarist, had a sophisticated appreciation of the sort of rhythms and drum patterns he wanted to hear when recording his new band. A more experienced drummer would bring support to Doc, but also put pressure on him as the bass player to lift both his playing and musical connection.

Perhaps one could also be cynical and observe that this was also possibly too good an opportunity to pare the band back to the three key creative members. George had told the three songwriters repeatedly, 'You *are* the band.'

There was also by now the somewhat uncomfortable recognition by the Brewsters that when the band had faced financial oblivion, it had been Bernard—the least flush of them all—who had put up the money to keep things going for a few more months. He could now be more forceful with John and Rick on both the ownership and musical direction of the band.

It was also agreed that any replacement band members would be employees and have limited earning and creative involvement prospects. The seeds of future discontent had been planted and this decision would ultimately become a key factor in the years of rancour and disagreement between the band members.

———

When experienced Adelaide drummer Graham 'Buzz' Bidstrup walked into the office at Adelaide's Thebarton Theatre in July 1976, he knew that he had seen the three guys waiting for him before. They were unmistakably members of the Moonshine Jug and String Band he remembered from a few years previously. His heart sank.

Buzz had only landed back in Australia a few weeks earlier after eighteen months in the UK. He had done the rounds of Adelaide looking for possible work opportunities but was keeping his options open. 'An agent rang and said a Sydney band were looking for a drummer and was I interested,' he remembered. 'They had a record contract. But the agent wouldn't tell me who it was, saying they would be in Adelaide the following week and I could talk to them then.'

Now he was in a spot—he had been really hoping to jag something a lot better than the acoustic outfit he had seen a couple of years back at the Suffolk Hotel. He did know that the band had electrified since then and he'd been told they'd improved considerably. At this first meeting they told him excitedly about their recent appearance on *Countdown*.

Buzz agreed to a rehearsal at a hall in Kensington Park. The jam went surprisingly well and they seemed a good bunch of guys, but musically they were all over the place. Their jug band origins were still dominant in their sound; the ever-changing blues and swamp rockers, Little Feat, were obviously a strong influence and Buzz found Doc's bass playing extremely difficult to follow.

He knew from experience that the bass player had to connect the band musically and make everyone else sound good. Doc's role was to get the pulse going between his bass guitar and the bass drum, but it wasn't happening. Buzz felt he would certainly have his work cut out, but he figured that a regular pay cheque and an immediate move to the much bigger opportunities on offer on the east coast were better than banging away in the limited Adelaide scene. There was also a good vibe about the band. He was happy to accept their invitation to join, and the boys welcomed him on board warmly.

Then it was straight to work, Buzz setting up his blue Ludwig drum kit at the Arkaba Hotel for the band's last gig on their Adelaide visit, before hitting the road back to Sydney.

Arriving in Sydney, Buzz moved in with Doc and Dzintra for a few months before taking turns boarding with both Rick and John Brewster. This enabled him to get to know his fellow band members, although it was with Doc that he developed a real connection as they spent lots of time listening to music together, discussing and exchanging details from their extensive knowledge and experience of bands and vibes. Buzz had a portable professional tape-player that could play the day's recording from the studio, and they were able to go over these again and again to understand and learn from the process.

Buzz and Doc also had very similar musical tastes. Buzz had done some session work while he had been in the UK, but his main mission had been to check out what was hot. The emerging punk music scene quickly got his attention; he had caught gigs by the Sex Pistols, The Clash and The Buzzcocks at London's Oxford Street 100 Club in early 1976 and immediately recognised them as a distinctive next-phase evolution.

The early Pistols, with Glen Matlock at the hub, had revived the old Eddie Cochran, Small Faces and Who standards, over-laying them with fearsome jams of blistering raw noise. They had quickly developed into a tight, ferocious live band. Full of attitude and characterised by wild vocalisation styles, they were capable musicians experimenting with overload, feedback and distortion, pushing their equipment to the limit. The Pistols' musical template and DNA would inspire a generation of followers, but in 1976 they were then still at the small-gig, spectacular private-party stage and their anarchic theatre would quickly become way too real, both captivating and appalling audiences across Britain, as unforgivably brilliant as they were short-lived.

Arts graduate Matlock had a tall gangly frame, a Rickenbacker guitar and inspired stage mannerisms and costume—his dress shirt, Ascot tie and tailored dinner jacket contrasted with the leather jackets and street-feral look across the rest of the band. Leather-jacketed Doc, also with a Rick bass, was already well ahead of the rest of The Angels, who were still in hippy flares, butterfly motifs and denim jackets. Doc had also noticed the nod to Trevor Bolder in Glen Matlock's bass lines.

The early punk music scene was everything the traditional music industry wasn't. Its disruptive 'bootleg' business model had evolved organically; the improved quality of compact tape-recording allowed live gigs to be recorded and limited batches of 45s cut and distributed by small independent entrepreneurs.

The Angels were all pushing hard. 'We had a huge work ethic, always listening to stuff and bouncing ideas around,' recalled Buzz. 'It wasn't a typical way for a young band to work at all. We were constantly working on the songs in the studio and trying to improve them by playing them live on stage, long before recording an actual album.'

This was exactly the methodology employed by the Pistols, whose only studio album was actually a compilation, recorded after months of playing live. But unfortunately, by this time Glen Matlock's musical prowess had been lost to the line-up and his replacement bassist—spiky-haired, leather-clad Sid Vicious—even with studio muso back-up, failed to capture the magic and brutal musical intensity of the early bootleg live-show recordings.

At first Buzz and Doc's entreaties to the Brewsters to listen seriously to the tapes of the Pistols' bootleg singles brought only casual interest. Initially the brothers didn't really get the Pistols' raw energy, their salvos of descending chords and garage-band naivety. They preferred instead to focus on the band's anti-social behaviour as much as the perceived lack of musicianship and musicality in their post-Matlock recordings. Nevertheless, Doc and Buzz's persistence eventually convinced the Brewsters to take the Pistols' driving rhythms to the next level, incorporating new drumming and high-hat cymbal patterns. This resulted in the development of what was to become The Angels' distinctive sound.

Doc showed Rick Brewster how to control the dynamics of a song by putting a piece of foam under the strings by the bridge of his guitar to replicate the Pistols' damped-down, chugging, Eddie Cochran fatter-sounding style of playing that he had learned in The Innocents all those years previously. Rick's dexterity immediately allowed him to dispense with the foam, and just use his palm to damp the strings when he needed it. What evolved was a tight, hard, rhythmic sound with little sustain, all downstrokes, now played slightly faster. Doc's syncopated Trevor Bolder-like bass lines were driving the bass drum and rapid-fire, staccato tish-tish from Buzz's high-hat cymbal. This distinctive driving back beat would provide the infill and counterpoint between Doc's angrily spat lyrics—about social injustice and relationship angst—and the raunchy ringing riffs and power chords that filled the Brewster brothers' duelling guitar solos.

The Angels had a Sound!

Now they needed an Act, a Look and a Hit Record.

Buzz encouraged Doc to step up and take on the role of front man. With a pleasantly distinctive voice and drama school background, surely he was the ideal for the role. But it was just going to be too difficult a challenge to try to combine the increasing demands of being a contemporary bass musician in a connected rhythm section with singing and creating a highly differentiated musical offering.

The band needed a new bassist, and Buzz knew just the man.

———

Chris Bailey was Adelaide rock royalty, with a formidable resumé as bassist. He'd played in a number of legendary Adelaide bands from Tattered Sole to heading up political activists Red Angel Panic, to blues rockers Headband and being bandmates with Bon Scott in the Mount Lofty Rangers. Buzz had been closely involved with Chris for a number of years—in two bands and, as a duo, they had been a pair of rhythm-section top guns available for studio work. Chris was certainly not impressed when Buzz had gone off to Sydney with The Angels and left him without a studio partner. But they had kept in touch and Buzz's regular updates and demo tapes, backed up by Chris's attendance at some of The Angels' Adelaide gigs, had made him think that there was definitely something with potential going on.

When Buzz suggested Chris for the band, Doc, John and Rick Brewster were stunned. 'Chris Bailey? Are you serious—he won't leave Adelaide for us!'

But with Buzz's encouragement, Chris did join them, arriving in Sydney in January 1977. There were no auditions. Almost immediately the dynamic of The Angels' sound changed and lifted. Chris went straight to work, in the studio and on the road with the band's new sound. He was a real pro, a walking textbook of bass lines, licks and runs from rock and blues legends and jazz and Motown. 'Chris was our secret weapon,' reflected John Brewster on the record production process. 'We always mixed up his bass very clear. His great talent was to add a melodic beat to full-throttle hard rock.'

Finally, in May 1977, John Woodruff arrived back in Australia. Doc, John and Rick didn't appear to have held any grudges, despite having been virtually marooned in Sydney and left to their own devices for seventeen months, as they waited at Mascot Airport to welcome their manager home. If anyone could help get the show on the road, it had to be the indomitable, barefooted, chain-smoking Woody!

Moving in with John Brewster, Woodruff attempted to ramp up the band's forward bookings. He pulled the band away from booking agent Jim Towers and directed them to his colleague and burgeoning agent Chris Murphy, who was shifting the focus of his long-established family-owned booking agency from theatre to rock music acts. Chris was astute and well connected across the entertainment industry and would go on to manage some stellar groups, including INXS. But it quickly became apparent that the band needed time to develop its new audience. The hoped-for lift in earnings simply didn't occur, and with Woodruff not hesitating to resume taking his management fees, the band was in an even worse situation than they had been in before his return.

There was no money to pay a manager, so Woodruff decided to leave it to Chris Murphy to build the band as their booking agent, and he stepped back from management and returned to Adelaide, where he drove cabs and managed the stage production of *Ned Kelly* for the next few months.

The band's second single, the rather melancholy soft rock 'You're a Lady Now', was released in July 1977. This was followed a month later by the self-titled debut album *The Angels*. Both received a lukewarm response. Nothing the band was doing seemed to be working.

In early October 1977 John Brewster, in his role as band bookkeeper, took a hard look at their finances. The situation was grim: after the Christmas and New Year's holiday gig and party season, their forward bookings were falling off a cliff. A wind-up of the band's activities in the first few months of 1978 appeared inevitable.

———

The Sex Pistols' compilation album *Never Mind the Bollocks, Here's the Sex Pistols* was released at the end of October 1977 and Buzz immediately bought a copy. Due in part to the Pistols' notoriety, the album debuted at number one on the UK charts and went gold a couple of weeks later. Virgin Records in Sydney sold out of their entire stock within hours. It remained a bestseller for over a year, spending sixty weeks in the Top 25. If Doc and Buzz needed any further endorsement of their gut feeling that The Angels needed to capture this emerging high-energy musical revolution, this was it. The Brewsters finally capitulated, agreeing to collaborate with Doc in writing a couple of songs that they hoped would capture the new-wave punk vibe.

Around this time, George Young seemed to want to move on from his full-on mentoring role with the band. John and Rick Brewster had been eager learners in the studio and George encouraged them to take on the role of producers. To support this, he engaged Mark Opitz as an apprentice sound engineer/producer for them. Mark quickly slotted into the team, throwing in additional ideas. He supported the idea of the band taking on a more punkish vibe and joined Doc, Buzz and Chris in extending their influence on the band's musical direction. Once everybody was on board, things quickly got going. It was a real team effort.

Professor Wal Cherry was Head of the School for Dramatic Arts when Bernard was at Flinders University, and Doc had sought his counsel on developing a unique stage presence. Professor Cherry had been at his most eloquent and brilliant when delivering lectures on German impressionism and the 1930s revolutionary playwright Bertolt Brecht. Bernard had absorbed every detail of his lecturer's animated presentations. 'Prof Wal is undoubtedly way too clever for the establishment politicking in the Adelaide scene,' he would say. 'Without doubt he will end up in London or New York. A fascinating guy on his special subjects, and I really appreciated being in his classes.'

Wal Cherry was pleased to catch up with his former pupil and readily offered his advice. 'Bernard, you must develop a character that you can step into for your performances, just like an actor every time he goes on stage. Start working on Doc as a separate identity who goes out before an audience and performs a role that you've designed for him.'

With Glen Matlock as an inspiration, Bernard suggested he could enter the stage dressed up like a toff in a dress shirt, dinner jacket and Ascot tie exuding an air of superiority. Wal agreed, but wanted him to develop the concept much further. 'How about, as the show warms up, have him discard the coat, loosen the tie, pull out the shirt tails and undo the buttons,' Wal offered. 'Have him disintegrate into a dishevelled mess, and in the end he staggers off into the night—bloodied but defiant, undefeated. A very romantic figure. They'll be howling for more.'

Doc was intrigued, but not entirely convinced. He certainly got the concept of a tall mysterious theatrical figure prowling the stage, contrasting with the stationary guitarists, but would this work with audiences?

Doc took up and tested many of Professor Wal's suggestions, including pulling back from the audience and then employing his hands to expand his visual space. On several occasions he even performed under a white bed sheet for greater theatrical effect.

Almost immediately the band had new songs they could test on gig audiences. 'Coming Down' was a single release in March 1978, ahead of the *Face to Face* album. It was driving and upbeat with a punkish feel; it was the shape of things to come.

The fans reacted enthusiastically. The song's catchy chorus precipitated the chanting audience participation that would soon become The Angels' trademark.

Other similar songs came rapidly. 'I Ain't the One' reinforced and developed the band's new sound; its percussive syncopated vibe drew together, refreshed and updated those driving dance-able rhythms that began way back at the Big Bang of Rock. Doc exploded from the quietly spoken, somewhat reserved Bernard Neeson into a mesmerising dramatic onstage Superman. Wearing an elegant dinner jacket, dress shirt and Ascot tie, his towering, mysterious and intimidating figure stared into the middle distance shaking his maracas. The transformation was complete. A frenetic dervish, whirling, jumping and strutting into new undiscovered realms that were abstract and unrestrained. 'Doc was a crazed alien, trapped in a cock-eyed world,' he was to explain.

Behind him, the thunderous surging of the Brewster brothers' powerful ringing guitar riffs and high-energy power chords overlaid the pounding hard-driving Chris Bailey and Buzz Bidstrup rhythm section. This was no tentative, half-formed jug and swamp blues cover band . . . this was a full-on freaking rock tornado!

The Angels had arrived. And straightaway their bookings started to improve. Their live performances were quickly winning fans, and those fans were coming back and bringing friends. Any reservations Doc had had about Wal Cherry's counsel soon evaporated as gig audiences enthusiastically embraced the new songs and his new persona. It was word of mouth bringing the audience. Within days media, music industry people and promoters descended upon their gigs and emerged shell-shocked, mesmerised by Doc's mercurial persona as he hurled himself backwards and forwards across the stage, his face twisted and contorted, his hands and arms extended.

Chris Murphy swung by the band's 1977 New Year's Eve gig at the Stagedoor Tavern and was stunned. They were now a stand-out band on the cusp of greatness, and he needed to put some serious weight behind them.

National tours as a support band for Meatloaf and David Bowie in 1978 provided the exposure needed to properly break their next single, 'Take a Long Line', which was to spend nearly three months on the Australian charts. Their *Face to Face* album followed and spent more than a year in the Top 100, eventually achieving four times platinum with a shipment of 280,000 units.

Both Meatloaf and Bowie encouraged their support band in ways that were to provide exemplars for The Angels' later careers. 'Welcome to my tour,' Bowie greeted them at the first meeting in Adelaide. 'I really like your music. Please join us for dinner.'

'Bowie was fantastic,' enthused Doc. 'He treated us as his guests. He came down to our very first sound check and he offered us everything on stage in terms of lighting except for one [especially fragile] light that he wanted to keep [safe].'

To coincide with this support slot, The Angels issued their first extended play, *After the Rain—The Tour*. Fans appeared to hold them almost as an equal billing to Bowie. *Face to Face* was rocketing up the album charts and The Angels were top of the bill for their own shows all over the country, lauded and pursued by a media that wanted to know all the details about this unstoppable phenomenon.

Bernard was trying to come to terms with Doc's new-found fame. Plucked from his relative anonymity, he suddenly found that being the focus on stage quickly transferred into his everyday life, more so than for the other members of the band. Female attention during and after the shows became unrelenting, and the temptation to stray came with the territory. His private life quickly became compromised.

In late 1978 the band released a maxi single with 'After the Rain', 'Who Rings the Bell' and the Lou Reed-reminiscent 'Coming Down'. The following May they were on the road again and still touring when the *No Exit* album was released. A successful single, 'Shadow Boxer', came with it and in November 1979 the band struck the charts again with a twelve-inch EP called *Out of the Blue*, which was to be The Angels' last venture with Alberts.

They were labelled the 'New Centurions of Rock' in the press and Doc was hailed as the 'King of Aussie Pub Rock'. With stadiums overflowing, The Angels were now commanding up to $10,000 for a big show (the equivalent of $40,000 in 2021).

Then came the epic 1978 free New Year's Eve concert at the Sydney Opera House. The organisers lost control of an inebriated and riotous crowd estimated at over 150,000 strong and the show had to be stopped. Doc and Chris ended up in hospital from injuries caused by flying bottles and hurled sections of street signs.

Music industry recognition and accolades finally followed. In the 1978 and 1979, The Angels took more awards than seemed possible in *RAM Magazine*'s readers polls. In 1978 the band finished within the top three in eleven of thirteen categories. In 1979 the band took the top spot again with six category winners.

By now though The Angels had their sights set on America.

Chapter 11

On the back
of an alligator

John Woodruff watched incredulously from the sidelines as The Angels' circumstances dramatically changed. He realised that if he were to take charge of them again and develop their burgeoning career, he would have to change the way that bands were booked across Australia. So he threw himself into organising an alliance between the managers and booking agents representing the country's most popular artists; his aim was to renegotiate what was a totally inequitable balance of reward between the artists and the venue owners.

This wasn't the first attempt by a manager or booking agent to improve the cut for local bands and to make it commensurate with their drawing power, but it was the first time booking agents and managers had banded together to push back against what had become an entrenched issue in an exploitative industry. Woodruff saw an opportunity for the exciting new live shows and the harder-edged songs that had now evolved to position themselves as a unique entertainment offering—Australian pub rock.

He argued that bands playing in huge beer barns or licensed clubs where several thousand could easily roll up should receive part of the admission charge from every punter who came through the door rather than a flat fee. This would mean a huge difference for the musicians; instead of $500, the band might now take home $5000.

Such changes did not come easily. Most publicans, well aware of the huge bar take they enjoyed when a top-flight band was playing, eventually agreed to share the spoils. The licensed clubs, on the other hand, resisted these changes with a passion. Counting and recording patron numbers would make their off-the-books skimming much more difficult, and as for the ludicrous suggestion of now paying thousands of dollars to a few layabout musicians . . . Well, that was a complete anathema.

Woodruff's leadership in the revolutionary restructure of the industry, and the formation of his somewhat appropriately named Dirty Pool Management organisation, did not come without personal danger, and Bernard appreciated that threat far better than most. He had learned in the 1960s that entertainment businesses generating large amounts of unregulated cash attracted standover merchants, racketeers, conmen and thugs, who would protect what they saw as their entitled little earn.

'Rock-and-roll, despite the glamour, is still a hard, serious and ruthless business, peopled by highly creative opportunists, egotists and untogetherists. As well as the blatantly dishonest and the badly deranged,' Bernard was to observe. He included undercutting to secure contracts by the highly competitive booking agents and managers in this sentiment. And, just quietly, they also did very well out of Woodruff's initiative.

———

Woodruff then turned his attention to the contract that he and the band had signed with Alberts. There had been some misgivings, supported by legal advice, that the financial terms of the agreement were one-sided and heavily in favour of Alberts. But at that time, with just a small local recording history this was a fantastic opportunity any Adelaide band would have signed with their eyes shut!

While the deal had enabled them to develop from being a knockabout Adelaide cover band to the highest-paid entertainers in the country, it no longer seemed reasonable. Woodruff not only wanted to revisit the financial arrangements of the contract, but he also wanted to see plans to break the band in the US. As he later recalled, 'To me the US was the be-all and end-all. We didn't have a release anywhere outside of Australia and New Zealand. Alberts seemed far more interested in getting AC/DC heard overseas.'

Woodruff was galvanised into action by the rapid rise in the US charts of Australian harmony soft rockers Little River Band following a US tour and after signing with EMI Australia's US stablemate, Capitol. He wanted The Angels to immediately follow Little River Bands' ground-breaking trail. He requested a meeting with Ted Albert.

Woodruff was the son of a wealthy Adelaide eastern suburbs doctor; Ted Albert the youthful and polished scion of Alberts' four-generations-old music empire and a resident of Victoria Road, Bellevue Hill in Sydney, arguably Australia's most prestigious address. Their meeting was never going to go well. 'He intimidated me,' Woodruff would say later. 'He reminded me of my father.'

However, from Ted Albert's not uncharitable perspective, Woodruff had done absolutely nothing with or for the band during the seventeen months he was away. He had left the country immediately following the signing of the contract and, to cover his absence, he had made a sloppy interim management arrangement that had immediately fallen over. He had returned to the scene after all the work had been done to transform the band into a stampeding, highly creative, hard-rock musical juggernaut.

Ted believed The Angels were succeeding because of their talent and hard work in the pressure-cooker atmosphere of the Alberts studios, backed up by the company's efforts to promote and market the band and by the astute and capable mentoring of George Young and Harry Vanda. With still a year to go on the contract, Alberts had plans for another Angels album, with recording sessions scheduled ahead of a mid-1980 release date. The Angels would follow the same route Alberts had mapped out for AC/DC: opening in the UK and Europe, and then going on to the USA. Ted was emphatic. 'John, let's talk about it when we are ahead on the investment that we've made.'

But Woodruff was impatient. He reminded Ted that AC/DC's manager, Michael Browning, with the support of Alberts, had signed a deal with Atlantic prior to their move to the UK and had prepared the way for them in the US a full two years before the band played its first US concert. Ted proposed that as it had done for AC/DC, Alberts would fund an apartment and a phone for Woodruff in the US and provide him with contacts. He could take it from there.

––––––

If John Woodruff found the usually genial Ted Albert intimidating, he quickly learned that doing business with corporate America was like jumping into a shark tank. Nevertheless, after spending time in the US and doing the rounds of the US music companies, he had an international offer on the table from formidable global hit-makers

Epic, whose acts included The Hollies and The Yardbirds, and ABBA, Boston, Cheap Trick, The Clash and The Jacksons. Epic's small subsidiary label, CBS, represented them in Australia and Epic recordings were also issued by EMI under the Columbia label.

Epic's offer included financial support for US and European tours, record promotion and a substantial advance for the production of new material. However, a critical condition was also included: the band would be required to immediately break its contract with Alberts and sign locally with CBS.

John Woodruff was caught between a rock and a hard place: Alberts had financially supported his plan to broker an international record deal, but in order to accept the Epic offer he would have to break a contract that still had a year to run.

He put the Epic offer to the band, first outlining the shortfalls in the contract they had originally signed with Alberts regarding royalty payments. Given their low profile, the-then Keystone Angels had accepted a royalty of 5 per cent of the retail price. But there was also a 10 per cent deduction to cover breakages when records were vinyl, which meant the royalty pool for the performers was 5 per cent of the 90 per cent, from which John Woodruff as manager deducted 20 per cent before the balance was divvied up. Hence the Brewsters and Doc, as performers, ended up with a fraction over 1 per cent of the recommended retail price of each record sold.

There were further issues with the deal they had signed with Alberts. Alberts owned the copyright for all music recorded during the duration of their contract and received 100 per cent of the songwriting royalties.

The Epic offer was much better: they would pay 12 per cent of 90 per cent of the retail price to the performers and would split 50-50 the copyright income with the songwriters.

The band had mixed views about the Epic offer. From their direct experience of trying to live on gig income since their move to Sydney 18 months earlier, the financial benefit of the Woodruff-led industry restructure stunned them. The difference to their previously desperate circumstances in only a few months was unbelievable. Woodruff was nothing short of a fricken genius. He was the man! At last, they had records that everybody wanted to buy and an act that everybody wanted to see.

'We trusted him implicitly with that side of our career,' John Brewster said. 'So when he laid it on us that Alberts were short-changing us and we should go for the better deal that Epic/CBS offered, well, we didn't feel good about leaving, but he presented the scenario in such a way that we said, "Yeah, OK, John. If you think this is the way to go, then let's do it."'

Bernard was somewhat ambivalent about the proposed Epic deal, but his long friendship with Woodruff meant that he could be talked into or out of most things. He had never been happy with the low royalties in the Alberts contract and even at the time he had encouraged Woodruff to try harder. Woodruff reminded Doc of all this. With a significantly better deal in his hand, he hammered the somewhat hesitant Doc to take a leap of faith with him. He promised that the new deal, together with Epic-facilitated US and European tours, would bring them immediate international success.

There were further complications. During the band's early grim days in Sydney, Doc had been looking at other options and had put out feelers for acting and film roles. This had resulted in scripts to read and, in the case of the film *Monkey Grip,* based on Helen Garner's bestselling book, a screen test. To his delight and astonishment, Doc had been offered the lead role of Javo.

This was no small achievement; he had beaten off a promising little-known actor named Mel Gibson, who was just about to start filming a small-budget bikie movie called *Mad Max*. But to accept the offer Doc would need to take a two-month break from the band, and filming was due to start during the period Epic had pencilled in for the band's first US tour.

At the forefront of Doc's mind was the memory of the difficult conversation he had had with his parents before they finally agreed to act as guarantors for the loan that had kept the band alive. It did not seem to weigh with them that he had helped support his family financially while he had been at home and during his military service—he had felt as if he was still a teenager asking his mother if he could buy his first guitar. He never wanted to have to do that again and broadening his career aspirations into film had been his attempt to establish an independent and sustainable future.

Buzz and Chris were more circumspect. Both had a lot more recording experience with studios other than Alberts and understood the significance of the unlimited studio time that the contract with Alberts offered. According to Buzz, 'As it turned out, the Alberts deal was better for a band like us, that needed a lot of studio time, because Alberts paid for our entire studio time and engineering. After we left, we had to pay for that ourselves.'

Buzz, who had been largely sidelined from the Brewster-Neeson-Brewster songwriting partnership and thus from a potential income stream, had directly negotiated with George Young to pursue his personal songwriting and recording aspirations. He even had his own key to the studio. There was little benefit for him or Chris in the Epic proposition.

Nonetheless, the songwriters, being three-fifths of the band, concurred with Woodruff and so the deal was done. Adelaide's *The News* stop-pressed in block type:

POP GROUP IN $2M DEAL

Former Adelaide band The Angels has signed a record
$2Million contract with American company Epic Records.

This deal is one of the biggest ever signed by an Australian
group.

Alberts, quite understandably, felt it had been dudded. There
was a tense meeting between Ted Albert, John Woodruff and the
US attorney acting for Epic/CBS. The two Australians never spoke
again. Ted and George were extremely disappointed with the band's
decision, but they blamed Woodruff entirely.

The wash-up was not pretty. Alberts imposed a contract-break
fee of $125,000—effectively a penalty of $25,000 on each member
of the band. This more than wiped out Epic's $100,000 produc-
tion advance, especially after Woodruff deducted 20 per cent from
it, forcing the band into debt on their first album under the new
contract. Alberts also rescinded the verbal offer it had made to pay
a producer's royalty on at least one of the albums the band produced
themselves.

The upside was that America beckoned, and if anything like
the local chart success of *Face to Face* and *No Exit* could be replicated there the vastly improved royalties would quickly redress these
losses and return a river of gold to the band.

It soon became clear, however, that in the music business when
you got out of one unfair record contract you didn't necessarily get
into a fair one.

What became almost immediately apparent from the move
was that the band had traversed from what had been a largely
independent and supportive environment at Alberts to a corporate
relationship with Epic, known for good reason as the 'Mafia of the

American Recording Industry'. And as for recording studio time, production and engineering . . . well, that was now something the band would have to pay for themselves.

The Angels' contract was just one of the almost fifty global signings that Epic made in 1979. Of these, perhaps five would still be on foot two years later. For most artists flocking to the music industry majors for a breakthrough, in retrospect securing a record company contract was widely seen as something akin to crossing a river on the back of an alligator.

Chapter 12

Campaign America

With the Epic contract signed, things moved very quickly. But with The Angels' management almost completely inexperienced in dealing with the smooth-tongued self-interest of the US music industry, the band members were like babes in the woods.

They were immediately pressured to accept an ambiguous fine-print clause in the new agreement that compelled them to allow their two bestselling albums to be subjected to a costly and time-consuming remix and reconfiguration to 'suit American tastes'. After some negotiation, it was agreed that the band's production team would work with top US producer John Boylan, who was vice-president of Epic, to effect the desired changes.

No less a luminary than The Beatles' manager Brian Epstein had recognised in 1964 that remixing tracks for 'American taste' was an expensive and arguably unnecessary record-company gouge. In an almost exact re-run of the treatment meted out to UK bands in the 1960s, The Angels were launched into the American market with a hybrid greatest hits album that was also called *Face to Face*. It comprised what Epic considered the best songs from the two albums, remixed and cobbled together so that arguably the tracks lost their continuity of sound and style; the running order completely disregarded any concerns the band had about coherence and song sequencing.

This process denied American fans the unique album-to-album creative progression, the mix of light and shade so obvious to the band's Australian followers. Arguably it contributed to a confusion over musical style and genre, which ultimately led to the loss of highly curated radio station support during their second and subsequent US tours.

The band's new single 'Marseilles' would be released into the US and Europe, and 'Coming Down' would be tried as a single in the UK.

———

Planning for their first two US tours, even allowing for the firm direction of their record company, brought into focus the band's management's relative inexperience with international touring.

When the Little River Band and AC/DC had set out to conquer the US, LRB's Glenn Wheatley and AC/DC's Michael Browning were already internationally experienced promoters in their own right. They had each independently tested the US market with a few targeted support gigs and had been able to use that experience to influence record company's plans on the marketing and the duration and promotion options for future tours.

AC/DC's first American radio exposure had been two years before they played their first US concert. Under the guidance of booking agent Doug Thaler of American Talent International, and later the management of Leber-Krebs, they gained invaluable experience of the US stadium circuit. Although AC/DC found it virtually impossible to get onto the big-name tours, they found a niche as support for leading rock acts and co-headlining with collaboratively inclined and upwardly mobile bands.

None of this was an option for The Angels—their deal with Epic was much more structured. They lost the freedom to run their own lives. It was the Epic way or the highway.

Epic's next demand was a name change, supposedly to avoid possible confusion and legal hassles with a minor-league US glam band called Angelz. So they became 'Angel City' after an idea that they might make Los Angeles their future home base. It was a name that all the band members took an aversion to from the get-go.

———

By now Epic had established the order of battle: before the band left Australia they needed to record a new album, which would come to be called *Dark Room*. The Epic plan meant that the album would be recorded in somewhat impatient haste as the band prepared for its first overseas tour.

Epic wanted its VP John Boylan involved again, this time as producer. This did not sit well with John and Rick Brewster, who felt passed over after having produced the previous two bestselling albums, so it was agreed that they would do the production. Mark Opitz would be brought in as recording engineer and John Boylan would be 'Production—Consultant'.

There were other emerging tensions within the band regarding the recording of this new album. Buzz and Chris had both contributed significantly to the melodies and arrangement of songs on the original Australian *Face to Face* album, but the production of *No Exit* opened up areas of conflict when Buzz and Chris realised that they had been effectively excluded from any share of future royalties in the Epic contract. They no longer saw a reason to contribute their creative input and diverse experience to record production. If they were going to be treated as session musos and employees, then that's what they would be.

A compromise was apparently suggested that the melody stream of the royalty be divided between the Brewster–Neeson–Brewster songwriting partnership and the Bidstrup–Bailey rhythm section, but the matter remained unresolved.

The band had just completed a whirlwind 25-date tour around Australia, so a change of tempo was welcome. Compared to the many months of work in songwriting, development and production for the earlier two albums, there would only be ten days allowed for songwriting and rehearsals before two and half weeks of recording sessions at the Paradiso Studios in Kings Cross. Doc did, however, have his ever-present notebooks stuffed with carry-over lyric material, so a disciplined songwriting process did not take long to produce a number of new songs.

With recording finished there were just a couple of large farewell concerts and then, aligning themselves with the Epic master plan, the band was straight on the plane to commence its first US, Canada and UK tour.

———

Epic's first tour itinerary for Angel City was to be launched like a military campaign, with the record company's heavy-gun promotion and pounding air support fanning out across the US and Canada, backed up by a coordinated record release, media ads and radio interviews.

For the band there was an exhausting and demanding performance itinerary: first, a two-month, strongly orchestrated campaign of mainly support gigs covering all the main regions of the US and Canada, to be followed by showcase events in the UK and Europe. The support gigs were arranged as part of a record company pay-to-play deal, whereby Epic advanced promotional money to headlining acts on big tours in return for being able to offer the opener spots to their up-and-coming bands. The cost of this was then deducted from future Angel City royalties earned in the US, Canada, Europe or the UK.

An immediate casualty of the tour arrangements was Doc's film debut in *Monkey Grip*. With Epic driving the tour itinerary, there could be no accommodation for individual projects. He had to take one for the team and cancel his plans. There would be other opportunities, he hoped.

———

There was also a looming complication in Doc's private life.

Coe Uttinger had arrived on the scene a year or so previously as one of what he euphemistically described as 'flirtatious dates'. The vivacious twenty-something blonde divorcée had attracted him at a gig at Sydney's legendary Civic Hotel and their clandestine relationship had developed rapidly from there.

The daughter of an American military attaché based in Canberra, Coe was a graphic artist of considerable renown. She had famously designed the Weiss clothing logo and the cover for Peter Carey's hugely successful first novel *Bliss*.

Coe mixed in circles that fascinated Doc. A highly talented graphic artist, a singer, musician and songwriter, she had aspirations in Sydney's artistic and musical set and lived at Adereham Hall, a block of neo-Gothic Manhattan 1930s-style apartments in Elizabeth Bay. Social pages reported on glittering parties hosted there by its wealthy residents. Coe's arrival immediately set alarm bells ringing among the band's principals and management, who were concerned that she was leading Bernard away from the expressionism of Weimar cabaret that characterised The Angels.

Doc ushered Coe into the band's inner circle—even into the studio, where no other wives or girlfriends were ever granted access. When her influence extended to advice on musical arrangements, John Brewster was quick to put a stop to it. 'Coe came into the control room. She stood listening for a while and tapped me on the shoulder and told me to turn down the backing vocals and raise the level of Doc's voice. I got up out of my chair, opened the door and said, "Coe, this is a door. It's time for you to go through it."'

It was the band's Yoko moment.

Doc had managed to keep the details of his double life away from Dzintra by explaining away the nights spent at Coe's apartment as long sessions in the studio. But he was about to come terribly unstuck.

———

On 25 February 1980 Doc, John Woodruff and fellow Dirty Pool director Ray Hearn flew to the US for two weeks. Their main objective was to meet with the Epic chiefs ensconced on the thirteenth floor of Black Rock, their black granite and black-glassed skyscraper headquarters on New York's 52nd Street, and be briefed on arrangements for the upcoming Angel City tour.

Doc also recorded station IDs for rock stations across the US and Canada and met with representatives of the West Coast agency that would be placing the band. He flew back to Australia in early March to prepare for the US tour, which was due to start four weeks later.

With John Woodruff and John Brewster already in the US, the rest of the band and the support crew took off for America in two parties. Doc flew with the tour manager and the sound mixing and lighting team. Woodruff had managed to wangle them upgrades to first class from economy, where they expected to be. Seated in front of them were Everest conqueror and Antarctic explorer Sir Edmund Hillary and future Australian prime minister Bob Hawke. It was a trip to be savoured.

Doc was distracted during the flight, however. His departure from Sydney had finally brought his relationship with Coe Uttinger to the surface. She had turned up at the airport to farewell him and her effusive greetings of love and affection stunned and perplexed Dzintra, his fellow band members, their families and friends. His lame explanation that Coe was just a besotted fan was never going to placate his suspicious spouse.

When they landed in LA, Woodruff was waiting for them in a black Lincoln limo with darkened windows for the drive to the Beverly Laurel Motor Hotel. They settled back into the leather seats. There was a faint smell in the car reminiscent of petrol or kerosene, and the four arrivals looked at each other, smiled and looked back to Woody. There was something of a little ceremony about to begin.

Woody started scooping white powder out of a small plastic bag that he had pulled from his briefcase. A grin seeped around the outside of his aviator sunnies as he cut out four huge lines with a credit card on the shiny glass top on the bar unit next to his seat. He paused, sat back and his grin broadened.

'There you go, fellas,' he said. 'Welcome to America!'

———

The tour commenced on the US West Coast. After a couple of days' rest from the flight, they were driven a few hours south to San Diego for two late-addition warm-up gigs. The first of these was at the Roxy Theatre. As a result of good media, and 'Marseilles' being promoted hard by local radio station KGB, they received an enthusiastic response.

Then it was back to LA and the full-on tour launch, a weekend extravaganza involving two shows a night at the world-famous Whisky A Go Go on Sunset Boulevard. The Whisky is LA's iconic rock music nightclub in West Hollywood. Performing there has been a rite of passage for rock bands since the 1960s when The Doors were the house band.

A couple of hundred hand-picked high-profile music industry doyens and press were seeded among the capacity 'doors closed' crowd on the Saturday evening to witness a somewhat more reserved and subtle version of The Angels/Angel City phenomenon so familiar to Australian rock audiences.

The band roared into action, elevating the enthusiastic crowd that included not only Australian government luminaries from the LA trade office but recently relocated Oz-rock legend Billy Thorpe, as well as members of new-wave bands UFO and Pretenders. The finale brought the band to a truly sensational sound-and-light-filled climax and the audience begged for, and received, three encores.

Backstage in the dressing room, the record company presented the band with an enormous cake moulded into the shape of

America—rivers, mountains and plains iced in glowing technicolour. It was a symbol of the territory to be invaded and hopefully conquered.

———

The tour then kicked off in earnest, a cavalcade of cars and trucks swinging in a huge thousand-mile arc over the mountains to Denver and one of the Poison Apple discos. It was a rather odd gig, considering the disco-rock wars raging at that time and that they were supporting a Detroit pop band, The Romantics, whose recent hit was 'What I Like About You'.

Another long drive took them to the lake lands of Michigan, where they opened for the recently formed Joe Perry Project, a solo spinout for the former Aerosmith lead guitarist and occasional vocalist. Suitably impressed, he invited the band to work with him again. In the audience were Robin Zander and Rick Nielsen of Cheap Trick, for whom they were going to open the following night. Cheap Trick had previously toured in Australia and had struck up a friendship with The Angels. They had driven 80 miles to see Angel City support Joe Perry.

The Cheap Trick gig was a sold-out show at the downtown Joe Louis Arena, Michigan's largest area for indoor concerts. It held 14,000 people that night, the largest gig on Angel City's tour to that point. But it was also something of a letdown. When the band made its entrance onstage, the crowd was still filing into their seats and the house lights were yet to dim. This was not unusual in the US, where audiences time their arrival to coincide with the arrival of the headliners on stage. The Angels made the best of a situation that was largely beyond the control of either band; the broader shared experience was to lead to lifetime friendships among the musicians.

The touring schedule became an unyielding grind very quickly. The band travelled at night by hire car and truck, sometimes for hours and hundreds of miles after a gig, in order to make it to their next scheduled city. The cycle of travel-rest-perform-travel was repeated day after day.

Epic's well-practised routine awaited them at every town and their arrival was foreshadowed with anticipation and excitement. They were getting airplay on 130 stations, and with their compilation *Face to Face* album sitting at number 27 on *Billboard* they were receiving high rotation across the States. 'Marseilles' was on maximum launch exposure at local stations and there were regular press ads for their forthcoming concerts.

During the earlier trip to see Epic in New York, Doc had done individual station IDs for dozens of AM/FM radio stations. Epic publicist Gloria Johnson had telexed him in advance. 'Approach these station IDs as an acting exercise. Energy and sincerity are the keys. Use your flair for the dramatic and crazy and have fun with them. I know that when you are here to record you will be great!'

They were greeted by record company reps on arrival at each new town or city where they were booked to perform. The publicist would arrive with the photographers—*Stand here! Sit there!* There were pictures with local promoters, with fans and with event organisers—*Smile! Click click . . . Different pose! Click*—then maybe a station interview or lunch with a radio jock.

Doc was the band's undoubted master of ceremonies, the media king. That honeyed Irish accent and his piercing blue eyes had them from 'Hello . . . I'm Doc Neeson.' As he later told it, 'After each show the dressing room was filled with people: shaking hands, meeting this person, that person, smiling for the camera, posing with music industry people, journos and record store people. That's what these tours are all about . . . Meeting people and having a chat. You do one show on stage and another in the dressing room.'

'It's their whole American "push-a-band" trip,' he observed, seemingly in awe of Epic's coast-to-coast organisational prowess and single-minded focus. 'If they like something, they're full-on into it.' But Epic wanted to see reciprocal commitment and results from their new signings. 'By the same token if they don't like something, it gets dropped like a lead brick.'

———

After Michigan the band doubled back east to Chicago, where they were booked to headline at leading mid-west promoter Arny Granat's legendary Park West Club. This 750-seat venue in Lincoln Park had built an impressive history by nurturing relatively unknown bands from the ground up and The Angels, aka Angel City, were pumped to produce an outstanding show. What they could not have foreseen, however, was the chain of events that transpired after their truck, containing all their equipment, was stolen from a downtown Chicago parking station within hours of their arrival.

Hearing radio reports of the theft, Cheap Trick's Rick Nielsen was immediately on the phone—he was 150 miles away, but said he'd meet them at the Park West Club with a bunch of guitars from his personal collection. Woodruff rang Arny Granat. The promoter promised they could use the house PA system and then followed this up by calling the show's openers, Survivor, to ask them to lend their equipment to the Australian headliners.

A receptive and sympathetic crowd gave Angel City an amazing reception. Rick Nielsen joined the band on stage for a triumphant finale and the gig became part of the Park West's fabulous history.

The loss of all their musical equipment, however, was a disaster of major proportions. Filling out police reports and establishing the legitimacy of their insurance claim took days, delaying the whole tour. Four fully booked gigs—in Milwaukee, Pittsburgh, Washington and Philadelphia—were cancelled while the band regrouped.

The next stop on their itinerary would be New York, where they checked into the famous but time-worn Gramercy Park Hotel that had played host to the likes of Bogart, Cagney and the Kennedys in better days.

The band was booked to headline two nights at an Iggy Pop hangout, Great Gildersleeves in The Bowery. John Brewster recalled, 'That was in a really tough area, we had to walk through all these street bums and very weird people. You got the feeling that if you looked the wrong way, said the wrong thing, you'd be in a lot of trouble. But those two gigs were hot ones for us. We had a few celebrities coming backstage to say hello including Ian Hunter from Mott the Hoople and Karla De Vito, who we had met on the Meatloaf tour.'

The next gig after they left New York was a club in Newhaven, home of Yale University. Tour manager Mark Pope remembered: 'As usual the band blitzed the joint, left them standing on chairs and tables yelling for more! The next night we were booked into the Paradise Club in Boston. Epic had lined up a full day of media, so we jumped in the cars, lit up a few numbers and drove on to Boston.'

Then it was over the border into Canada and a long fifteen-hour drive north-west to Toronto. The top radio station there, 1050 CHUM, had had 'Marseilles' playing for days and the band's headline gig at the El Mocambo nightclub was a full house.

The 'El Mo' club is quite a local legend. The two-storey blues and rock music venue featured Buddy Guy and Muddy Waters as regulars. U2, Elvis Costello and Blondie had performed at the El Mo as up-and-coming performers. In common with Australian pub-rock venues, drink sales determined which bands would return. New bands would start out downstairs, and if the revenue they generated increased they hoped to graduate upstairs. Angel City's performance had the club's owners immediately wanting to book a return gig.

The tour then took them back over the border into the US and west to Detroit. The promoter of the Cheap Trick concert had been so impressed that he had booked them to appear at his Detroit club Centre Stage and had promoted it hard, selling out two shows.

Then there was a run of club dates down through Cincinnati, Columbus, Milwaukee and a long two-day drive to Seattle, before heading down the West Coast. After a Portland gig, the band arrived at San Francisco and appeared at promoter Bill Graham's Old Waldorf club, where AC/DC had played on its first US tour. This famous club on Battery Street had hosted some of the biggest names in the music industry, such as Dire Straits, Iggy Pop, Blondie, Metallica, Pat Benatar and U2.

Another long day's drive back down the coast to LA, where the band caught up with Epic, the William Morris Agency and their bookers.

There were lots of high fives and excitement. The Epic reps were elated and upbeat over the gig feedback, the extra radio airtime the band had received and the record sales figures filtering through. Astonished that the band had managed to recover from the theft of its equipment and wanting to maximise the momentum generated, Epic offered Angel City the support slots for Canadian 'Guitar God' Pat Travers, whose band would be playing 5000- to 15,000-seat venues.

John Brewster recalls, 'We were about to fly to London and Epic and William Morris the agents were saying, "For fuck's sake, get straight back here after that because it's happening here and we can get you opening sets on some big shows." We had airplay for

"Marseilles" on over 170 stations, some of it on high rotation and seriously charting in places like Seattle, Portland and in Canada.'

Everywhere Angel City played on that first American tour they had been getting an overwhelming response. As well as being picked up by over 170 US AM radio stations, FM and college radio were also getting right behind 'Marseilles' as the favourite album track. But management inexperience, plus conflicted planning and decision-making, meant they had to interrupt that surging momentum and return to Australia after the London shows for the planned national tour promoted by Dirty Pool.

———

In retrospect, it certainly wouldn't have been impossible to postpone their Australian plans. The role of their management company was critical in all of this. Dirty Pool had changed the way in which the Australian music industry operated forever: by combining the artists and their management as promoters of their live shows, they had effectively imposed on the performing artists the financial risk for their own tours while management took their cut as booking agents and promoters.

If The Angels had had a manager advising them solely in their own interest, the force majeure clause would have been invoked in both the US and Australian tour contracts following the theft of their equipment in the USA. That event had resulted in the loss of more than a week from their touring schedule, including four radio-sponsored gigs across four cities, with the consequential loss of tour momentum and record sales. The opportunity presented to support the Pat Travers tour offered them a serendipitous solution to that loss and it should have been seized immediately.

It was left to John Brewster to rail furiously and impotently at their helpless predicament. 'Woodruff insisted we get back to Australia after London for the release of *Dark Room* and to play the tour he had organised to support it. To me it felt like the space shuttle thing—you've got that window. If you get that window, you are back on earth. If you miss that window, you bounce off and disappear into the wild blue yonder.'

———

The UK and European legs of the first tour included showcase events where the band was presented at key venues in support of its record release.

After overnighting in London, they took off to Amsterdam for the locally popular Hemeltjelief Ascension Day Festival, which offered a rather esoteric 24-hour musical and theatrical line-up. Their gig started at midnight on an elevated stage at a city football stadium, where they rocked on to a friendly crowd and a cacophony of screeching whistles, hand-held hooters and fireworks.

Then it was back to London for a Marquee Club appearance. Doc had looked forward to playing the legendary club where all his teenage heroes had trodden the boards. It was a sold-out crowd of mostly expat Aussies from nearby Earls Court; with sparkling new replacement kit and their sound-and-light show, the band was on fire.

A couple of days later it was off to Paris and two hastily arranged small regional gigs preceding their headline show at the pagoda-like Le Bataclan theatre, years later the scene of the infamous terrorist attack. On that balmy evening, the band was warmly welcomed by an enthusiastic, largely walk-up crowd whose numbers stretched in a long queue down Boulevard Voltaire.

Considerably impressed, Epic's Europe chief took the band on a progressive dinner extravaganza that saw them walking in an increasingly unsteady fashion between multi-hatted Paris restaurants.

The following day it was back to London and the long flight home. They were nailed for excess carry-on baggage for their guitars. The bill was more than the value of the instruments. The tour had provided some very expensive lessons.

The release of *Dark Room* in Australia and a very profitable coast-to-coast tour to promote the album produced good local sales. Four months later they were back in the US to do it all over again.

But even four months is a critical period of time in the music industry. It can certainly cut short the zenith of an artist's career. Timing had meant everything in The Angels' success to date; now that compelling force, when opportunity and coincidence collide, appeared set to desert them almost irreversibly.

———

Doc's relationship with Coe Uttinger hadn't come to an end at Sydney Airport. The affair continued on his return and for a time he left Dzintra and moved in with Coe at Adereham Hall.

Doc had a lot on his plate. The following year would be an exceptionally busy time for the band, with tours around the country and recording commitments, followed by a return trip to the US, Canada and Europe. There was also a smorgasbord of other romantic opportunities. This did not represent the sort of life that the intense Coe had envisaged, and the grand passion soon appeared to be over.

Ultimately Doc reconciled with Dzintra and went home.

Chapter 13

Truth and consequences

The second Angel City fifteen-week international tour began in Detroit on 8 September 1980. Instead of the hire cars and trucks of the first tour, the entourage had graduated to a 'band bus' and driver engaged to transport them throughout North America. After eight weeks the band would leave the bus in New York on 1 November while they went to the UK and Europe to support a Cheap Trick tour, and then board it again three weeks later for the final four weeks of concert appearances that would in total wend a meandering journey across 20,000 miles of the US and Canada.

It would prove to be a monumental challenge of endurance.

The band bus that was to be Angel City's home for most of this period was similar in size and appearance to a Greyhound passenger coach. Polished gleaming silver and chrome, with black-tinted windows, it provided seating and sleeping accommodation for twelve, had a bathroom and huge underfloor lockers, accessible from the outside, for their luggage and musical equipment.

On arrival at each destination they would take just one room at a hotel—a 'day room', as travelling bands described them—where they could use the shower and facilities while the coach parked outside.

On the US segment of the tour, the band was scheduled to support 1960s UK rock legends The Kinks on three legs of their third US stadium tour after they had been banned from the US between 1965 and 1969. But The Kinks weren't just pulling crowds on the back of their earlier hits; they had released a new album that connected with the world-weary cynicism of the times. Clever marketing of frontman Ray Davies as the unique but ornery 'Godfather of Punk' meant the band was offering a somewhat updated message.

Angel City would be promoting *Dark Room*, the album they had hastily recorded just prior to their first overseas tour four months earlier and which had subsequently enjoyed success in Australia. One of its tracks, 'No Secrets', had been released simultaneously with the US tour as a single.

'No Secrets' was a different song for the band. Doc had written some enchanting lyrics based on a conversation with a young woman he'd given a ride to after he'd watched her miss a bus. It was a catchy number but, as released, it was undeniably a toned-down transition from the trademark hard-driving rhythms and those glorious bell-like peals of cascading guitar that saturated songs like 'Marseilles' and 'After the Rain', which US audiences and record purchasers had loved and so clearly identified with on the previous tour.

'No Secrets' was selling well in Australia, on the back of the band's exciting live show and TV performances, but trying to reconquer the US hard-rock radio stations proved to be a totally different proposition.

On their first day in Detroit, Doc was picked up from their suburban motel by the local Epic rep for media interviews to push the new album and to spruik 'No Secrets' to leading rock station WRIF. But he was stunned when the station DJ didn't pull any punches, telling him that the new single was 'soft' and did not fit the station's hard-rock format. The DJ wasn't impressed with the rest of *Dark Room* either—it was too different from their much harder-edged *Face to Face*.

Doc was immediately forced to recognise that this was going to be a lot more of an issue than just an unfortunate band and management oversight. From the perspective of the US hard-rock music stations, the *Face to Face* and *Dark Room* albums were poles apart. It wasn't a progression in the same genre; it was chalk and cheese.

It was also plain that the new album reflected the band's somewhat conflicted vision of their underlying musical identity. Doc, Buzz and Chris, along with engineer Mark Opitz, had all shared the view that The Angels as a band adapted musical trends to their signature sound. The Brewster brothers, however, still appeared to see the band as more of a roots-oriented rock and blues act in the tradition of their early jug band days. With Doc increasingly distracted by his turbulent personal life, and with Buzz and Chris no longer providing input into song production, the deadline-driven creative output on *Dark Room* had been, at best, confused.

And, of course, the fickle world of popular music had not been standing still. The hugely volatile market dynamic had sliced and diced existing genres into sub genres and hybrid genres. During the few months since the band's first tour, the so-called punk inspiration in the US had mutated and fragmented into more aggressive hard-rock sub genres.

One iteration, dubbed 'new wave', involved rebranding punk to avoid its negative anti-social connotations—it incorporated more pop and electronic sounds. Another iteration of punk music, calling itself 'hardcore', had also started to manifest itself. Hardcore was a faster, louder and more stripped-down, distilled version of the first wave of punk rock—its songs were not as melodic, but they were rhythmically intense and short.

From the perspective of the strictly curated US hard-rock radio stations in late 1980, Angel City no longer fitted with their focus on the evolving mutant hard-rock sub genres. Although the band had never wanted to be categorised as punk and had tried to avoid the baggage that came with it, they had certainly ridden the punk/new wave vibe and many of their followers and fans saw and aligned themselves with what that represented. Unfortunately, the band was always going to face a challenge regarding its 'authenticity'. Punk was meant to be the voice of the dole queue and the educationally deprived, but that was something that the articulate Angel City guys—university and private-school educated—obviously were not.

Epic too had recognised the changes with the *Dark Room* songs. The band had missed the opportunity to capitalise on 'Marseilles', their emerging hot single of the first tour, and instead of their next album becoming harder and edgier and thus suiting the progression in musical taste of their US fan base, their songs had become softer and more melodic. The Epic rep was intrigued why *Dark Room* had been released in the US so soon after *Face to Face*, telling Doc that more support and record sales for the band could have been achieved if they had continued with the punchier rock songs, which suited the tightly scripted genre requirements of the hard-rock stations. They could then have subsequently developed a different promotional strategy to suit the softer-format radio stations that would curate 'No Secrets' and the *Dark Room* album.

It was a dilemma that should have been recognised. It is amazing that John Boylan, their high-profile US consultant-producer on *Dark Room* and vice-president of Epic, did not appear to have even remotely faced up to these issues. Where had his counsel been on the plainly obvious? The cherry-picked *Face to Face* album was always going to be a hard act to follow, but it had established a successful song template that the radio stations, audiences and record purchasers loved. Some songs are like the Rosetta Stone, the key to a breakthrough. 'Marseilles' was certainly one of those songs. All they had to do was to put their heads together and write more songs like it.

———

Rock station WRIF was a promotional partner of Detroit's first and infamous punk rock venue Bookies, where Angel City were to appear. The Bookies 870 club had quickly become the hub of Detroit's punk, new wave and underground rock-and-roll scene.

A roster of emerging national and international acts had played Bookies, including Iggy Pop, Ultravox and The Police. Local bands, such as The Romantics, Sonic Rendezvous and The Sillies, made Bookies their second home. National magazines like *Life* ran stories about the club. Even David Bowie and his band came down after playing one of the big arenas, as did Elvis Costello, Blondie and other major stars. As a result of the popularity of this venue, radio stations and record labels in Detroit that had previously ignored local punk and new wave acts began to pay attention.

Despite the downer received from WRIF earlier that day, Bookies became a memorable gig for the band. Three encores did not satisfy the enthusiastic crowd. Doc realised how quickly the dynamic club music circuit had trended since the band's previous visit; just as they had experienced with the Hydaway Club members back in the 60s, niche pockets of followers here were right in the vanguard of what would undoubtedly eventuate as mainstream. The band was encouraged those enthusiastic fans from their previous visit had returned wanting to hear the older songs again live in the club setting. Angel City was a live band and it soon became clear that *Dark Room* would have to be sold through live performances rather than on radio.

However, it was also obvious that American and Canadian audiences, without having the exposure to Angel City that Australian radio and TV audiences enjoyed and yet to experience MTV, were going to take some time to 'get' what Angel City was all about. But they certainly understood the X factor wild frontman Doc provided—he stunned and intrigued audiences immediately.

He was unique. His pleasantly different voice could change from punchy spat lyrics to deep and husky, or to falsetto. His constantly changing theatrical stage persona was from another dimension— leaping outstretched from stage side or appearing from under a bed sheet—with a weird kaleidoscope of contorted facial expressions that ranged from benignly superior to the fiendishly Mephistophelian. Arms clasped around himself or outstretched beseeching, with wide-handed gesturing. Dancing, leaping and parading. A weird third-person monologue between numbers, stage clothes that changed from dinner jacket and Ascot tie to flying-suited test pilot.

Even the Epic promotional blurb, which described Doc's 'lightning stage manner' as 'manic, dynamic, powerful and possessed', gave up in the end—it concluded that he 'defied adequate verbal documentation'. Comparisons to Bowie, Jagger or Mercury were inadequate—Doc Neeson was really freakin' AMAZING!

———

The morning after the Bookies gig it was into the bus to commence a short series of club dates en route to the first Kinks gig in Chicago.

First off was Cincinnati, Ohio where the band was to appear at the 250-seat club and restaurant Bogart's, which was known as a proving ground for upcoming bands.

Cincinnati had provided a good reception on the first tour, to the extent that local radio Rock 96, which had heavily promoted 'Marseilles', was sponsoring their gig. But Doc's promo visit to the station again fell flat, with the DJ telling him that neither *Dark Room* nor 'No Secrets' were being played. 'Sorry, man, nothing there fits our format.'

The reception at Bogart's, however, was much better. The intimate setting offered an up-close experience, often allowing the audience to flow onto the stage. Angel City opened the set with a first-tour favourite, 'After the Rain', and Doc was described by local reporter Chris Williams as 'a raved up thumper'—'Neeson in black waiter tux cavorts about from stage right to stage left. Like a graduate of the Dwight Frye School for Wayward Rock Stars.'

The band had by now set out to sell 'No Secrets' properly and the song got a special workover for the pumped-up audience. As Williams reported: 'Neeson begins this number like an out-of-touch Sinatra amid blue lights and soft music. Snapping his fingers and hanging on the mike, it's a certainty that you're in for something more. Then the band lets loose and watch out.'

Another good gig. Another enthusiastic audience that moved tables and chairs so that patrons flowing onto the stage could dance.

The following day they travelled north to Madison, Wisconsin for a booking at Merlyn's Night Club, which had previously hosted many live-music shows including an up-and-coming U2. But local radio again had difficulty positioning *Dark Room* in their closely scripted playlists; the station jock described the album as 'a lighter brand of heavy rock; or a heavy kind of light rock . . . with elements of pop style new wave, or is it new wave style pop?'

Then it was on to Chicago on 17 September 1980 for their first support gig on The Kinks One for the Road tour, with two shows scheduled at the Uptown Theatre, a massive, ornate movie palace and concert venue located in the Uptown neighbourhood of Chicago and boasting a staggering 4381 seats. After that there would be a break while The Kinks went to Kansas, Baton Rouge and Dallas, before Angel City joined up with them again for concerts in Boulder, Seattle, Vancouver and Portland. These would be followed by gigs supporting The Kinks in Oakland, Inglewood and San Diego in California. Then there would be another break of about a week and they would join The Kinks again for a string of shows on the east coast, where they had not previously played.

——

Looking back now, after just over 40 years, it's almost impossible to imagine that there could have been any doubt whatsoever in the minds of Angel City band members or their management that the opportunity to provide support for The Kinks' One for the Road tour was going to be risky, with a high probability that some sort of incident or disruption might occur.

Ray Davies, The Kinks' brilliant songwriter and social commentator, frontman and band leader, was by then renowned for possessing a violent temper. He was subject to mood swings and to controlling and eccentric behaviour. He was capable of scheming and manipulative mind games. He had been promoted as an anti-establishment, feisty, aloof figure, and what you saw was what you got.

The frequent violent fights and exchanges of invective with his brother Dave, as well as with other band members, were already legendary; there should have been no doubt in the minds of any band contemplating the role as their undercard entertainment that they would be entering a bizarre and undoubtedly dysfunctional environment.

The tour was the third since The Kinks were allowed to return to the US, following an altercation that had led to their four-year ban from touring, imposed by the American Federation of Musicians in 1965. By 1980, The Kinks had managed to partially revive their commercial fortunes by adopting a much more mainstream arena-rock style, and the band's first studio album for Arista, the *Low Budget* album, showcased a rather opportunistic punk realignment with their 60s hits.

But their third tilt at the US was not going to be spoiled by absolutely anybody, and a number of reports had already surfaced of prickly relationships with their support bands mainly because The Kinks were of the fervent and emphatic belief that the show was entirely about them, showcasing Ray Davies and the lyrics of his songs.

Davies was also well known for being a tightwad, unwilling to spend money to progress technically with equipment, amplifiers and lighting. Also, The Kinks were already getting tired of touring; the effort required to be constantly on their game, to crank up the tired old standards, meant a regular turnover of contract musos and

backing singers. Their long-suffering road crew were in the unfortunate position of having to carry out the behind-the-scenes scheming
of the truculent Davies brothers. Where there was any chance of The
Kinks being shown up by a musically superior, better-equipped or
louder support band, their roadies were expected to be as unhelpful
as possible to the support outfits, limiting their electrical connections, lighting and power. The Kinks, and especially Ray Davies,
were not going to be upstaged or feel artistically threatened by
anybody. It was a simmering, watchful and petulant dynamic.

As a band, Angel City were comparatively well equipped. After
replacing all their gear following the theft on the first tour the
band had close to the latest, best and most powerful of everything.
They had a brilliant state-of-the-art lighting system and, long before
the development of in-ear monitors, they had the latest in fold-back
amplification. Doc even had one of the latest remote microphones,
which enabled him to walk down into the crowd as he sang.

Angel City's well-tested line-up arrived at their Kinks tour debut
quietly confident of their ability to put on an exemplary support
performance that would advance their goals and aspirations. They
were emphatic that they were not going to be intimidated by anyone.

There was, however, a significant, but at the time unknown, wild
card in the overall equation: Ray Davies, although still married to
his second wife, Yvonne Gunner, had recently embarked on a closely
guarded secret relationship with Pretenders' initiator and songwriter
Chrissie Hynde. Davies had expressed an interest in Hynde during
an interview in the rock magazine *Dark Star*, after her band covered
The Kinks' 1964 hit 'Stop Your Sobbin' and it became their breakthrough entrée to the charts. As well as a nice little earner for Davies
from the songwriting royalties of his old hit, the song did much to
generate interest in the whole Kinks back catalogue.

Davies and Hynde eventually agreed to meet in May 1980 in New York at the Trax nightclub. Hynde had been a Kinks fan since her teens. Although Davies was to say later, somewhat ruefully, 'I'd rather people liked my songs from a distance rather than try to meet me,' it certainly appears that his affection for her was for a time quite genuine. Hynde, by her own admission, was quickly besotted. Their clandestine relationship had gone from there.

———

For their first show at Chicago's Uptown Theatre Angel City arrived for their sound check in time to hear The Kinks in rehearsal, giving an updated shredding to some of their early hits. When The Kinks finished, they nodded at the members of their support band and walked off the stage and out through the theatre to their waiting limos, leaving Angel City to their set-up and to open the show.

It appears certain that The Kinks did not return to the Uptown Theatre in time to catch their support act but local reporter Bill Kitchen, writing a few days later, certainly did.

> Angel City is one of the most exciting and watchable groups to hit the new wave scene. Its performance, triggered by the wild antics of lead singer Doc Neeson, resulted in two encore demands. Neeson was vibrant from start to finish. His actions and the talent of the group should propel Angel City into the forefront of their field.
>
> Neeson, a cross between David Bowie and Mick Jagger, was literally all over the Uptown. He sang from the rafters, the balconies, the floor and even on top of the huge stage speakers. On one number he draped himself in a cheese cloth!

It wasn't until the following day that Ray Davies caught up with his support band. The 750-seat Park West Club, where Angel City had performed previously, had snared the band for a late-night supper show and The Kinks had been invited back to party on after the earlier performance at the Uptown.

Ray Davies was obviously disconcerted by the warm reception Angel City had received during the Park West sell-out show, and he attempted to get the band replaced for when The Kinks' tour was due to resume in two weeks. But contracts had been signed and he would simply have to put up with the upstart colonials.

One thing that Davies was apparently unaware of was that the first eight destinations where Angel City were playing as support for The Kinks were in cities where Angel City had been well received on their first tour—where the radio stations had been supportive and good record sales of their debut album had been achieved. The stadium crowds there were delighted to have the band return.

At the next show, at the 11,000-seat Boulder Events Centre in Colorado, the band arrived to learn that Davies had left instructions with his road crew that their power outlets for lighting and sound were to be cut back. He personally was going to be on hand to see exactly what these Angel City guys got up to on *his* show.

The Kinks meant different things to different people, and in Boulder there was all of them in the audience—from ageing hippies to the modern-day punks and punkettes checking out the legends whose riffs and power chords had inspired a whole new generation of US garage bands. But it was obvious that their appeal lay in the 21 songs from their heyday. Sadly, these were rushed through and handled so mechanically it was embarrassing. A few songs from the late 70s were slipped in, but these just served to emphasise that nothing held a candle to the golden oldies.

This was The Kinks' inherent problem. Ray Davies had lost his showman's verve; all his campy humour, theatrics and charisma were gone. Suffering from spinal issues that restricted his movement and made him look old, he was saddled with a sad and tired band that really could no longer deliver the goods.

Angel City, on the other hand, had no past to revive, just an ambitious vision: the fierce back-beat songs, like 'Shadow Boxer' and 'Long Line', set the cadence of their future. Doc's energetic approach to performing kicked down the doors that the tired old warhorses from The Kinks were trying to keep shut.

And so they progressed to the West Coast, where Angel City had been well received on their first tour a short few months previously. In Seattle, The Kinks delayed and dithered though their sound check, spending twice their allotted time, leaving Angel City only a few minutes before the doors opened. And their sound levels and lighting were again reduced by half.

In Vancouver 15,000 fans reacted to Australia's strongest live act in a decade with an ecstatic reception, holding aloft thousands of lit matches and lighters.

For the show in San Francisco additional restrictions were placed on the band. Their performing area was outlined by white tape stuck to the floor each side of the microphone, with instructions relayed from Davies by an embarrassed road crew that Doc was not allowed to move beyond those lines. Their lighting was cut down so severely that the promoter's ground staff had to appeal for common sense and courtesy. Doc ignored the white-tape borders and took his mic into the audience for a mesmerising three-encore show.

The LA show was a stormer for the band, with chanting demands from the audience for more encores. Buzz pleaded with his fellow band members not to further antagonise the now obviously incendiary anger of the headline act that was due to follow. He recalled calling to Doc and John, 'Don't do the extra encores, leave the audience wanting more.' But the rest of Angel City, including Doc, were impatient—nobody could tell them what to do. They would blow The Kinks off the stage.

At the 10,000 seat San Diego Sports' Arena, Angel City had their sound cut by half again, but they still got three encores. Yet it was a situation that could not go on. Ray Davies and The Kinks, as the headline act, held all the cards.

Then the axe fell.

The news came through from the tour promoter that Angel City would not be required for the final series of five stadium gigs on the east coast. They would be replaced by two girl bands for the Buffalo and Providence gigs; a very early John Cougar (before he became John Cougar Mellencamp, and when he was being positioned as a sort of glam Neil Diamond) would do the Philadelphia, Yarmouth and Hempstead dates. And for a second Philadelphia show, local pop band The As would support.

The aftermath of Angel City's sacking brought repercussions and over subsequent years a largely revisionist version of events has emerged, an elaborate story about the band's tragic misfortune in being denied the opportunity to play New York's iconic Madison Square Garden, the holy temple of rock-and-roll for touring acts and a guaranteed fast-track stairway to success. But contrary to this widely held belief, there never was an Angel City support performance scheduled at Madison Square Garden on the 1980 Kinks tour. Angel City did not miss out on playing MSG; there wasn't an MSG concert on the tour schedule.

The only New York City date on this tour was at the Nassau Coliseum in downtown Hempstead. This was an upmarket venue that had played many top acts, but it was not the centre of the musical entertainment universe the way MSG was. The Kinks did eventually play Madison Square Garden, but not until the following year, on 3 October 1981, during their Give the People What They Want tour. A new bestselling album, plus updated equipment and better sound, lighting and marketing, had by then improved their act considerably.

Doc was widely blamed for the tour sacking and, undoubtedly, he should have been more courteous, more respectful of the opportunity to support the legendary act. But in reality, an almost reckless bravado seemed to permeate the band and this is where responsibility lies. They all—the band, management and road crew—pushed back hard against what they felt were nonsensical restrictions.

It's highly unlikely that Doc would have ignored the emphatic and repeated directions from The Kinks without receiving management counsel. Where was the support for Buzz, telling his bandmates that it was better to leave an audience wanting more rather than aggravate, delay and diminish the arrival on stage of the main act?

The wild card was that through all this time Ray Davies was caught up in his affair with Chrissie Hynde. The Pretenders had just played the last venue in New York of their own lengthy tour. There were undoubtedly intentions for the pair to spend time together in New York between Christmas and the New Year. The Kinks had scheduled a very special and intimate New Year's Eve concert at the New York Palladium and the couple then planned to take a European holiday together. It was at this point that the international press would finally get wind that they were an item. In the calm before that media storm broke, Ray Davies was undoubtedly happy and very pleased with himself: Chrissie would be with him at The Kinks' New York City gigs, and he would put on the best performances of his life.

He certainly didn't want a tall, dark, handsome, younger and obviously much more athletic support act cavorting around with a microphone schmoozing and diverting attention from the main man. Perish the thought! Doc Neeson and Angel City were always going to be collateral damage. Nothing and nobody would be raining on his parade.

In the end Angel City suffered little real loss. Epic was quick to spin the sacking as the result of the band being too good, and the William Morris Agency and its bookers immediately threw themselves into arranging new dates across the US, up to Canada then all the way back to a monumental sell-out show at the iconic Ritz nightclub and concert venue in New York's East Village. Epic even organised a meet and greet with company heads after the Ritz show and Angel City's reputational damage from The Kinks tour fiasco seems to have been largely remediated. There were, in fact, so many gigs pushed into that frantic last hurrah of the tour's first leg that the road crew had to make up signs for the stage to remind the band where they were.

Certainly the club gigs did not provide stadium-sized crowds, but the band was developing a very useful fan base for the future. And by then it was November and time to leave the band bus in New York for three weeks while the tour progressed to the UK and Europe.

Chapter 14

Band bus blues

On the other side of the Atlantic, Angel City provided support gigs for Cheap Trick on their All Shook Up tour, which took in Birmingham and London, and Paris, Lyon and Nice. The Trick were headlining arena shows on the back of their earlier hits 'I Want You to Want Me', 'Surrender' and their relatively recent 'Dream Police'. The Cheap Trick guys generously provided Angel City full support and encouragement, even on occasion to their own detriment.

The Trick, however, were in something of a career lull at this time, certainly as far as their UK and European audiences were concerned. Their Beatlesque shows were seen as dated. *Music Week* reported on the Hammersmith Odeon gig in London: 'Cheap Trick laboured under the strain of coming on after a group who were better than they were.' Doc got the plaudits and the reviewer compared him favourably to Mick Jagger.

In France, which had been the third biggest market for Angel City record sales after Australia and North America, there was a similar vibe at the Paris Hippodrome. Doc was amazed to find the fans knew all the words of their songs and that they laughed good-naturedly at his French pronunciation in 'Marseilles'. The band performed to thunderous ovations. However, the Paris audiences were seeking something fresher than the Trick's old numbers and covers of classic 60s hits and were underwhelmed by the headliners.

There were similar responses at Lyon and Nice, but nonetheless Angel City was invited to join the Trick in their encores as the two bands delivered pounding renditions of AC/DC's 'Highway to Hell'. The audience's foot-stomping applause and flashing cigarette lighters just about brought the house down, and both bands celebrated their combined success before parting company. Angel City were driven to two gigs in Holland, while Cheap Trick went off in the opposite direction, to Portugal. Angel City then headlined club gigs in Amsterdam, Wiesbaden and the iconic Top Ten venue in Hamburg, where The Beatles had held residencies back in the day. They returned to London for a packed show at the Marquee Club before flying back to the US on 24 November for the third leg of the tour, which included concerts in New York, followed by shows in Atlanta, Nashville and Chicago then dates in Winnipeg, Seattle and Portland.

———

By this time the band members, the tour management and crew were becoming physically and mentally exhausted from a routine that closely resembled Groundhog Day. But they knew they needed to hang in there, boots on the ground, for as long as it took. AC/DC, The Kinks and Queen each toured the US relentlessly for years, eventually achieving success, yet even as bankable cashed-up star entertainers those groups found the going tough.

The Little River Band had broken the ground for Angel City in the US, but LRB was strongly focused on its brand of laid-back country rock. They were tightly disciplined musicians, and the band's management was more experienced, better focused and certainly less conflicted as promoters and booking agents than was the case with Angel City.

The Angels had originally found success in Australia through being a hard-working touring band doing 300 shows a year, head-lining their own shows under the Dirty Pool model and making a lot of money. They had developed a unique offer in a market where there was not a lot of real competition at the top end. But in the US, the band faced too many temptations, lacked focus and there was, at best, mixed commitment. As support artists, they were not earning big money. They had to secure a pathway to their own shows.

John Woodruff was also become increasingly conflicted between strategic decisions regarding the future direction of the band and his role as promoter and booking agent with Dirty Pool. Wearing his booking agent hat, his view was that future US tours needed to be based on reciprocal exchanges with US and European artists and their incorporation into the lucrative Dirty Pool Australia/New Zealand tour circuit. This meant that the promoter's commercial interests were likely to be put above any consideration of the best interests of the band.

As the band neared the end of the long grind on the US and Canada section of the tour, their original enthusiasm for life on the road had long since vanished. Their tour bus they had been initially so impressed with had proven to be time worn, uncomfortable, mechanically unreliable and unsafe.

It was obvious that some sort of watershed moment was about to occur. Despite the fact that the response to their concerts and their following were building strongly, there had yet to be any financial return from all the money they had made in Australia because it had been re-invested in touring and supporting their record company's overseas promotion.

Relationships were becoming increasingly strained between the tour party in the closely confined environment of the tour bus. Aggravations and niggling tensions, which had built up over weeks, were now spilling over into disagreements and arguments. Multiple issues—relating to perceived status, hierarchy and tour management process—now divided the band members, tour management and road crew into factions and cliques.

There was also a rapidly growing concern by their tour management over hard-drug use, which had quickly become integral to the band's touring scene, even affecting their day-to-day schedules. Record companies were very used to the colourful lifestyles of rock stars, but hard-drug dependency by artists had become alarming in the popular music industry worldwide. Deaths from drug overdose had cut a tragic swathe through the biggest bands of the day, and Australian artists and musicians were no exception. Record and band management deals were significant long-term investments, and record companies in particular were becoming increasingly risk adverse.

The long hauls that overseas tours entailed had also contributed to destructive and emotion-sapping relationship breakdowns. John and Rick Brewster had wives back in Australia who had selflessly supported them through the early days, but the intoxicating attraction of besotted fans, groupies and camp followers provided the perfect on-tour environment for misbehaviour.

There was also rivalry, even envy, of Doc's high visibility and his growing entourage of female fans. His marriage to the long-suffering Dzintra was collapsing under a veritable tsunami of infidelity, and he had left some major unresolved relationship issues back in Australia. Self-medication with alcohol and prescription drugs became his response to cycles of exhilaration and guilt.

———

The attraction of groupies and camp followers held little interest for either Buzz or Chris. Both were in committed relationships and just about over the touring thing. They were prepared to continue, but were both deeply dissatisfied that, after patently demonstrating their creative value to the band, they were unable to arrive at a revised commercial arrangement with the BNB songwriting partnership so as to provide them with a stable financial future.

They had raised this issue on several occasions at what they felt had been appropriate moments during the tour, but on each occasion the subject had been changed or the conversation moved on. There was still no benefit to them in helping promote and sell records if there was no future royalty income. It made no sense at all for them to endure the long hard life of the US tours. They felt they had become little more than low-paid hired help. This even extended to them having to accept a lower quality in their travel, daily living and meals arrangements. The camaraderie of the early days was gone. The 'all for one and one for all' spirit had all but vanished.

Doc had been sympathetic to reviewing a revised royalty split on the melody component of the songwriting, but he was out-voted. Finally, Buzz took his grievances to Woodruff, who went to the Brewsters.

John and Rick Brewster had become fine musicians by watching and emulating AC/DC. Their talents as songwriters were widely acclaimed as considerable, but they were now in Rock God and Guitar Hero Land. They saw no reason whatsoever to accept the argument that Buzz and Chris's collaborative and collective creative contribution in the past had helped drive the band to greater success and thus made the whole financial cake bigger.

Now pushed by Woodruff to deal with the issue, the Brewsters were emphatic: there would be no changes. The royalty shares were non-negotiable. Buzz and Chris were employees; they could take it or leave it. For Buzz that was the end of the road. He would work out a reasonable period of notice and be gone. Chris would hang on for another few months but, without Buzz, his enthusiasm was gone.

So now there was a real problem. With Doc increasingly distracted by a storm of emotional entanglements, Buzz and Chris effectively rejected, The Angels, aka Angel City, were creatively dead in the water. They were directionless. Their mojo was gone, and their creative wings were flapping vacantly. Meanwhile their competitors had recognised that the constantly evolving music industry in North America was changing its direction again—punk, new wave, hardcore and their multi-fragmented derivatives were just about done as mainstream genres.

The new direction, which Angel City had certainly helped precipitate, was going to be a resurgence of elements of the 60s power pop. It re-emerged as a more aggressive form of pop rock, based on catchy, melodic hooks and ringing guitars. This would be very much the sound that Angel City had pioneered with 'Marseilles' and 'After the Rain'—songwriting that combined their Eddie Cochran-inspired back beat with the influence of 60s icons The Who and The Byrds.

But would The Angels be able to meet the challenges that these developments presented, or would they become a victim of their own success? Would another band pick up the baton that The Angels had within their grasp and run with it? After all, a band's sound and its songs are almost never completely original creative compositions. You can't copyright a rhythm pattern, bass run or a chord progression, only a melody or lyric. And even then the boundaries can be pushed, so it's whatever you can get away with. The simple fact is plagiarism drives rock music innovation.

The future for the band was unclear, and some of the issues they now faced were complex and troubling. There were to be very difficult times ahead. What would later be viewed as the classic Angels line-up, which had held together through all the long hard years with Alberts, was about to end.

Buzz stayed on for the planned Back in Black tour around Australia with AC/DC then departed the band. For him it was a bittersweet moment. He had grown considerably during his years with the band, and he was proud of the band's achievements and his contributions. But he had met Kay, and he wanted to fully commit to their life together. He was excited to get to the next stage of what would become a fantastic musical career, closely linked to his family and other personal interests.

His departure from the band was announced to the media in a short statement that said he had left due to 'musical differences'. The band now had to look for a replacement, and a stream of well-known Australian musicians showed interest in the role. Eventually a quietly capable New Zealander auditioned. Brent Eccles had more than natural talent—he had come well prepared. He had learned the songs, rehearsed them and studied Buzz's fills. The band was impressed. He was in.

It was a good decision. As well as his drumming skills, Brent had an intelligent and capable business head on his shoulders, something that would greatly enhance his value to the band in the years to come.

Chapter 15

Mislaid mojos

The new year of 1981 provided The Angels with the opportunity for a fresh start in many ways. It was a chance to regroup after what was a rancorous, argumentative and weary close to the two long international tours of the previous year.

There were local and interstate tours to look forward to, concerts with AC/DC, trips to Darwin and New Zealand, a new album to make and an opportunity for the band to review their progress during the past year and plan the next stage of their attempt to break through into the US. But first the fallout from the previous year's US and European tours required resolution.

Bassist Chris Bailey was unhappy at losing his friend and long-time colleague Buzz Bidstrup, which meant it was only a matter of time before he departed as well. Hiring new musicians might cover live-show requirements, but the creative input, diverse experience and organisational memory that had helped drive the success of the *Face* and *No Exit* albums were not going to be readily plucked off the streets. The overseas tours had also prompted criticism of the band's management from vocal members of the support crew. While manager Woodruff might tolerate and work to remediate the concerns of his band, he was not going to allow dissent from lighting and sound people to go unsanctioned no matter how talented they were. However, despatching skilled but resentful technical support specialists who went straight to Cold Chisel to help that band look and sound truly brilliant and amazing was effectively shooting yourself in the foot.

The contribution of recording engineer Mark Opitz and the experienced overview and mentorship of the Albert Music people, together with George Young and Harry Vanda, had also been lost in the move to Epic.

To many industry observers and fans, this was confirmation that The Angels' opportunity for a stellar future was in real danger of being shredded and lost forever.

Nowhere was this risk more evident than in the US.

———

The Angels' opening commitment of 1981 was to support a national tour by AC/DC, which was to be that band's first return visit since leaving Australia four years previously. Although The Angels had now reached the stage where they no longer played support acts in Australia, they had welcomed the invitation from their old friends to open for them. The AC/DC tour would provide a swansong for drummer Buzz Bidstrup, who would leave the band at the conclusion of the tour. It would turn out that these would be the last concerts in which they would play in their original line-up until The Angels' reunification 25 years later.

AC/DC's world tour to promote their *Back in Black* album was a logistical extravaganza. The always high-wattage band had been amped up considerably—gargantuan sound, lighting rigs blazing and, as the centrepiece, 'Hells Bell', a cast bronze bell pitched to the note of A and weighing a tonne or more. By the time they arrived in Perth on 13 February 1981 they had played almost 150 concerts on a gruelling eight-month global journey, taking in Europe, North America and Japan. They were returning triumphant to Australia after conquering the world.

For The Angels, the concerts provided an opportunity to pit their musical prowess and showmanship as Australia's most popular working band against the hottest global rock-and-roll act of that time. For Doc striding onstage in Sydney, resplendent in red silk shirt and white scarf streaming, it was an opportunity to pay his own tribute to friend and AC/DC frontman Bon Scott, who had died tragically the previous year. It was very important to him that his performance fitted the moment. This was not a US tour pay-to-play gig. The band was there for the audience, who not only knew who they were but the words to their songs.

Doc remembered The Angels audition for Alberts at Chequers, and way back when the Keystone Angels played support for some of the first AC/DC tours.

It was an opening act that fans would long remember, with some suggesting it was a performance equal to that of the head-liners. Even AC/DC gave them big grins and thumbs-up as they left the stage.

———

Epic had originally created a marketing plan for Angel City in the US that was quite different to the plans that produced success for the Little River Band and AC/DC. The Angels strategy had been to start with 500-seat clubs, come back within six weeks to do 3000–5000 seaters then come back again to do 10,000–15,000 seat venues; throw in some pay-to-play support gigs on big-name stadium shows; and back up with promotional support from the dedicated US rock-music stations and high rotation airplay of album and single releases. But this had not panned out as they had expected, and the original battle plan needed a rethink.

Epic was undoubtedly losing interest. Despite some encouraging initial sales for the US *Face to Face* album, the Epic view was that the opportunity for maximum sales of this first US release had been lost due to the band's return to Australia following the heavily abbreviated first tour. Their delay in returning and the hastily released follow-up, *Dark Room*, had gone against the evolving direction of the US market and was lacklustre compared to *Face*.

Total US album sales for the band were described as 'subpar'. The US industry's performance benchmark was that 300,000 US album sales were needed if there was to be continued music company support; sales of Angel City albums were nowhere near that.

Epic had been patient and put plenty of boots on the ground and songs across the air to support the first two tours, but Angel City and their management had been tested and up to this point had, frankly, been found wanting. The sales of their next album and the feedback from their third US tour would be watched and listened to very closely.

———

In January 1981 Ronald Reagan rode to the US presidency on a tide of sentiment for an earlier, simpler time. The US music industry too was going back to the future, refocusing on the broad-spectrum power pop and pop-rock genres of the 60s. The US chart-topping artists for the year were to include resurgent 60s power-pop origi-nators The Who, followed by post-punk/power-rock Pat Benatar and post-punk/pop-rock The Police.

Then on 1 August, MTV, billed as 'Rock-and-Roll Music Tele-vision', exploded on air for the first time and completely disrupted the American music industry, which immediately turned away from cultivating expensive alliances with rock-music radio stations to spending millions on music videos. Within a couple of years MTV was in nearly every American home and just about every-thing that was cool in the 80s could be sourced back to MTV as a pop-cultural phenomenon.

Down Under, music had moved on too: The Swingers from New Zealand, Kim Wilde, Kim Carnes, Roxy Music and, among the locals, Men at Work were some of 1981's chart toppers with various shades of pop rock and post punk/power rock. Australian pub rock had found its niche, progressing from Billy Thorpe's New Aztecs, with their ear-blasting repertoire of blues-based boogie rock and simple repetitive riffs, giving way to the quite different sound that The Angels had made their own—unashamedly primaeval pounding kick and snare-drum thumping rhythms, solid connected bass lines, power chords and cascading duelling riffs. It was energetic, urban and predominantly male.

Doc's oblique poetical lyrics, alternating from dark reflections on society to relationship angst, at times mirrored his personal agonised relationship journeys. His dark poetical interludes between the songs startled and delighted his audiences.

Australian pub rock's heavy danceable beat drew big crowds of enthusiastic and often happily intoxicated fans to the pubs and clubs in Australia and New Zealand, but in the US this style did not translate to big record sales, nor did it pack theatres and stadiums. There was a market to be had in the US club scene where, as in Australia, performers were judged by alcohol sales, but, unlike in Australia, it was highly competitive at the top end and the patrons were selective and fickle.

American and Canadian audiences had shown definite interest in Doc's unique and exciting mock Weimar cabaret-styled offering, but it took effort and energy to present and the band and its management failed to recognise the impact and enormous opportunity that MTV would provide to bands with a highly visual stage act and presentation. It became quickly obvious that, thanks to this new medium, how a band looked mattered as much as if not more than its sound.

———

With the AC/DC tour over, The Angels undertook trips to New Zealand and Darwin; then it was back to the club and pub circuit for a few months, working up their act with new drummer Brent Eccles and recording what was to become the highly successful local release live EP *Never So Live*.

Brent's drumming was to bring an entirely different musical personality to The Angels. His pulverising rhythms now almost dominated the mix, with a steady hard-hitting groove, but he was not as sophisticated as Buzz, whose style had swing and a Ringo-like finesse of balancing the percussion sound to the song and complementing the composition.

Given their intention to return to the US in February 1982, plans then got underway for their next studio album. John Woodruff successfully negotiated to engage LA-based producer Ed Thacker in a joint deal with Ray Hearn, who wanted Thacker to record his band, Flowers. This move was attractive to Doc because Ed Thacker had earlier worked with a favourite artist and fellow Weimar cabaret fan, Marianne Faithfull, producing her highly acclaimed *Broken English,* a new-wave rock album containing elements of punk, blues and reggae.

Thacker was keen to see the band live the moment he arrived, so a special gig was organised at Blacktown Workers Club. Then it was into EMI's iconic Studios 301, Australia's long-standing tier-one studio and even then one of the top half dozen recording studios in the world. For the band members it felt surreal to be recording there at this time; Stevie Wonder and David Bowie were also recording under the same roof.

The band took the opportunity to catch up with Bowie. Doc and David talked animatedly about what each had been up to since the Thin White Duke tours; they compared notes on touring the US and David congratulated the band on their progress.

——

There has been much conjecture over the years on where The Angels' relationship with Epic went wrong. Was it Doc's supposed fling with the girlfriend of a senior Epic/CBS executive? The behaviour of the other band principals? For record companies band peccadilloes are occupational hazards—issues, but unlikely deal breakers. The truth, unfortunately, was pretty basic. In the US and Canada, Angel City record sales were not enough for the band to remain commercially attractive to their record company.

In the case of the critically important *Night Attack,* the make-or-break album for their February 1982 US tour, it was undoubtedly rushed through to meet an Australian Christmas 1981 show and record-store deadlines without any real effort and commitment towards their US obligations. At least a couple of the songs in the album had been written months previously, during the 1980 overseas tours, and half a dozen of the new songs had been well tried and tested on the subsequent tour to New Zealand and on the three-week run of gigs from Darwin to Sydney with the band and crew enthusiastic about on-road performances of the new material. However, matching that excitement to studio recordings is another matter entirely. As new drummer Brent Eccles recalled, there was a 'never-ending drive to get the right phrasing, the right lyric and the right emotion. I had never experienced that kind of angst or intensity, it was serious.'

On *Dark Room,* with Buzz and Chris creatively furloughed, the 'grade stick' (recording-industry jargon referencing relative market-ability) was wielded by the band's three principals, John, Rick and Doc, with specialist technical input from co-producer John Boylan and recording engineer Mark Opitz. Manager Woodruff would never go into the studio and interfere: he would always let the band get in and do it, and then he'd go out and sell it.

The *Night Attack* sessions were to generate some argy-bargy as to whether the album was good enough to take US record sales to the next level. Doc had considerable anxieties as work on the new album got underway that neither John nor Rick Brewster seemed to understand the seriousness of their predicament with Epic. Something really amazing needed to be pulled out of the box to underpin the album's intended international release by Epic-CBS and the proposed global support tour. Doc felt there was too much emphasis by Ed Thatcher on what the local pub and club circuit venues demanded and not enough focus on what Epic-CBS and the US rock-music stations wanted to hear.

Doc's parents Kathleen and Bernard James Neeson in Belfast, 1942.

LEFT: Two-year-old Doc with his first girlfriend, Helga, in Austria, 1949. RIGHT: Young Doc in Bordon, England, 1953.

LEFT: Bernard at a pyjama party in 1964. (Alan Hale) RIGHT: Brenton Spry gives Bernard and Jon and impromptu music lesson at Noarlunga Beach, South Australia, in 1964. (Alan Hale)

A Hydaway Club poster, 1964. (Jon Bradshaw)

Jon working a part-time job at the Mobil servo, Elizabeth West, 1964. (Jon Bradshaw)

Bernard in the pose on the 1966 Sink Club poster with his remodeled Maton guitar and plasticine nose as a nod to Pete Townsend. (Jon Bradshaw)

Dzintra Neeson.

Doc the sound engineer while
recording *No Exit* in 1979.
(Philip Morris)

Doc and Buzz recording *No Exit* with The Angels in 1979. (Philip Morris)

The Angels in concert in the 1980s. (Bob King)

Doc with Rick, Buzz, John and Chris in the early days of The Angels. (Grant Matthews)

Doc on the Night Attack tour, Friday 9 April 1982 at the Old Waldorf Club in San Francisco. (Geej Castillo)

Messianic Doc at The Venue, St Kilda, in the early 1980s. (Kevin Moss)

Doc in full flight, 1985. (Bob King)

Doc at the Seattle Paramount Theatre, 1985. He was very popular in Canada.
(Bryan Woodwick/Woodeye Photo Seattle)

Doc with Judy Mermaid on the night they met in Canada in 1985 after he leapt into
the audience and carried her back on stage. Judy ended up making one of Doc's
most famous pieces of stage gear, a flying suit he wore for many performances.
(Ken Orr/*Edmonton Journal*)

Kym Pymont and Doc, circa 1987.

Doc having a bubble bath, in Santa Barbara, USA, 1989.

LEFT: Annie Souter in 1997. (Margaret Wentworth) RIGHT: Tina Power, Doc's secret companion. (Avi Ohana, Celebrity Vogue Photography)

Doc, Kylie and John Farnham at the Tour of Duty concert, Dili, 1999.
(Newspix/Scott Radford-Chisholm)

LEFT: Doc being given the Australian Service Medal by Lt General Sir Peter Cosgrove at Springwood Public School's Twilight Fair, which Doc opened in 2000. (Jason Webster, Top Notch Video) RIGHT: Doc serving champagne to bestie Bob Bowes dressed as a World War I fighter pilot, circa 2001. (Anne Souter)

Doc with an acoustic guitar. (Deb Martin)

Doc signing the album *Out of the Blue* for friend Tone E. Murphy. (Tone E. Murphy)

Doc in Baghdad on his tour of the Middle East with Doc Neeson's Angels in 2007. (Mitch Hutchinson)

Doc with Doc Neeson's Angels in Kevlar body armour inside an armoured Humvee in Iraq, 2007. They are about to negotiate Route Irish, the most dangerous road in the world. (Mitch Hutchinson)

LEFT: Doc with Mitch Hutchinson at the Hard Rock Cafe. (Pete James) RIGHT: Doc in Hobart with The Angels, 2010. (Deb Martin)

Doc with his brother Anthony and sister Maureen at the Lord Mayoral reception for The Angels, Adelaide, 2010. (Deb Martin)

Sno Brewer's 1998 portrait of Doc for the Archibald Prize.
(Sno Brewer)

Doc with his portrait painted by Pietro Calvitto, circa 2012. (Anne Souter)

Doc and Annie at Padstow RSL, on St Patrick's Day 2012. (Deb Martin)

Doc with Dame Marie Bashir when he received his Order of Australia, Government House, Sydney, in 2013. She said she was a fan. (Rob Tuckwell Photography)

Doc giving his infamous 'death stare'. (Deb Martin)

Doc had wanted the band to use Peter McIan to produce some of the tracks for the new album as his assistance had proved invaluable during preproduction of 'Fashion and Fame', which subsequently proved to be one of the band's most popular songs. US-based McIan was in Melbourne at that time producing what was to become Men at Work's US and Australian number-one album, *Business as Usual*, which would become one of the biggest international-selling Australian-produced albums of all time. Peter's high-level skills in musical arrangement were exactly what was missing in the process of turning an average Angels song into a brilliantly successful one.

'There were a lot of good ideas that weren't realised,' Doc said later. 'We didn't finish writing the songs properly before record-ing them. We took on too much. We were in such a hurry to do them that we did not turn them into good songs. It's not one of my favourite albums.'

An understandable sentiment. For much of the album his vocals, his oblique poetic lyrics almost unintelligible, drown in the mix.

———

The recording sessions for what would become the *Night Attack* album finished on notes of high drama and bruised egos. Doc, as one of the three band principals, felt entitled to contribute and have his views respected, but the reality was that he was continually out-voted and out-gunned; his attempts to bring other advisers such as Peter McIan into the creative process were viewed as disrespectful to the Brewsters, as well as to producer Ed Thacker.

Given the feedback he had received from doing dozens of radio interviews on the first two trips to the USA, Doc was also strongly of the view that their new offering needed to be correctly 'positioned'.

But the Brewster brothers clung to the belief that all the success of the *Face* and *No Exit* albums had resulted solely from their collective vision. They were deeply concerned that outsiders would try to change what they saw as their unique guitar-band signature.

With the tracks finally completed, it was time to take the master tapes to the US for final mixing to so-called 'American standards'—the addition of reverb, the subtle refinements and final polish before handing over to the record company. Ed Thacker and John and Rick Brewster flew off to Hollywood's Cherokee studio, which Beatles producer George Martin had once called the best studio in America. Everyone who was anyone—from Ringo Starr and Michael Jackson to David Bowie and Frank Sinatra—used the place. It came with a price tag to match.

But the final mix is only the last 500 metres in any album's marathon production journey. It certainly won't get your record onto the podium if you haven't undergone the right preparation and hit every milestone along the way.

Their vulnerable situation was almost immediately confirmed when, soon after John and Rick Brewster returned to Australia, John ran into Epic's VP John Boylan, who was in Sydney on business. Brewster played the mixes for the new album to Boylan, who listened politely, paused reflectively and commented somewhat cryptically that it sounded like the band 'didn't have its creative captain anymore'. Boylan's view was that if the songs had been more like 'City out of Control' it would have been a great album. That was The Angels; the rest of the album wasn't.

John Brewster was stunned.

But, despite this gnomic assessment, Epic's local distribution partner, CBS Australia, was well in tune with the local market and the burgeoning pub and club rock vibe and was very happy and

excited by the new album. Its local release was immediately scheduled for 30 November 1981.

A stunning coal-black cover provided the background for
a wheeling dervish outlined in vermillion—Doc, with his arms and
legs flung out, a momentarily transfixed anti-Christ. On the reverse
were the attendant Brewster disciples and the whirling drumsticks
of Brent Eccles.

Night Attack would subsequently come close to top ten in
Australian album sales at this time; its songs would enthuse the
punters at the beer barns and clubs across the country, who saw it
as a return to a heavier sound. But, sadly, it wouldn't attract the US
radio stations or be convincingly commercial enough to win friends
and influence the hard-nosed suits high in the towering New York
headquarters of Epic.

'Fashion and Fame', arranged by Peter McIan, was to become
the only song from this album to feature in both the top 10 and
top 40 of all-time Angels' gig favourites.

———

The Angels flew off to New Zealand on 28 January 1982 to play
a spot at the annual Sweetwater Festival while John Woodruff went
to the USA to finalise arrangements for the release of *Night Attack*
in February and the promotional support tour. It was obvious that
Epic VP John Boylan had immediately acted on his lack of enthusiasm for the new album. Instead of an international release and global
tour, Epic would instead support the US release with a six-week
run of 500-seat club and 700-seat theatre dates, plus some 1000-
seat auditoriums and a couple of 2000-seat arenas up the US West
Coast and Canada, where the band had been previously popular.

Then, a few weeks before the tour was due to commence, Chris Bailey was advised by a specialist that an injury to his left eye sustained when a bottle was thrown at the riotous Sydney New Year's Eve concert was now seriously threatening to become a detached retina. Because he needed a delicate operation and a month's recuperation, he would not be available for the first two weeks of the tour. To keep to the tour schedule the band would need to engage a stand-in bass player.

With little time to spare John, Rick and Brent flew to the US to find a replacement. They drew a blank with the first applicant, but the second—Jim Hilbun, an LA studio muso—immediately impressed them. Quietly capable, Jim had bought the *Face* album and learned the songs. Without even needing to plug in his amp, he nailed the audition. A talented musician and vocalist, Jim played not only bass guitar but a mean saxophone and electronic keyboards. And not having heard of the band before the audition, Jim was soon amazed at what he had got himself into.

———

The first gig for the third US tour by Angel City was 8 April 1982 at Warnors Theatre in Fresno, California, where they had made a huge impact on both previous tours. More than just a theatre, Warnors is a 2000-seat late-1920s Spanish colonial pile with a massive pipe organ boasting 1000 odd pipes with 720 keys, pedals and pistons that sits in the orchestra pit in front of the stage area beneath a flimsy cover designed to protect the pipes. 'Whatever you do,' the theatre manager implored Doc, 'don't tread on that!'

Of course, with that warning, Doc jumped down onto the cover to serenade the audience during the show, only stopping after the manager shrieked from stage side that he would surely fall through the cover and impale himself 'like a sausage on a skewer' on the organ pipes below.

Then it was on to do a double show at the Old Waldorf Club in San Francisco, the popular venue on Battery Street where they had been well received on the earlier tours, and another gig back in Fresno at the 750-seat Tower Theatre. After that, a semi-trailer was loaded with all their equipment, sound and lighting gear for the concerts in the north–west.

Booking agents William Morris had managed to capture the enthusiasm for the band that had made this corner of America the biggest generator of their record sales in the country. The *Face* album and single 'Marseilles' from the earlier tour had created huge interest and months of high-rotation airplay, so the band easily filled a string of concert venues from Portland and Seattle, across the border to Vancouver, Calgary, Edmonton and Anchorage in Alaska.

The intensity of these performances and the pressure to go out day after day, both on stage and for promotional interviews, was unrelenting. And it was obvious that the support from Epic had been pulled back. Staff on the ground seemed somewhat casual and disinterested as the tour progressed—'Oh, are you guys in town?'— despite the enthusiasm of the concert crowds.

With Chris Bailey now ready to return, the concerts in Alaska were Jim Hilbun's last of the tour and a send-off party for him was held at the hotel before they boarded the plane for the long flight back to LA. Jim had fitted in well; it seemed certain that they would work together again.

Back in LA there was a two-show sell-out at the iconic 500-seat Roxy Theatre on Sunset Boulevard. At the first of these a host of high-profile expat Australians—including Bryan Brown, Mel Gibson and Billy Thorpe—and a busload of Epic heavies from the LA office added to the press in the VIP area of the smoke-filled nightclub. Chris Bailey arrived with minutes to spare after being delayed by a lockdown at his nearby motel resulting from a shootout in the street below.

The band hit the stage for a mesmerising show, ripping into life with the hard-edged riff of 'Long Night' before Brent Eccles started pounding the skins, demonstrating that The Angels were back with a new album with a forceful new energy. Doc, in his element and energised by both the music and the sea of faces in front of him, cavorted from stage left to stage right singing, shouting, whispering and cajoling his way through the set list.

Afterwards, in the small backstage area, the band squeezed for greetings and photos with the celebrities and gladhanding with the local Epic people, who 'enjoyed the show a real lot'. Enthused by the high of the show and the rush of excitement, the band was filled with hope that, despite the obviously diminished interest from Epic and an uncertain future, all they had to do was continue to deliver their stunning live shows and they would get through in the end.

———

After only a few days back with the band and missing his long-time colleague and friend Buzz Bidstup, Chris Bailey had had enough. Chris had lived and breathed The Angels from the early hardship days with Alberts, but it was now time for him to do something different.

A sense of profound despondency settled upon the band during the last days of the tour. Jim Hilbun was offered Chris's bass role and accepted it, but it was becoming evident to all that the band members had entered a totally different phases of their lives. There was a real need for many things to change.

It was increasingly apparent that the band would be dropped by Epic International. But in Australia the situation was completely different: the band had an enormous country-wide following; the popularity of their music would ensure local record company CBS's continuing support, at least for a while. The club and pub scene was vigorous and the Dirty Pool business model for popular touring artists was successful and highly lucrative for all involved.

But the personal relationship between the three principals was becoming problematic; there were even increasing tensions between John and Rick Brewster. There was considerable uncertainty and doubt as to whether the band could continue to successfully function at all.

The events of 1981 were to foreshadow what was the start of a monumental period in Doc's life. He certainly felt the loss of Buzz's consistent artistic support during recording sessions; frustrated and feeling increasingly marginalised, he was already indicating outside of the band that he was seeing The Angels as a useful stepping-stone to a future in the Australian film industry rather than as a career in itself. In fact, he had already initiated and been steadily developing a circle of colleagues and friends useful to that career progression, some of whom would play an increasingly large role in his life.

Chapter 16

A different swansong

The despondency surrounding the last few days of the third US tour prompted considerable soul searching by Doc. Apart from the band's issues, his recent 35th birthday and the physical demands of continually wheeling out the dramatic, constantly moving exertions of his alter-ego had strongly reminded him that nothing lasts forever, and his current energetic stage act definitely had a use-by date.

He reflected on his schoolboy aspirations to become an Australian Rules footballer where the average career of a player was just eight years and the usual retirement age, after perhaps 200 games, was 35. Yet he had completed over 1000 concerts during the previous five years; these were only marginally less physically demanding than the stress on a footballer's body and most of his gigs were conducted in the unhealthy, overcrowded, choking, smoke-filled fug of clubs and pubs.

By comparison, the next most physical performance in the band was that of the drummer, but at least he remained seated.

The theatrics of the guitarists in an Angels show was as a foil: they remained almost stationary and theirs was a relatively unstressed routine, apart from the risks to all of the band from unpredictable, hot and sweaty, beer-swilling crowds.

If the instruments of the other band members broke down or wore out, they repaired or replaced them. But Doc's instrument, his voice, was already permanently damaged by overuse and required frequent painful injections to augment and repair vocal cord scarring. Lengthy and repetitive practices and rehearsals, arguably unnecessary for a vocalist, became excruciating. On top of this, his temporary hearing loss from the effects of loud music was progressing to a permanent condition and, without any of today's ear-monitor technologies, this made it increasingly difficult for Doc to gauge his own performance.

Despite the infectious enthusiasm of the band's new members, the relationship between the three principals was becoming increasingly argumentative and Doc recognised this was probably terminal. Nevertheless, he was optimistic enough to see this provided an opportunity for change. It could be the spark for inspiration or the seed for transformation.

Following the end of his affair with Coe Uttinger a year or so previously, his home life away from the band had stabilised considerably. Dzintra had accompanied him on local tours, and they had recovered their relationship with shared friends, interests and activities outside of the band. He was receiving considerable support and encouragement from her towards the next stage of their life together, whatever the direction, and there were even, at last, thoughts of a family.

Sadly, however, this reconciliation was soon to be subjected to new stress. While Coe was now largely on the fringe of Doc's life, their feelings for each other were still somewhat unresolved. And then came tragic news.

Bjarne Ohlin, keyboardist with the Divinyls and a friend of Coe's, recalls: 'Sometime in May 1982 Coe had returned from a retreat where no one realised that she was turning yellow from jaundice. She assumed her weight loss was the result of a diet/fitness regime. I visited her with my partner Anthea, was shocked at her condition and promptly had a doctor mate do a house call. He immediately called an ambulance and had her admitted to hospital. Tests quickly revealed cancer in most of her vital organs with no hope of recovery. We saw Doc after an Angels gig and told him she was terminally ill, which appeared to knock him hard.'

Doc was devastated. Coe had had a profound influence on him. A muse, an inspiration, the embodiment of a surreal aesthetic that for him equalled instant and continued attraction. He was horrified by her rapid physical decline and immediately committed himself to spending much of her few remaining weeks at her Elizabeth Bay apartment looking after her as her condition deteriorated. But in late July she had to move to palliative care.

Coe died on 9 September 1982. Bjarne Ohlin said, 'After she was cremated, we organised a bus with her parents and a group of us who had cared for her while she was ill, and drove to Kangaroo Valley. Doc was able to attend. We all passed our hands through Coe's ashes as we spread them into a hole we had dug in preparation of planting a tree.'

There is no doubt that Coe's tragic death had a profound effect on Doc for the remainder of his life. His surviving diaries record heartfelt reminders, the anniversaries of their meeting and of her death. He corresponded with her parents for decades and they seemed to look upon him almost as a son.

Coe had provided Doc with an entrée to Sydney's wider art establishment and introduced him to a world that was exciting and new. To people who were interesting, erudite and affluent and who respected and feted him for his talents as a songwriter, musician and entertainer. Her bright-red manicured fingernails epitomised much of her personality: daring, dramatic and outgoing. She certainly didn't shy away from being forthright in her views and opinions. In one of Doc's notebook jottings his anguished words write of blood-red nails, and of tasting ashes in his mouth.

Doc quietly took over the lease of Coe's apartment and it appears that from this point, surrounded by her possessions, he began to live two separate lives: his return to a semblance of normality with Dzintra at their tastefully renovated inner-west Sydney home and his clandestine half-life in the shadows of his affair with Coe in the refined art-deco elegance of her old apartment at Elizabeth Bay.

Rick Brewster recalled: 'From Coe's death on, Doc carried a small shrine in his suitcase—a hoard of photos and mementoes—and set it up in his hotel room with candles, where he drank and howled for hours after gigs. So much so that it sometimes disturbed other guests and brought the manager to the door to see if he was OK.'

———

Even before the third tour to the US, Doc had become involved with CBS on the artwork for the *Night Attack* album. This had resulted in him working towards a refresh of the visual images associated with their five-year-old live show. The plan for the rest of 1982 included finalising these updates, recording a new album and the development and preparation of promotional film clips to support the single releases from their next album. With MTV, music clips had become increasingly like mini movies, involving talented creative directors, storylines, highly developed sets and support actors. Radio audiences accustomed only to hearing artists sing could suddenly see them too.

Doc immediately realised he could develop and promote his interest in a future film career via these new developments. But John and Rick Brewster were reluctant to support what they thought was a selective investment in Doc's profile. It became a new source of friction between the band's principals.

————

The new Rhinoceros studio in Surry Hills was purpose-designed and managed by engineer Andrew Scott to attract the cream of local and international musical talent. It was to become legendary for its role in creating some of Australia's all-time great albums, from the likes of INXS, The Angels and Cold Chisel just to name a few.

Early to move to the Rhinoceros studio was Mark Opitz who, after joining the creative exodus from The Angels, had produced the seminal *East* for Cold Chisel. In July 1982 he recorded three songs for INXS that their manager, Chris Murphy, used to broker local and international record deals for the band, including with Atco, a subsidiary of Atlantic Records in North America.

Impressed by the new facility, The Angels followed INXS into the Rhinoceros studios in September 1982 to record what would become the *Watch the Red* album. The plan was that they would schedule recording during the week but keep the money coming in with gigs at the weekends.

Watch the Red is often described by Angels fans as the album where the band lost direction. Musically it is certainly the most incongruous and diverse in the band's entire discography. It seemed as if they had decided to dip their toes into completely different styles, songs and song structures—there were shades of Tom Waits, Queen and Van Halen, and other tracks featured a French horn, an organ and sultry saxophones. It was certainly not The Angels of old.

Gone too was the pounding percussive backline of *Night Attack*. The drums sounded completely emasculated, an audible shadow of their former dominance. In fact, there was something tinny and frail about the whole thing. The Angels were a muscular guitar band and they needed to sound muscular on record.

The title track, 'Watch the Red', was about being cheated by a sleight-of-hand sideshow game at New York Central Station. 'Eat City' was based on Doc's recollection of watching a group of young Americans scoff down enormous calorie-laden sundaes. These were pages from a US tour scrapbook and more of an expensive indulgence than anything like a seriously focused songwriting attempt to capture US chart success. 'Stand Up', penned by Jim Hilbun, was a pop-rock number and it was rushed to be released as a single so it could be in the record stores for November 1982.

———

Doc's work with CBS's marketing department in Sydney meant that he was soon driving the production of videos to support the single releases from the new album. He was also quietly scoping the possibility of a larger project. His widening social network had brought him into contact with an arts collective called the Macau Light Company, which was based in one of the expansive old residences on Lang Road fronting Sydney's Centennial Park. This was a loose group of artists, writers, musicians, dancers, designers, actors and filmmakers. One of their leaders, Susy Pointon, a New

Zealand-born filmmaker, had just made an art film about the life of the terminally ill poet and self-styled mystic John Walker, who Doc had met and become friendly with.

At this time Dirty Pool and some of its industry partners were organising a large musical event to be held on New South Wales's Central Coast. The Narara Music Festival was to be Sydney's attempt at a Woodstock-type rock-and-roll event—albeit fourteen years after that iconic event in upstate New York. It would extend over the 1983 Australia Day weekend and feature an all-Australian music bill, including Men at Work, The Angels, Cold Chisel and INXS.

John Woodruff had negotiated that The Angels would perform a set of eleven songs on the Saturday night. He was also talking about recording the set for another live-album release. Doc immediately saw an opportunity to film the concert.

Although Doc couldn't secure much interest from Woodruff and the rest of the band, he explored the idea of filming their set as a commercial proposition. He was spurred on by his sense of history and by the real possibility that the Narara concert might well be the last chance he had to preserve images of himself as the frontman of The Angels at a highpoint of their popularity.

He also saw the opportunity to present the new show format to a wide audience, both locally and internationally. He felt very strongly that The Angels were a lot more than just a band, an issue that divided the three principals. He was clearly seen as the lead figure in the band so, implicitly, The Angels were *his* band. This clearly rankled with John and Rick Brewster, a situation that undoubtedly discouraged the brothers from offering anything more than lukewarm support for the idea of filming the concert. The round of pre-Christmas tours, during which Doc was frequently accompanied by Dzintra, only served to increase the animosity. Small issues exploded into open hostility, which was not helped by Doc's growing dependence on alcohol and the routine use of cannabis and methamphetamines by the other two.

The other members of the band were also by then becoming increasingly anxious about Doc's state of mind. His secretive behaviour and his friendship with John Walker had them imagining that he had taken up with a strange religious cult. When he invited the tall saffron-robed figure, who wore a white Akubra and was on crutches, into the Rhinoceros studio, John Brewster had a fit. The band was paying $2000 a day for the studio and the presence of 'Doc's Swami' was a major problem. Ultimately Doc acquiesced and John Walker left the studio.

———

In early January 1983 touring started again. Doc felt lousy, marginalised and alone, and the atmosphere between him and the Brewster's was increasingly toxic. Alarmed at his report of being 'obsessively depressed', Dzintra joined Doc on the road in country New South Wales. This was just the support and reassurance he desperately needed to formally advise of his decision to quit the band—effective after his commitment to the Narara concert and completion of their current album.

A huge row with Rick ensued. When things calmed down, Doc went to each band member and apologised. John and Rick tore strips off him, he said; Jim and Brent wished him luck.

But later that day there was something of a circuit breaker. The gig was raided by the drug squad, and Rick and Jim were busted. With charges being laid, a truce was required.

Back at Flinders University, in a drama production, Doc had played the part of a small-town lawyer. To get into the role he had spent a few days doing the rounds of the city's courthouses with an Adelaide solicitor. He had absolutely aced the theatrics of that onstage role and subsequently he stepped up to the plate with a freshly pressed suit, eloquence and that brief previous 'legal experience' to extract the band members from their drug charges. Rick was on five charges, Jim on three. Dope and speed. Doc's efforts secured them three months to pay their fines.

———

Doc started to shop the idea of filming The Angels' Narara set around Sydney's FM music stations and TV stations. Within a few days Rod Muir, the owner of two-year-old Triple M, had agreed to buy the radio broadcasting rights and to support an approach to commercial TV stations for a simulcast.

Now Doc needed to organise a film crew. On 19 January he asked Susy Pointon for her advice, and she recommended he talk to Bernie Cannon. Bernie had been the producer of *GTK*, the wildly successful pioneer ten-minute rock-music program on ABC-TV. Cannon was keen to cover the event and offered a hot-shot four-man film crew. He would direct and Doc would be executive producer, in association with Triple M.

It all came together very quickly. A day later Channel 10 was on board. All Doc now needed was the $12,000 ($30,000 in 2021) to cover the cost of filming and film stock. Time was running short. The Narara concert was just days away.

Meanwhile the band was juggling recording studio and inter-state tour commitments. The pace for the last week of January 1983 was frenetic: the weekend in the Sydney studio, then to Tassie for a hot gig at the Kingston Sports Stadium in Hobart followed by Melbourne's Bombay Rock, where Doc literally passed out from suffocating heat and nervous exhaustion. He also felt both conflicted and guilty over his grief at losing Coe and distress at how upsetting the whole episode had been to Dzintra.

He then flew to Merimbula for a couple of days, a welcome break and recovery after the horror gig at Bombay Rock. Doc talked with Woody and Brent about the future, still wondering about what would happen after the Narara concert.

All the while the two new band members, Brent and Jim, were anxiously working behind the scenes to see if the conflict between Doc and the Brewsters could be resolved and if Doc could be persuaded to stay on. Maybe things could be done differently.

With Doc seemingly in a better place after the break, Dzintra returned to Sydney but it was less than a week before the Narara concert and Doc needed to resolve whether the band would support his filming proposal. During the drive back from Wollongong he put the proposition to John Brewster that the band invest $12,000 (equivalent of $35,000 today) to cover the cost of film stock and engaging the camera crew. John advised that he was concerned about the band going over budget on the album and declined. Doc rang Woody who couldn't see any way of financing the film either. Doc told them both that the band could not afford not to commit to the project, but with no lifeline in sight the film crew was stood down.

Filmmaker Susy Pointon, however, encouraged Doc to push on, pointing out the importance of getting the footage in the can. Edit and finance later. Then on the drive home Doc witnessed a huge prang on Parramatta Road. It was a light bulb moment! He knew that Narara was going to be spectacular and realised that being there when the action was happening was a once in a lifetime opportunity.

With only hours to spare, Doc immediately seized the moment, rang his bank and arranged an overdraft against his house in

Adelaide for security. He gave Bernie Cannon the go-ahead to get the crew and film stock together. Showtime!

———

It was a hot day at the Narara concert and an audience of around 50,000 people settled in for the drawcard events of the Saturday evening. The site was well organised with a fantastic sound system. Rick pitched their tent in the holding area for upcoming acts and this became band HQ. Doc and Dzintra strolled and filmed the crowd and Doc went for a warm-up while INXS was on the stage.

Top of the bill was Men at Work, all pumped from their US Billboard chart-topping album success with *Business as Usual*. Second on the bill was The Angels. Theirs would be a performance silhouetted against a blood-red moon rising over the stage behind them. They would be followed by Men at Work with the closing set for the evening.

John Brewster was more than a little anxious about The Angels following an in-top-form INXS. 'On the night INXS were on before us and put on a blinding show. We said: Woops, we'd better play well and just went for it.'

The Angels delivered an absolutely blistering performance; reviewers acclaimed it as one of the finest shows of the band's career. It was later released as an album titled *Live at Narara*.

During 'Marseilles', Doc called again on the skills he'd learned all those years ago servicing PMG telegraph lines and started climbing the scaffolding on the speaker towers. The band anxiously watched him steadily ascend, microphone in mouth, till he reached the top.

Doc later recalled, 'I wish I had organised a camera up there. I asked the fans to light their lighters and suddenly there were all these pinpricks of light across the amphitheatre. It was a starry night and it looked like I was seeing right out to infinity.'

The delighted crowd called the band back again and again for encores. It was an amazing show and Bernie Cannon's team had captured it all.

Coming off drained and exhausted after their performance, the band passed a group of CBS execs totally riled that poor programming had resulted in The Angels' high-energy show effectively trouncing the more laid-back Men at Work before they had even made it onstage. And CBS was The Angels record company too!

Finally wending their way home after a long day, an exhausted but exhilarated Doc reflected over a nightcap joint with an elated John Woodruff; INXS had gone down well, but the Angels had creamed it. Their three cameramen had got the best and only professional footage of the entire concert.

Doc had been friends with John Woodruff for a long time, back to his uni years at the shared house at Glenunga. Over the few days following the Narara gig Woodruff was able to convince Doc that his best course at that point was to remain with the band. Bookings for The Angels stretched out for months ahead. Any new career that involved roles in theatre, film and television in Australia would mean a fragile existence and he had just hocked himself for a large overdraft for the film project that would take some time to complete and see a return.

With this, the immediate crisis had been resolved. However, there were still deep-seated issues within the band that were much more serious and would surface again. Doc too was entering dangerous territory with his personal affairs and 1983 would prove to be incredibly traumatic for him and those who chose to share his life.

Chapter 17

Tangled

Doc's time during the weeks immediately following the Narara concert was filled with tidying up the loose ends associated with his last-minute filming arrangements. He needed more funds to cover the editing and his bank overdraft was increased to $15,000 (2021 equivalent $40,000). He made arrangements for a business name to be registered and, after forming a company with Albert Music to promote the film, he organised the lease of a temporary office in the Alberts building.

A sad anniversary was also on his mind: 7 February was the day he had met Coe. He recalled in his diary her last words to him on the night she died, 'You'll see me'. He wrote that he loved Coe but a few lines down he scribbled the name Susy Pointon, her address and her phone number with the words 'Life goes on'. Sometime around this date he had commenced an affair with the New Zealand filmmaker.

A couple of weeks later John Woodruff confirmed the news the band had been expecting. Epic Records formally advised that it would not be going ahead with its option to distribute *Watch the Red* in the US and its relationship with The Angels/Angel City was therefore officially terminated.

Somewhat surprisingly, though, Epic's local distributors, CBS Australia, had agreed to take up its options for the Australian and New Zealand markets and would release both the album and selected singles, despite many in the company believing that the band had lost its way.

Doc does not appear to have been too concerned about the news from Epic. It was early autumn, and the band was very busy but he was anxious to enjoy the remaining warm days of the season. Daylight saving had just finished and he woke early after a late night.

He tells himself to USE THE DAY! He hires a dingy and small outboard at Balmoral Beach for a cruise under the Spit Bridge with Dzintra at the helm. They enjoy a quick swim on the nude Chinaman's Beach, then a sumptuous seafood lunch, and a couple of bottles of Traminer at the Monterey Guesthouse in Mosman.

During March and April 1983 Doc was heavily involved with the editing of the Narara film, often relying on Susy Pointon's advice and connections. John Brewster was helping mix the soundtrack for the film at the EMI Studios 301 in Sydney. There were meetings with Rob Muir, sometimes accompanied by John Woodruff, regarding the commercial exploitation of the broadcast. Add in The Angels' local concert commitments and it was an intense and exhilarating period.

In late April 1983 Doc was still spending a lot of time at Coe's apartment. He arrived back one night after a meal with friends to find that there'd been a break-in and almost everything of value had been stolen. He was overwhelmed with distress at the loss of virtually all of Coe's personal possessions. Gone were the tapes of her voice and the film of their time together, her clothes, her shoes . . . her crazy blue metallic wigs that he regarded, among other things, as his 'talismans'. Everything!

———

'Eat City', a second single from *Watch the Red*, had been released in conjunction with the Countdown Awards back in March and on 2 May 1983 the whole album was released in Australia by CBS. *Watch the Red* first charted on 9 May, peaked at sixth position and stayed in the charts for 24 weeks. Supported by the new stage show, it maintained the strong sales record that The Angels' album releases had always achieved on home turf.

But for those who had known Bernard a long time and only saw him irregularly, the vaguely imperceptible changes to his personality from around this time certainly had more impact. Initially there was little you could put your finger on, but gradually there were signs that all was not well: personality changes during which he morphed from someone you knew into someone you didn't; introspective self-analysis; uncharacteristically troubling incidents; and a refusal to play by the rules in relationships. He seemed almost compelled towards entitled infidelity.

Doc would later rationalise his state of mind by offering that he was emotionally vulnerable and that the timing of his relationship with Susy Pointon was very much in line with his psychological neediness. When Susy came along he was attracted by her adventurous spirit, and he admired and respected her commitment to filmmaking. She showed him another way to be, a different option for life partnership and a different career direction that was initially very attractive to him.

By the end of May 1983, both Dzintra and Susy knew they were pregnant.

Dzintra, at that time utterly in the dark about her husband's secret life, was delighted—at last Bernard might recognise he had family responsibilities and change his ways.

But Susy's feelings were considerably more complex. She recalls: 'We became close but then, and I think this may have been typical, just as intense as had been his presence, he was gone. I continued with my life until I learned to my great surprise that I was pregnant. I decided to keep this to myself while I worked out what to do. Then one day Bernard turned up at my apartment with the news that his wife Dzintra was pregnant and he was going home.'

At the time Susy was extremely angry. She felt she had been deceived. Doc had presented himself as having separated from Dzintra, living on his own in the apartment he had been sharing with Coe before her death. Susy had felt their relationship had been special and that they shared similar career goals and aspirations. She had no idea she was just one of a number of liaisons Doc had been conducting at the same time as he was supposedly responding to Dzintra's attempts at reconciliation.

For Susy the fallout was agonising and raw. Doc wanted to ignore her predicament and move on, but her friends couldn't wait to tell her which attractive females he'd been seen with. She felt she was paying for some sort of weird game he'd been playing with his wife. She felt misled, used and discarded.

More recently—with the passage of time and since Bernard's death—Susy has revisited these events and the decision she made.

'We had a serious discussion—I had decided I could not dishonour the child I was bearing and would take full responsibility for it without any obligation from him. I promised Bernard I would not ask him for anything, or put any pressure on him and his family, and I have kept this promise for the past 35 years. Of course I was subjected to a range of negative judgements—people said I had got pregnant on purpose to entrap him or to get money. But none of this was true.

'After Aidan was born, I realised I did not want him to be raised in that kind of toxic environment—he deserved much better—so regretfully I left Sydney and returned to New Zealand, where my mother was seriously ill. Of course, it was hard. I lost my career and my friends and was forced onto a benefit, living and looking after Aidan in a simple bach in the bush outside Auckland. Meanwhile I continued with my writing but, when Aidan was two, I married an American filmmaker and we set up a studio in Appalachia on the border of West Virginia in the US.'

———

Late June to mid-July 1983 was a busy time for the band. The Angels' Watch The Red tour hit the road, supported by the deafening blues-rock outlaws Rose Tattoo and Alberts' recent signing, hard rockers The Choirboys. It was a remarkable local tour for the time. Three of the biggest and loudest rock-and-roll bands in the country, accompanied by two semitrailers with all the equipment necessary to support the massive tour, circled the eastern seaboard playing sell-out indoor concerts.

To coincide with the tour, CBS Australia released The Angels' 'Live Lady Live' in two separate single versions, a 7-inch version and a 12-inch collector's edition with a photographic cover. Combined sales of both reached number 43 on the Australian charts. It was also during this time that the band encountered the infamous 'No way, get fucked, fuck off!' chant for the first time.

On his return to Sydney at the end of July 1983, Doc made arrangements to give up Coe's Adereham Hall apartment. He had enjoyed living there and leaving was a wrench. On what was likely his final night at Elizabeth Bay he cannot sleep. Lying in his bed unpacked and feeling homeless and hollow, he murmurs a prayer, 'Goodnight, Namaste Coe'.

Meanwhile the Narara film was in the final stages of completion. It had involved a lot more work than Doc had ever anticipated but that, plus the band's touring commitments and other diversions, kept his mind occupied. At the last moment there were high-level and somewhat frantic discussions as a bidding war unfolded over which TV station would receive first screening rights. *The Angels Live at Narara* simulcast finally went to air on the Nine Network and Triple M Radio on Wednesday, 14 September. It received the highest viewer rating for a simulcast up to that time and the video of the event was released soon after.

But things were not going so well with their record company. CBS Australia had released a fourth single, 'Is That You', from the *Watch the Red* album and it had failed to chart. With the support tours and associated promotion for the album concluded and sales tapering off, the word came down in November that CBS would not be re-signing The Angels in the new year. The band was surprised at this news; they believed that local domestic sales had always been good and they were still packing out local venues, indicating a solid base for future releases.

Nevertheless, both Epic and CBS had previously expressed their concerns, even misgivings, over the lack of clear vision in the band's musical direction. Apart from Epic chief John Boylan's earlier comments, the stellar Artist and Repertoire (A & R) head of CBS Australia, Peter Karpin, had to push hard to get 'Small Talk' onto the *Night Attack* album. But Rick and John Brewster both felt it sounded too much like what they had done before. In their view, it was just 'too Angels'. To this Peter had retorted, 'Too Angels, eh? Well, I've got news for you—you are the fuckin' Angels!'

CBS had also been disappointed that the band hadn't used producer Peter McIan while he was in Australia engaged by Men at Work. There was also anxiety about the damage wrought by the toxic relationships between band members, the personnel changes and the loss of what had been a diverse and uniquely talented creative partnership.

The record company was also concerned about the recurring media reports of drug convictions by band members and anecdotal stories filtering back that at least one member's cocaine dependency had earned him the sobriquet of the 'Snow King' among hard-living members of Sydney's entertainment set. CBS Australia had been down this sad path a few short years earlier with Dragon who, after exploding onto the Australian music scene, had all but destroyed themselves with a heroin- and alcohol-fuelled descent into oblivion, leaving three members dead from drug overdose or related causes.

The Angels now represented a distinct risk to any further record company investment, to say nothing of the possibility of reputational and brand damage. In CBS's view, other emerging Australian bands represented better value and prospects without being difficult to manage or creating controversy.

Chapter 18

Brave new world

Change is a constant, a fact that The Angels manager John Woodruff appreciated better than most. He appeared to be not too dismayed that his band had been dropped by both Epic and CBS. He'd had a couple of months to consider the anticipated loss of both contracts and was ready to move forward with someone else. It was also convenient timing in a way, because in the last weeks of December 1983 he closed the Dirty Pool booking enterprise. He would retain his interest in band management, but his aspirations now lay with tour promotion, arguably even more of a conflict with band management than being a booking agent.

Woodruff had heard that Irving Azoff, a US music industry hot-shot band manager and promoter, had been appointed to head up the rescue of the near-bankrupt LA-based entertainment conglomerate MCA Inc and to stop the haemorrhage of its top-selling artists to more progressive labels. He had immediately cut the deadwood from the MCA artist roster and set its A & R team to sign some more acts. Without delay, Woodruff opened his Teledex and started to work the phones.

The Angels had been using EMI's Studio C in Sydney to write and record some demo songs. 'Small Price' had emerged from one of those sessions. It would be used to represent the band to US and Australian music companies, but it was hardly the killer track that could take on the likes of Van Halen, whose 'Jump' was then currently holding the top spot on the US Billboard charts.

Nevertheless, the pitch John Woodruff made to MCA's A & R folk was certainly effective, and it didn't take long to have them interested. MCA was well aware of Angel City's popularity in the US north-west and felt that with the right album and proper support the band could finally achieve broad US success. MCA was not impressed with *Watch the Red,* but an album that reflected the band's earlier successes and contained similar high-quality songs would secure a contract.

So the deal was done. An advance against future royalties of US$200,000 (about $500,000 in 2021) was paid. After Woodruff's commission, plus legal and other expenses, this left the band with about US$130,000.

And then began what was to be the most expensive album production experience of the band's entire career. But it never really needed to be that way. EMI's Studios 301 in Sydney had already pitched an open-ended, no time limit, flat-fee offer of $56,000 for Studio A, plus $4000 if the band wanted to use Studio C for songwriting. John Brewster recalled: 'The demos we had done [at Studios 301] were really good, so it wouldn't have been hard to take them upstairs and do them for real for the album. But Woodruff said we should record in LA. He had done the deal with MCA and wanted us to be on their doorstep. He wanted their active involvement. I said EMI's Studios 301 is an amazing studio; it was good enough for Bowie, Duran Duran and Stevie Wonder. But Woodruff insisted he could get a top studio *just as cheap* in LA and convinced us to go.'

Woodruff was obviously well prepared by MCA to counter any resistance from the band; using a top-line studio in LA and a name producer would have been regarded by MCA as essential for the band to progress to the next level. To create music for a world market, where the real money was made, the band would need the best of everything.

―――――

By the time the band flew out of Sydney on 1 May 1984 bound for LA, all thoughts of containing album production costs to 'just as cheap' as EMI's Studios 301 seem to have been pretty well forgotten. Also relegated was the idea of a tight schedule. This was definitely not going to be another frantic re-run of the *Dark Room* album. Production would take as long as it took.

Top-flight UK producer Ashley Howe, a favourite of hard-rock legends Uriah Heap, had been engaged at $50,000 against percentages, plus first-class air tickets from the Old Dart and 5-star accommodation for him and his wife for the duration. His brief: to produce an album that would relaunch Angel City in the US. The band was booked into the swish Oakwood Apartments at Toluca Lake in downtown LA, just a few easy steps from Universal Studios.

Once settled in the band needed transport, and with the local LA sales yards full of big cars at bargain prices, John and Doc both indulged their 1960s rock-star fantasies. John was first off the mark, purchasing a white 1964 Cadillac De Ville, which was duly named

'Caddy White'. A few days later Doc also picked up a Cadillac, a 1967 gold De Ville with a black roof and a six-litre V8 that was christened 'Doc's Caddy'.

The renowned Record Plant Studio in LA was also a long way from being considered 'just as cheap'. Its long and rich history included recording sessions with a veritable pantheon of rock icons, from Jimi Hendrix and John Lennon to Fleetwood Mac's *Rumours* album and, rather unsurprisingly, Irving Azoff's own band The Eagles, who'd produced *Hotel California* within its fashionable surroundings.

Their band's first two weeks there were spent in the rehearsal studio, writing songs and testing out ideas. When they moved to the recording studio and Record Plant's house engineers started to mic the instruments, there were immediate issues with Brent's drumming. In the engineers' opinion it didn't 'swing'. Sometimes called 'groove' or 'shuffle', swing is the addition of tiny delays to every other hit of a beat.

A lot of drummers raised on rock just haven't internalised the syncopated feel of a jazz back beat that was supposedly essential to the recording process. No swing, no essential groove and the studio engineers were helpfully suggesting that Brent be replaced by a local LA session musician. But the Brewsters were not having any of that. Brent was the band's drummer, he had played on the two previous albums and the demos and they were not changing him.

The engineers played around with Brent's drum set-up for another couple of hours before an exasperated Howe decided to call in the big guns. He picked up the phone and maestro sound wizard Lee De Carlo arrived. De Carlo was the superstar of studio engineers; he had worked on *Double Fantasy* for John Lennon, but he came at a hefty price. He straightaway provided his complex and impenetrable mic set-up for the drums and they sounded amazing, but there was one problem as John Brewster later explained: 'It was fantastic, but it didn't go down on tape. We paid for him to get the sound and he got it. But then he disassembled it at the end of the session. He said, "That's my drum sound. If you want to get it back, you have to hire me." So Lee De Carlo was on the payroll and some monster celebratory lines of coke were set out and consumed.

Then they got on with the mic set-up for the other instruments. They were all *boosted*, and everything was *charging*. Occasionally they'd pause for a cheeky champagne to calm the buzz. Much later, their eyes wild, the band was ready for the long night of recording ahead. Such a blitz was pretty standard stuff at the pointy end of the LA recording business, where the whirring cogs of power and money that keep that frenetic-paced city running hot thrived on those little stripes of white powder.

At that time, recording at top-end US studios was a painfully slow and expensive process. Studios were booked for weeks, if not months, for the recording and mixing of an album. Under the direction of specialist producers and engineers, prospective songs and melodies were broken down into their separate parts. Individual instruments were recorded, played exactly the same and re-recorded, one take on top of the next, to build up layers consolidated into a so-called big sound. Then all the component parts of the song, including the vocals, were reassembled like a jigsaw and mixed for a final musical profile.

Ashley Howe showed himself to be a first-class audio engineer, with a terrific ear and the stamina to be able to work with the creative tension of record production. His calm attention to detail and his patience to bring out the best in each band member while still focusing on the end result was a great asset. Even when the nights stretched into the following morning and everyone was dog tired, he was meticulous about what went down on tape. Ashley's attention to detail was always evident. 'Great take. But just a couple of small changes!'

After finishing each 'keeper track', Doc would break out the champagne. There would be a few more lines all round, and then work would resume again.

And so the recording process continued. Then there was a slight hiccup—another band had been scheduled into Record Plant, so an alternative studio was booked for three weeks and the whole box of tricks was moved over there.

Slowly the pile of 'keepers' amassed—'Underground', 'Run for the Shelter', 'Razor's Edge' and a reworked 'Small Price'. Spare moments were filled with collaborative ideas for album names and cover sketches. A day was spent on Doc's margarita-soaked vocals for 'Between the Eyes'. But progress continued to be snail-like. Yet another move was necessary, this time to MCA's Whitney studio for final vocal and guitar fill pieces and patch-ups. The drum track for 'Sticky Little Bitch' was sorted just as flights were being booked and the return to Sydney became imminent.

Finally, after almost three months, the band was on the way back to Sydney. Ashley would remain in LA to complete the mixing. The Angels' seventh studio album, *Two Minute Warning*, was finally completed.

But when the finished tapes arrived in Sydney a couple of weeks later the band was aghast. That final LA mix had changed the whole album completely. Critically, the sound was completely different to the 'Small Price' demo tape supplied to MCA at the outset that had been the basis for their contract.

The tapes had to be completely remixed. This required the band returning to EMI's Studios 301 in Sydney, where they ate crow and engaged the engineers there to help them. When everything was totalled, the 'just as cheap' LA recording exercise cost an astounding $450,000 (around $1 million in 2021).

The worst part of it was the band knew in their hearts, even before they left LA, that while the album would undoubtedly sell pretty well in Australia they didn't have a killer track. It was simply not going to be good enough to break them into the US.

————

On their arrival back in Australia the band needed work, and fast. John Brewster knew they were in a precarious financial position; the outlays from recording in the US would take months to recover. He was fast becoming disenchanted with both the band and John Woodruff.

With the demise of Dirty Pool, Woodruff had made the decision to return to Sydney's Harbour Agency and its Melbourne sister, Premier Artists, the bookers he had unceremoniously dumped back in 1978 when Dirty Pool was formed. These two agencies threw themselves into the task, booking The Angels into pubs and clubs, town halls and theatres. They even lined up an appearance on *Countdown*.

Tony Grace of Harbour Agency recalls: 'They were playing everywhere, anywhere and pioneering lots of new areas. They took around fifty grand [$130,000 in 2021] on a typical week. They were definitely one of the hardest-working bands of that period. I used to call Doc "The Prince of Pub Rock"—he owned that space!'

Not that the band saw much of that money. With 20 per cent for management and 10 per cent for the agency off the top and then wages for the crew, production, promotion and accommodation, a lot of money was sliced away. Then a chunk had to go to pay down the LA recording debt.

That The Angels would gravitate towards Michael Gudinski's Mushroom Records to handle their distribution in Australia and New Zealand was never much in doubt. The father of the Australian music industry, Gudinski had long believed that Mushroom could do a far better job for the band than CBS in Australia. A distribution contract was soon signed for *Two Minute Warning* (*TWM*), the name finally agreed to for the new album.

The contract with Mushroom Records was sealed with a $75,000 advance payment on royalties which, after deducting management commissions, also went to paying off the LA folly. *Two Minute Warning* was released in Australia and New Zealand on 28 November 1984 and reached number two on the Australian charts by Christmas, after which interest in it waned.

TMW was released by MCA in the US on 12 December, scoring a mention on the front page of US recording industry mag *Tip Sheet*. It was supported by the re-released single 'Be with You' from the first *Face* album. Together, these twin releases piqued the interest of a dozen or so rock radio stations. Nevertheless, in the face of the genre-transcending almost-simultaneous monster releases of Bruce Springsteen's *Born in the USA*, the anthemic *Pride* from U2 and the jaw-dropping *Purple Rain* from Prince, the overall US chart response to Angel City was only ever going to be lukewarm at best.

However, MCA wasn't too perturbed; it was still keen to see the band tour in North America and drive US sales in the new year.

———

Doc had a lot on his mind in the first few months of 1985. In December Dzintra had given birth to his son, Daniel, and his personal life had changed considerably as a result. The heavy workload of dozens of performances that had become necessary to recover the band's financial position had also drained him both physically and mentally. In common with the other band members, he felt exhausted and increasingly apprehensive about returning to the US and Canada for another demanding tour. Based on their recent experience, another tour would be simply throwing more money away.

It also appeared to the band that, by establishing himself as a tour promoter, John Woodruff had effectively transferred many of the risks of touring directly onto the band. Poor tour scheduling, booking issues or related misunderstandings outside of the band's control would penalise them financially.

They listened somewhat unconvinced as Woodruff explained that the cost of the tour would be kept down because they were supporting hard-rock band Triumph, one of MCA's major bands, on an arena tour. They would be provided with their own promotions manager, and all the costs and expenses for the tour would be picked up by MCA and debited against future royalties rather than deducted immediately from the band's bank account. Significantly, Woodruff had engaged a new booking agent to replace William Morris whose role would be to set up a run of profitable top-club gigs to complement and balance the arena shows with Triumph.

Woodruff appealed to their sense of fairness. He soothed their concerns and reminded them of how far they had come on his watch. In the end, after a nice meal, some good wine, lots of bonhomie and a few celebratory lines, they agreed to go.

By 3 March 1985, however, when they joined the LA-bound flight, their unease began to return. Doc was concerned that not only had the re-released single gone nowhere on the US charts but their album hadn't kicked any goals either. In the highly competitive US and Canadian market, with some of the best-made music of a generation surfacing, perhaps they were simply too far off the pace.

On hand to meet the band at LA International was the welcoming face of Ashley Howe. He was back in town to produce another band, but he brought some concerning music industry gossip. The word around the traps was that there had been a staff rationalisation at MCA and a number of the previous senior executives had been shown the door.

What Ashley and the band were unaware of was that at this exact moment MCA had become the prime target of a country-wide criminal investigation by the FBI into alleged involvement with Mafia racketeering. The entire US record industry was about to be subjected to the scrutiny of grand juries in five American states.

Ultimately, organised crime was found to have penetrated the music division of MCA, with the involvement of reputed mobster Sal 'the Swindler' Pisello. This revelation would send unparalleled shockwaves through the whole US music industry. At MCA, many former executives were replaced by new people who either did not know, or did not want to know, about any verbal commitments made around previous contract signings. They had little enthusiasm for acts that they personally hadn't signed.

For Angel City, it was going to be a whole new ball game.

Chapter 19

Back on the road again

Angel City was back in LA. The first gig of their new tour was to be a show on 5 March 1985 at the iconic Golden Bear 300-seat nightclub at Huntington Beach, about 55 kilometres south-west of downtown LA. The Bear had started out in 1929 as a fine-dining restaurant, attracting Hollywood heavyweights including Humphrey Bogart and Lionel Barrymore, but from the 1960s it had become a rock venue par excellence.

Angel City's almost sell-out show at The Bear was well received. After the show, Tom Holser, the promised MCA promotions manager, and a few recently appointed MCA management types came by and chatted with the band. They appeared to have no idea of the tour arrangements that had been previously negotiated.

Rob Kahane from the Triad Artists booking agency introduced himself to Doc after the show as personally representing Triad director John Marx. Rob was well presented, tanned and suave; a couple of years later he would find fame and fortune as manager for

George Michael. He had come to check out the band and congratulated Doc on their performance. Triad was now positioned as John
Woodruff's go-to US booking agency and Rob would personally
look after the band as a key client.

———

The Angels hadn't heard of Triumph prior to them being invited to
open six of their twenty-three 10,000-seat arena shows during their
Thunder Seven album tour. Woodruff also hadn't mentioned that
Triumph was personally managed by Irving Azoff, the CEO of MCA
records, who had bought the band out of its previous contract with
RCA. Although they had received negligible exposure and had little
following in Australia, the homegrown Canadian band was now at the
peak of its popularity. Formed in Toronto in 1975, the trio had three
US gold albums (sales of 500,000 units) plus over 500,000 accredited
album sales in Canada. Its *Allied Forces* album, released at this time,
later achieved US Platinum sales of one million copies shipped.

Given that Angel City was already relatively well known and
increasingly popular in north-western America and Canada for its
dramatic over-the-top live concerts and club and theatre performances, even some as headliners, it was somewhat puzzling why
Woodruff had encouraged them to step back to new-band status
and accept MCA's offer to open for Triumph, citing a supposed
need 'to keep costs down while exposing them to bigger audiences'.

Opening for Triumph was always going to be an unequal live-
show match-up, creating a potentially awkward and uneasy role for
Angel City. Although obviously talented, Triumph was a three-piece
ensemble dependent on additional tour musicians for live-show
cut-through. They placed great emphasis on an elaborate laser- and

pyro-lit 'show' rather than the music, as they needed to replicate their much augmented, highly produced recorded sound on stage.

The attraction for Triad in the arrangement was that with 80 per cent of their 230,000-seat tour already sold, there was a nice opportunity not only to strengthen the bill but also to put some cream on everybody's cake by attracting the fans of an infrequently seen but relatively well-known and popular opener. The considerable risk for Triumph was that they might be upstaged and out-gunned by the bigger and louder-sounding opening act.

For Angel City, the arrangement would allow them to reconnect with their existing fans, albeit during a very brief three or four song opening set, and there was also the benefit of exposure to a significant base of potential new fans. The risk was a diminished performance because of restrictions that might be imposed on them by the principal act.

Given the events that followed, it could be speculated that Triumph reluctantly agreed to six gigs as a trial. If everybody played nicely together, there was the possibility of adding another dozen 10,000-seat arena shows during the next leg of the Canadian tour, which would start a week later. But if things didn't pan out . . . Bad luck, fellas! And under those circumstances there would be no time for Angel City management to organise a follow-on run of club dates.

The day after the opener at The Bear, Angel City headed off for its first support gig with Triumph at the 10,000-seat Cow Palace in Daly City, just south of San Francisco. This colourfully named indoor venue, originally built in the1940s for large rodeo events, had become a popular rock venue. Every group that could raise a decent crowd, including The Beatles and the Rolling Stones, had played its oval-shaped arena.

Saturday 9 March 1985 was cold, cloudy and windy. For the hundreds of hard-rock fans lined up outside Cow Palace, it was a long wait in temperatures that edged 5 degrees Celsius by the early evening. Delays in getting the crowds to their seats did not improve their mood, much less when someone in the Triumph crew thought it would be fun to further aggravate them by playing a couple of Michael Jackson songs over the house PA. The boos and catcalls in response were still resounding around the venue when Angel City entered the elevated stage area to open the show.

It's often very difficult for a band to get their sound levels right from just a pre-gig sound check in a big empty arena; furthermore, the sound at the mixing desk in the middle of a venue full of people is considerably different to that in the front seats. The musicians themselves, back behind forward-facing PA speakers, also don't cop anywhere near the full effect of the near pain threshold 125-plus decibels coming straight at the audience.

Angel City was always going to be loud compared to Triumph, but what resulted was a hail of coins directed at the band from the front seats. This was a totally new hazard to the guys They had faced much worse from well-oiled pub patrons back home, but this was unexpected and dangerous. Doc felt a stinging blow to his face from a coin and Rick had the lens of an expensive pair of shades shattered, but they played on. Finishing their set, there was some spirited clapping and calls for an encore, but the band had had enough. They didn't go back.

Also shocked by the incident was Tom Holser, who had been certain that the Triumph fans 'would love Angel City'. It was an aberration, he said, and he would talk to the Triumph crew about the Michael Jackson tapes and to the security detail. The band was emphatic, though: if it happened again, they'd walk off.

It wasn't a good weekend for the guys. Waking up on the Sunday morning, they found that their three-tonne Ryder hire van, containing all their equipment, had been stolen. Stunned, they were forced to re-live all the dramas of the previous theft almost five years before in Chicago.

The police were next to useless, and it was Monday before the van turned up behind a shoe shop less than a block away, stripped of all their equipment except for a few road cases. Although everything was insured, that was little solace for the loss of their cherished instruments and all the hired equipment. Worse, a showcase gig that evening had them booked to perform at a local theatre as part of a national 'Rockers Convention', a live-to-air radio station promotion that brought together recently signed artists with radio programmers and associated merchandising and promotion services from across the country.

Fortunately, as in Chicago, local artists came to the rescue with headlining metal band King Kobra generously lending their stage equipment and instruments to get Angel City up in front of an impressed crowd of a couple of thousand. The gig wasn't really a good fit for the band, as most of the artists on the bill were either heavy metal or country. Nevertheless, they had managed once again to bounce back from the jaws of defeat.

———

After the coin-throwing incident at the Cow Palace together with the dramas associated with replacing all their equipment, there was little interest from the band in continuing with the remainder of the Triumph support gigs. But the prospective loss of income, the lack of alternative show options and the likely damage to the band's reputation persuaded them to see out the five remaining concerts. They had talked to Triumph's show manager, who seemed concerned, and he promised to investigate the issues and to follow up with event security. Tom Holser encouraged them to view the Cow Palace show as a one-off. 'Wait and see how the next few shows go,' he said.

In Seattle, Angel City played to a hotbed of enthusiastic fans. They had headlined two full-house Paramount Theatre shows to 6000 fans on previous visits, but now they were playing three songs as openers for another band on their only appearance of the tour in the seaport city. Their fans gave them a noisy welcome and demanded encores. In their dressing room afterwards Tom introduced the band to Beau Phillips, legendary program director from KISW, the most popular rock station in the region. Beau was a massive Angel City fan; he had had 'Marseilles' on high rotation for weeks back in the day and was still playing the early albums. He wasn't playing anything off *TMW*, however. 'It's not really a fit for our demographic,' he told Doc.

The following night they were booked to open for Triumph at the Memorial Coliseum, an indoor arena located in the oldest part of the Rose Quarter area in Portland, Oregon. The Coliseum had hosted a massive concert for The Beatles back in 1965. Led Zeppelin, the Bee Gees and even Elvis Presley had all held multiple shows there over the years. MCA had lined up a big record-store promo on the morning of the gig so Doc, Jim and Rick, together with Tom Holser, took an early flight south to cover that while the rest of the band and crew made the 180-mile drive straight to the Coliseum to set up and run a sound check.

The fans waiting at the record store expressed great surprise that the sum total of the Angel City Portland visit was an overnighter supporting Triumph, where previously the band had headlined its own shows. Doc rang John Woodruff from the store alarmed that all their previous work building the band's profile in the north-west would be wasted unless they built their own shows. Why couldn't they plan a return visit to Portland on their own?

That night at the Coliseum, Angel City played an impressive opening set for the Triumph show. Enthusiastic fans sang along with 'Marseilles' and clamoured for encores. After the show Tom Holser brought in an excited Inessa Anderson, program director for the KGON rock-music station that covered Oregon and Washington State. Inessa, who had been a fan for years, said Angel City tracks had consistently achieved top five on their listener playlist, so she was keen to learn when the band would be returning to the local club and theatre circuit.

A furious John Brewster immediately rang John Woodruff when the band returned to their hotel, demanding to know why they were supporting 'this totally inappropriate band' instead of headlining their own concerts. A somewhat chastened Woodruff reiterated that they were reducing financial risk while playing to much bigger audiences.

At the three remaining support concerts—in Vancouver, Edmonton and Calgary—Angel City fans made the same inquiries: when would there be follow-up club and theatre shows across the north-west like the one that was already planned for Winnipeg? Meanwhile, the increasingly sullen Triumph crew cut their PA volume and reduced their lights.

In Calgary the coin throwers were back, and a clown threw a firecracker on stage that exploded in Doc's face. For the first time ever at a show, the band stopped. Bobby Daniels, their sound man, had seen the thrower. He jumped off stage and the perpetrator received a smack in the mouth for his troubles. John and Rick pulled their guitar leads. Jim followed. As the band left the stage, Doc rushed to the front. 'Thanks, arseholes—see you later,' he snarled at the bunch of bozos causing the problem. They didn't go back.

Triumph was about to take a week's break before the scheduled next leg of the tour, an eleven-stadium concert, 3500-kilometre-long spring sleigh ride through Canada. Further participation in the Triumph tour would have provided Angel City with the opportunity to extend its fan base in Canada. But that was not to be.

Instead, the band boarded a train for a 30-hour and 1200-kilometre spectacular journey across the Rocky Mountains to Winnipeg, where it was scheduled to headline its own show at the Pantages Playhouse Theatre. They relaxed into their seats and enjoyed the scenic journey and each other's company.

———

Arriving in Winnipeg, the band was delighted to learn that, as with their earlier visit, they had sold out not one but two shows—on 24 and 25 March 1985. These were the first concerts of the tour where they were headlining, and it felt good.

The number-one local FM radio station CITI had been a great supporter of Angel City since day one and Doc had done several interviews over the years with program director Roy Hennessy, who was at the vanguard of a radio revolution in Winnipeg and was later to become an American radio-industry doyen. Roy told Doc that there was a lot of interest in the city for the shows. With French ancestry solid across the population, 'Marseilles' had sat high in the local charts and on playlists for months back in the day.

The Pantages Playhouse Theatre is an early twentieth century former vaudeville theatre boasting a decorative facade with lights

across the front and columns, friezes and cornices. It had been well
maintained over the years and in 1985 it had just received a new
PA and lighting system.

With none of the restrictions that were imposed on the Triumph
support gigs, Angel City hit its straps. Doc sang his heart out and
the guys really got the joint rocking. Two enthusiastic full houses
called the band back again and again to reprise the old favourites.
Suddenly it didn't seem that hard anymore.

However, the band's elevated mood did not last for long. They
hit the road for the two-day, 1200-kilometre drive to Milwaukee
believing their new booking agency was in the process of arranging show bookings ahead of them. But in Milwaukee they sat in
their motel for five days waiting for the promised gig itinerary to
be faxed through from Triad. With the hungry horse of band and
crew, hired equipment and vehicles voraciously chomping though
the money they had made in Winnipeg, their situation was increasingly desperate.

Finally, a fax arrived directing them to a couple of small gigs
in Detroit, 600 kilometres away. Then one at Toledo, a further
60 kilometres on. Then they travelled another 200 kilometres to
Cincinnati, where they had a strong following nurtured by music
radio WEBN DJ Frank Wood Jr, the son of the station owner.

Doc had done station interviews previously with Frank, and both
Face to Face and *Dark Room* had remained on the station's playlists.
It swung solidly behind both *Two Minute Warning* and the single
'Be With You'. Despite the short notice, 500 concert tickets were
sold with the support from WEBN, and a relieved and appreciative
Tom Holser took Doc and DJ Frank Wood out to dinner.

The tour then moved to Texas, an 1800-kilometre drive with
some stops along the way for small-town gigs for 50 punters. The

band had been patient, but it was obvious that the Triad booking agency were not a patch on William Morris. Gigs were being booked and then cancelled at the last moment.

Arriving in Austin, which promotes itself as a live-music hotspot, the band again waited for promised gig rosters, all the while churning through its funds. It was only through Doc's promotional efforts with local radio station KLBJ that a 'dollar a ticket' show for several hundred people could be pulled together. This was no small achievement in this high-cost town, where really good bands played for tips on weekdays and for starving-artist pay at other times. Undoubtedly the city was getting a lot more from this arrangement than it was giving.

Things couldn't go on like that. John Brewster remembers: 'After the band and crew sat in the motel for five days waiting for a supposed run of dates, I'd had enough and rang Woodruff in LA. "You've got to come down and talk to your band, we're going fucking broke!" He flew down and we had this terse meeting in a disused room with old furniture stacked up and I let him have it. "You told me you wouldn't send us to America if it wasn't a good tour. Well it's a fucking disaster, which has probably destroyed our career here and we are going back to Sydney right now."

'He said he had changed agencies and they were setting up a new tour. But it was too late for that. We'd blown another bundle that we'd have to slog around Australia again to make back. I was over the whole thing.'

Doc had a separate meeting with Woodruff to discuss MCA's support, or lack of it. Woodruff was anxious about the band's mood and his increasingly fractured relationship with John Brewster; he wanted Doc's perspective. He had appointed a new booking agency, but it would take time for another tour to be put together. With

William Morris out of the picture, the best he could offer was an east coast tour, starting in Boston with an industry showcase event sponsored by rock radio station WBCN in four days' time, on 20 April. At this point, however, he could offer no further gigs.

Doc told Woodruff he was sure that this proposal—requiring them to spend thousands of dollars to travel 3000 kilometres to Boston, where they would sit around waiting again—was never going to fly. The band would be returning to Australia. If needs be, they could come back to the US later in the year.

The band's relationship with MCA was also coming apart. With the new executive team reluctant to revisit decisions connected to the odorous period of MCA's recent history, Angel City was unlikely to be re-signed.

So it was back on the road for the three-day haul to LA, then signing off their hired vehicles and equipment and waiting another four days for flights to Sydney to become available.

Finally, on the evening of 26 April 1985, the band joined Pan Am flight 815 for the trip home. This was the end of any attempt by The Angels to conquer America. They would later return to the US to record and for an occasional show, but the weeks and months of wearisome long concert tours were over.

Chapter 20

The warriors regroup

If Doc felt any sense of disappointment, much less defeat, following the debacle of the band's fourth US tour then he certainly wasn't showing it. On their return to Australia in the last days of April 1985, he was out almost immediately promoting a national homecoming tour to restore the band's ravaged finances. To avoid overexposure in the state capitals, shows were also scheduled in country regions where they'd never worked before. Not only was he promoting the band but—given the future's uncertainty—himself.

The range of merchandise to support the *Two Minute Warning* album was also expanded. Doc was organising posters and artwork, new stage clothes and props and he was working on the development of lighting and visuals for a new stage act.

This was Doc at his most capable and driven. But behind this bold and confident face, he was feeling increasingly exasperated, even resentful. During his interviews with radio DJs and

232

programmers on their US tours, Doc had received much valuable feedback about the musical direction and marketing of Angel City. But he had rarely been able to get any traction for those ideas within the band. Doc was tired of the endless wrangling. As a consequence, he revived his interest in a solo career if the band couldn't be saved from what he was starting to see as its downward spiral towards oblivion. With apparent encouragement from John Woodruff, and to John Brewster's annoyance, he began floating in media interviews the possibility of a return to the US that July for a revitalised promotional tour for *TMW*.

Woodruff was copping flak from MCA for reneging on the promotional tour commitments and his cosy new relationship with booking agency Triad was stressed as a result of its abysmal performance with the tour arrangements. He wanted the band back in the US to keep both relationships alive.

Since day one John Brewster had assumed the role of band leader. He had set the agendas, driven the outcomes and managed the finances. But now he had lost all confidence in John Woodruff. He felt the band had been compromised by the decision to change US booking agencies and it was patently clear to him that Woodruff, in his conflicted role as concert promoter, was no longer working in the best interests of the band.

John Brewster was now weighing up the situation and considering his own options. The dynamic within the band had surrendered any semblance of being a team. It was becoming every man for himself. The issue of whether they should have stayed in America and attempted to recover the relationship with MCA had divided the band against itself.

Up to this point the relationship between John and Rick had been indivisible and no one knew this better than Doc. As a member of the ownership triumvirate, he had been powerless when the brothers employed their combined muscle to steamroller the views of not just himself but everyone else in the band.

The other members, being employees, were not seeing the issues in the same way as the band principals. Bassist Jim Hilbun often referred to himself as the 'hired hand' and he was comfortable in that role—happy to do his job, enjoy a convivial joint and get on with everyone. Brent Eccles, however, was ambitious and commercially smart. Seeking more involvement in management of the band, he had built an alliance with Rick and was forthright and articulate with his suggestions and opinions.

Drugs and alcohol were fire starters for everyone. Rick's cocaine addiction had reached dangerous levels and with Brent had escalated into a series of daily rituals. Doc's alcohol dependency was growing worse, and his state of mind was clouded by prescription pain-killers and mood stabilisers. This was not the environment for calm thinking and rational decisions.

Nevertheless, within a few short weeks all the arguments about returning to the States were to become largely academic. MCA advised the band that despite early flickers of interest, both *Two Minute Warning* and 'Be with You' had bombed in the US. The company wouldn't be providing financial support for another tour until the next album.

———

Meanwhile Boomtown Rats frontman Bob Geldof was putting together Live Aid, the international super-concert scheduled for 13 July 1985 involving some of the world's biggest musical acts. Geldof had twisted the arms of TV network owners, including

MTV, arranged satellites and pampered rock-star egos, all of whom were playing for free. Live Aid brought together some of the biggest global names in music—including Queen, Elton John, Madonna, Mick Jagger, U2 and David Bowie—on massive stages in London and Philadelphia, plus concerts in a number of other cities including Sydney. The 16-hour concert would be linked globally by satellite to more than a billion viewers in 110 nations. In a triumph of technology and good will, the event managed to raise hundreds of millions of dollars for famine relief in Ethiopia.

In Australia, the four-hour Oz for Africa concert was held at the Sydney Entertainment Centre to an audience of 12,000 and broadcasted locally and internationally as part of the worldwide Live Aid performances. Due to the time difference, the Oz for Africa concert began 12 hours ahead of the main gig at Wembley Stadium in London, making it the first Live Aid concert in the world.

The Angels, billed as Angel City, were among a number of bands invited to appear, along with INXS, Men at Work, Little River Band, Mental as Anything and Australian Crawl—all of them well known to the international viewing audience. Each band was required to perform four songs, two of which would make the cut to the international and MTV broadcasts.

The Angels' set list deserved a lot more thought than it received. Incredibly, rather than including 'Marseilles', which had US Billboard form and was easily their most popular and best-known song in the US, they opted for 'Small Price' and 'Underground' from the recent *TMW* album, 'Eat City' from *Watch the Red* and 'Take A Long Line' from *Face*.

The Oz for Africa concert was a huge success, raising $10 million towards the international relief effort. Positive feedback from MCA and from US industry commentators on the MTV broadcast fed into the polarising undercurrent in the band about returning to America.

———

As the last few months of 1985 closed out with another big national tour, Doc was again thinking seriously of an independent career. Jimmy Barnes had shown that it could be done, having now produced two very successful solo albums. To move this idea along, Doc decided to make an early December visit to the US with the intention of writing with Chris Sandford, who had composed a number of songs with Barnes for his albums. He'd also made contact with Geoff Lieb and Gregg Tripp, two other recognised American songwriter/musician guns for hire.

Meanwhile, John Brewster had stopped participating in promotional film clips and overseeing sound checks during the tour. Instead, he would go off and play a round of golf. Someone else could step up.

There was also the matter of another album. Mushroom had put much effort and investment into promoting *TMW* but sales had quickly tapered off, leaving little optimism for the fast-approaching Christmas sales period. CBS Australia, with access to material produced under their earlier contract and seeing an opening in the market for a compilation album, had released *The Angels Greatest Hits Volume 2*. Riding on the back of Mushroom's promotional work and the live tours, it was selling well.

With no money to contemplate a new album and Mushroom pushing for something new, the band decided to produce another live album. Despite the internal discontent, it was agreed that John Brewster would be paid to do the mixing and production from earlier concert recordings. It was hoped that this project would enable everyone to move on from the US tour pull-out decision.

The evolving reshaping of allegiances within the band, however, meant that John had become an outlier. He felt jaded and over it. He even contemplated a return to Alberts. His outspoken concern over Rick's cocaine habit had driven a wedge between the two brothers, with Rick and Brent emerging as a new power bloc. Doc remained close and loyal to John Woodruff, who would have viewed any suggestion of a return to Alberts as an anathema.

The November concerts in Perth and the return of the band to Sydney marked the end of touring for the year. It had been a very arduous and intense period since returning from the US. The band was exhausted. Their bank balance had been restored, but the arguments and bickering over the circumstance of the US tour had continued.

The scene was set for an inevitable showdown but from Doc's perspective the band's decision to fire John Brewster on 26 November 1985 was something of an anticlimax.

After months of rancour and arguments precipitated by John's initiative to return from the US, the eventual decision had almost validated itself as a necessary circuit breaker and the only real opportunity for a completely new start. Doc thought that John took the news well, although the band certainly did not agree with John's suggestion it should just break up and do a farewell tour instead. He responded to this rebuff, according to Doc, by threatening to sue for $250,00 for good will if they didn't go ahead with this plan. Nevertheless, John was still invited to complete the mix on the live album.

———

Doc arrived in LA on 4 December for his fortnight of songwriting sessions. He'd booked into a downtown Hojos, one of a chain of ubiquitous orange and turquoise motel-restaurants that are found across America. He had arranged the use of a small local recording studio where he would work with Gregg Tripp, who had written songs for hard-rock bands LA Guns and Vixen and would later find fame as co-writer of the soft rock 'I Don't Want to Live Without You'.

The first session went pretty well, and they completed the writing of the chords for Doc's new song by early afternoon. Gregg had another appointment and said he would visit the studio the following day to get the music down on tape. Doc then had a session with Geoff Lieb. A songwriter, vocalist, keyboardist and guitarist, Lieb had worked primarily in the hard-rock/heavy metal genre. The previous year he'd had success with 'Gotta Let Go' for Lita Ford and 'Lipstick & Leather' for Yesterday & Today.

The following day Doc had an invitation from leading LA concert promoter and artist manager Phil Kovac to join him for a lunch barbeque with Blackie Lawless, leader and songwriter for heavy metal band W.A.S.P. Doc was interested in the possibility of collaborating with Blackie on songwriting.

The songwriting sessions continued with various people over the next few days, but Doc soon found that this was a rather more haphazard process than he had anticipated. Although the sessions with Geoff Lieb were eventually productive and a number of songs came together, Doc became frustrated when their work was frequently interrupted by Geoff's busy schedule. He soon came to realise that the new creative process was quite different to what he'd enjoyed in the early days of The Angels. There are in fact as many approaches to songwriting as there are songwriters. Where his responsibility had previously been mainly around composing lyrics, he was now being forced to appreciate the finer points of all the other challenges.

———

It was decided that John Brewster would play his last two Angels gigs at the end of January 1986. The first gig, as it happened, was the big farewell concert for Australian Crawl at the Myer Music Bowl. Then later that evening The Angels played their farewell with John at the Palace nightclub in St Kilda. The band put on a stunning performance. There were several encores and Doc gave a generous and gracious farewell speech to his band mate.

Then there was the matter of finding a new member of the band's line-up, but serendipity was about to step in. Ex-Skyhooks guitarist Bob Spencer had known Rick Brewster for yonks; they were both guitar geeks, friendly and competitive. Bob had recently been working at a small studio, Paradise B on Sydney's Oxford Street, as a studio engineer. Business had been quiet during the last months of 1985 and, with the calendar rolling over, he thought he'd ring his old mate and wish him a happy New Year, as well as sound out the chances of The Angels using the Paradise B facilities to do a bit of recording. When he heard that John had left the band, he was surprised and casually offered his help as a fill-in guitarist if they needed it.

The band's relationship with Mushroom had become stressed. After watching CBS Australia enjoy a big Christmas drink with *The Angels Greatest Hits Volume 2* courtesy of Mushroom's strong promotion but disappointing sales of *Two Minute Warning*, Michael Gudinski was going to be much more circumspect before doling out a big cash advance for the next Angels' album. John Brewster's departure did not help their cause and Gudinski wanted to see what the boys had up their sleeves in the way of new songs before signing any more cheques.

Doc's progress towards his planned solo album had all but stalled. He'd hoped that the US sessions would have produced enough songs for the project, but he'd returned with fewer than half a dozen songs and only half of those were anywhere near completion. However, John's departure had changed the creative balance within the band and Doc could expect to have infinitely more influence on musical direction.

This was not lost on John Woodruff, who hoped that Doc would again take a more prominent musically creative role in the band. He counselled Doc to put his personal aspirations for a solo album on the backburner and to step up with his new co-written songs. They would represent a positive and professional initiative for the band, an indication that at last they were receptive to accepting assistance from outsiders. This should be good enough to get their pitch for investment in a new album over the line with Mushroom.

Doc wasn't entirely happy about relinquishing his dream of a solo album. He had seen it as his ticket to the next stage of his career. Nevertheless, he could see something attractive in Woodruff's proposition for a new start and he soon acquiesced. He played the band the tape of 'Nature of the Beast', one of the songs he had composed with Geoff Lieb, and they rather grudgingly acknowledged it was a pretty decent song. After jamming on it for an hour or so, they had a demo for Mushroom.

Gudinski was now definitely interested. Even though he was still cautious, he booked the band into the Rhinoceros studio to record the song with renowned UK producer Steve Brown, who had recorded a comprehensive range of artists from Elton John to the Boomtown Rats, George Michael and Thin Lizzy. But Mushroom did not respond immediately after it received the tape; it was holding its counsel and playing it cool.

Doc had another couple of songs he'd composed with Geoff Lieb. The band thought 'All Night for You' worthy of inclusion in the new album. 'Look in the Mirror' was also worked up by the band but, to Doc's surprise and annoyance, they failed to arrive at a song arrangement they could all agree on. Nevertheless, the jam sessions prompted a creative outpouring from all the other band members, and new collaborative works and song ideas soon filled the project folder.

Doc also encouraged the band to think about including a cover in the new album. That would have been anathema when John and Rick had set the band's musical direction. Yet they had started their careers playing nothing else but covers, and the world's biggest and most successful entertainers all recorded songs by other artists and professional songwriters.

Doc suggested they cover 'We Gotta Get Out of This Place', the 1965 rock classic performed by UK legends The Animals, who had not written the song either. Every band that called Adelaide's deprived northern suburbs home in the 1960s could relate to this song. It was a set-list staple. Acutely aware of Australia's double-digit unemployment, which was then affecting even Doc's family in Adelaide, it could again become an anthem for the times. After they had refreshed the old standard with an intro of keyboards and brass and made other slight changes to the arrangement, they had a cracker of a song.

———

With The Angels' touring schedule for the year about to get underway, the band needed, at the very least, a temporary replacement rhythm guitarist. Rick recalled the offer from Bob Spencer.

Bob had started his career as an original member of Sydney rockers Finch in the 1970s and in 1977 replaced Red Symons as lead guitar in Skyhooks. He was an outstanding and talented musician and songwriter. As far as the band was concerned he was the perfect fit to replace John Brewster, but he would join the upcoming national *Tour De Force* caravan on something of a trial to see how things went on the road.

Doc had reservations. His anxieties weren't about Bob's ability, nor about how he would fit in musically or personally. But Doc was now within months of reaching his 40th birthday, the gateway from youthfulness. Was he ready to share the stage limelight with someone ten years his junior?

The main issue for Doc was that Bob was another showman. He certainly wasn't going to be playing in darkened shadows for much of the time as John had done. A slight, mild mannered, softly spoken Clark Kent by day, up on stage Bob was the complete antithesis. Under the spotlight he became the guitar super-hero, planting his feet, legs spread, guitar slung low and his arm windmilling or striding across the stage purposefully and restlessly, bounding athletically and effortlessly to blaze away from the top of his amp stack.

The other band members watched the face-off between the pair with barely suppressed amusement and maybe just a little *schadenfreude* as Doc tried hard to lift his routine to avoid being upstaged by the much younger man. Was there enough room for two bees in The Angels' bottle? Doc would eventually rationalise the situation as not dissimilar to another competitive pairing, that of his Who idols Pete Townshend and Roger Daltry.

In April, Mushroom finally gave the go ahead on the new album. It would directly fund production itself. The Neeson–Leib song 'Nature of the Beast' would be released in June and the band would be booked to head back to the Rhinoceros studio over May and June with producer Steve Brown to record the balance of songs required for the project.

Also engaged for the recording was Eddie Rayner, the talented and popular world-class keyboardist from Split Enz, who would provide a major enhancement to the band's sound. This was a huge coup: Eddie had just finished recording on Paul McCartney's *Press to Play* solo album.

Progress on the proposed live concert album was shelved for the moment. Looking forward, the band confirmed that Bob Spencer was now part of the team, and they would wait for an opportunity to add additional material to the project with their new line-up.

With Mushroom behind the scenes carefully managing a disciplined recording process for the new album, production went like clockwork; there were no studio-time over-runs and no nasty financial surprises. Songwriting and pre-production were done before the band got to the studio. Steve Brown had recommended that final mixing be undertaken at the Wessex Studio in London by Bill Price, who had engineered the Sex Pistols, The Clash and Pete Townshend's solo albums.

No further recommendation was needed. Rick Brewster was despatched to accompany the master tapes and watch master mixing craftsman Bill Price at work. Everyone was becoming more confident daily that with this album they had turned the corner and produced something to be really proud of.

———

Howling was released on 25 November 1986. With a stunning cover design and artwork from multi-talented Jim Hilbun and his photographer girlfriend Chrystine Carroll, the album went straight into the charts on its way to number six nationally. The single 'We Gotta Get Out of This Place' rocketed to number three.

That the Christmas stocking-filler had made it to market was testament to the professionalism of Mushroom's project management. Reviewers and fans alike welcomed the well-written and produced songs, the keyboards, plus the additional specialist musicians and backing singers overlaying The Angels' signature guitar-band sound. The numerous shortcomings and disappointing sales of the previous two albums were behind them. The Angels once again had a product that was being played and enthusiastically promoted by Australian radio stations; it moved rapidly off the shelves of local record stores and brought hordes of old and new fans to the live shows.

And so commenced one of the busiest concert-packed periods in the band's entire career. For the following sixteen months or so the very successful Howling Across Australia tour criss-crossed Australia every which way. The huge semitrailer-sized Pantech was loaded up with instruments, amplifier road cases, speaker cabinets, staging and risers, the mixing desk, lighting equipment and the gantry, all the paraphernalia associated with putting on gigs in every conceivable venue.

There was also the scaffolding to build 'Doc's World', Doc's black-curtained stage-side hideaway, and 'The Tardis', his phone-box-sized wardrobe of stage clothes. Before each performance Doc would indulge in a small ritual. Sitting alone with his face in a mask, in virtual darkness except for a couple of candles and glowing joss sticks and maybe a small light globe, he would breathe oxygen from a tank in preparation for his act in packed, smoke-filled venues. With a glass or two of wine or whiskey to hand and surrounded by his talisman and totems—photos and reminders of lost loves, absent and departed friends—he would immerse himself in his characters.

At small-town pubs, halls and footy grounds; at regional city theatres, recreation centres and gymnasiums; at state capital entertainment arenas and stadiums . . . wherever and whenever, their fans and media would always be waiting as The Angels' rock-and-roll circus arrived in town. There were almost a dozen mouths on the support team payroll to feed and accommodate: roadies and riggers, sound and lighting techs, merchandise sellers and truck drivers.

In March 1987, as the Howling tour was well underway, the band received a call from Jands, the lighting and sound professionals. A booking had just been cancelled for use of their mobile studio—the one that had been used to record the Narara concert. Were The Angels interested in a special deal?

This was the opportunity the band had been waiting for to restart the shelved live album project. With Bob Spencer now well settled into the line-up, they would have a solid mix of old favourites and new songs to add to the earlier concert tapes. A quick check was needed to see if ace recording engineer Andrew Scott, from the Rhinoceros studio, was available to do the honours. If he was, Jands could ink the deal.

A few days later the Jands recording van was parked outside a sell-out Howling tour show at the Bankstown RSL with cables running inside to the auditorium mixing desk. The concert was recorded as 800 happily inebriated punters enjoyed a fantastic live show to be put into storage for the future *Liveline* album.

But things didn't always go as planned. In Perth the band had sold out the 8200-seat Perth Entertainment Centre months in advance and a second concert, at the Herdsman Hotel, was scheduled. This second concert got pretty wild, and Doc sought to end the gig with a little competitive one-upmanship, making a show-closing stage dive into the audience. Somewhat out with his timing, he came down very hard on one fan, flattening him to the floor.

Doc picked himself up and attempted to climb back up on the stage. However, the very pissed-off punter grabbed Doc by the leg. Attempting to jerk his leg free, Doc ended up with torn knee ligaments.

Things went downhill from there. Doc was ambulanced to hospital and then flown back to Sydney to see Dr Merv Cross, the go-to orthopaedic surgeon for fixing footballers' knees. The band waited anxiously in Perth. Two shows were cancelled.

Then Doc phoned John Woodruff. 'Don't cancel the tour, I can still sing.' He was mobile on crutches and would be able to sing from an armchair. Then came the visionary theatrical master stroke turning defeat into a winning hand: he would sing from an old-time barber's chair. A 1930s vintage barber's chair was located. With its gracefully tapered cast-iron plinth base and chrome-plated frame up to its buttoned leather seat, its back cushions and its arm, foot and head rests, it was perfect. The show was back on the road again.

During the next two months, while Doc's knee came good, the band toured the east coast of Australia, Tasmania and New Zealand to sell-out shows. Every night, to an enthusiastic foot-stomping roar from the audience, the band's triumphal fanfare would announce the arrival of their tribal deity. Doc's elaborate throne would be ceremonially wheeled to the stage and placed up on the riser facing the mic. Dressed for the occasion with a large dead parrot at his side, he sang like a bird and the crowd loved every second of his performances.

Rick Brewster's verdict: 'Doc sang the best he had sung for years while he sat in that chair. Instead of running around out of breath, he concentrated on singing into the microphone and it was fantastic. He looked great and thousands of people who saw him never forgot those shows.'

During this time little thought had been given to the band's return to America. Nevertheless, John Woodruff had continued to be active in his concert promotion activities in conjunction with Triad. He had brought a number of US and European acts to Australia and New Zealand on very successful tours. It was just that breaking The Angels in the US was no longer a priority for him.

Little did Woodruff know that the impetus for a resurgent interest in the US was to arrive from a totally different and unexpected direction.

Chapter 21

Hitting their straps

Meanwhile, in a nearby parallel universe, The Angels rather than Angel City had, by a strange twist of fate, unknowingly entered the orbit of a couple of major-league US music industry movers and shakers.

Englishman Kick Van Hengel was the LA head of Capitol International and a renowned music-industry player. He knew everyone; he had once lived across the road from Jimi Hendrix on inner London's Upper Berkeley Street and had been neighbours with John Lennon in exclusive Montague Square. He would shortly explode Crowded House onto the global scene.

In late 1985 Capitol had taken over an entire hotel in Nashville for a company confab and Kick had been given the unpopular responsibility of ensuring that the several hundred company delegates surfaced each morning after whatever extracurricular shenanigans they'd undertaken the previous night. Having recently been given Angel City's *Dark Room* album by a colleague from the

London EMI office, he decided to use 'Face the Day' as his reveille call. He played it loud. Very loud. Intrigued by Doc's eyes staring out from the cover, *Dark Room* had gone into his flight bag for the trip back to LA.

US rock-band manager extraordinaire Alan Niven was at that time becoming the man of the moment when it came to picking up blindingly talented but hard-to-hold and explosively temperamental rock bands. Every band he'd ever committed to was considered out of step, unmanageable or incompetent by the 'experts' on Sunset Boulevard.

A Kiwi by birth, Alan didn't sit back and wait for things to happen. After he'd moved to LA in 1981, he signed Mötley Crüe to Greenworld and, during a stint at Enigma records, signed pop band Berlin. By his own admission he'd blundered into the world of management by connecting with Dante Fox, the hard-rock band that became Great White under his guidance. One day he received a call from his friend Kick Van Hengel, who wanted him to come by his office to share his latest find with him.

As Niven recalls it, 'Kick had a copy of the five-year-old *Dark Room* album on his desk. "Listen to this," he beamed as the opening notes of "Face the Day" filled his office. "Whatya think of that!"

'Of course, I appreciated the reveille style, but I heard something immediate and profound that totally suited my needs at that moment. I immediately had a sense of how it could be better recorded by Great White. It was perfect. It was so not-glam-Hollywood, it had the makings of great atmos. It had a brilliant rock-and-roll disposition—who the hell wants to face the damned day, literally or metaphorically? Reagan, Russia, rampant capitalism, being broke and bitchy demanding wives and girlfriends. Coke hangovers. It had brilliant dynamics.

'Long story shortened, "Face the Day" became the lead track on Great White's *Shot in The Dark* album, which I self-financed and self-promoted.'

All the main LA stations came to the party. KLOS designated Great White's cover their number-two Song of the Year, behind Steve Winwood's 'Arc of a Diver'.

———

The global orbits of The Angels and Alan Niven finally came together about halfway through the 16-month Howling tour on Sunday 12 July 1987 at the impressively colonnaded neo-Renaissance Wellington Town Hall on the main drag of New Zealand's capital city.

Niven had made a rare return to the country of his birth with a proposition for The Angels. He'd done his research. In the US—in fact, everywhere in the world with the exception of Australia and New Zealand—The Angels, aka Angel City, were in Limbo Land. MCA was certainly not doing anything with them. Niven believed that John Woodruff had made some fundamental strategic errors with the band in the US, and had all but given up on doing anything else other than maximising his returns from the highly profitable Australasian touring circuit.

The Green Room of an entertainment venue is where entertainers gather to await their call to the stage but, in the case of Wellington Town Hall, it did double duty and was one of the meeting places for the city councillors. It contained a large round boardroom table that, in a nod to its other role, was covered with a green baize tablecloth. Because John Woodruff wasn't able to join the band for the meeting with Alan Niven before the gig, Brent Eccles had been delegated to lead the discussion for the band. He sat with band members on either side facing Niven across the table.

Niven came straight to the point. His research had told him that the band had done nothing outside of Australia for almost two years. Their last album and single released in the US had bombed. Their American-market record company, MCA, didn't appear to be doing anything for them. He could see that Woodruff was managing the band in Australasia. He was offering management by his company, Stravinsky Brothers, for the rest of the world. They resumed their discussion post show in his hotel room.

'Post gig, a trolley with six bottles of Moët arrived at my room,' Niven recalled. 'Doc was no more than three steps behind. "Might as well have a drink," he suggested.

'"Should we wait for the others?" I politely asked.

'Doc eyed the bottles. "Nah. They can catch us up."

'We talked Angel songs. I asked him what had driven the formation of "Underground". Doc told me a sad tale of love and loss, and of the appropriation of Greek mythology. Discombobulated by 40 hours of flying, a gig and a few glasses of French sparkling wine caused me to lose control of my cerebral filters and I proceeded to tell Doc that the song had deeper sociological meanings and that he didn't really know what he'd written. Doc took umbrage. I stood my ground. We went to the mat.'

Rick Brewster arrived to find Doc wrestling with Niven. The furniture had been re-arranged. 'Oh, I see you guys are getting on alright then,' he said and immediately departed the room.

While their first meeting in the Green Room had been inauspicious, The Angels' performance that evening confirmed to Niven that the band and its material definitely had a unique personality, although creatively diminished from their early days of making the *Face to Face* and *Dark Room* albums.

It was agreed over the following days that Alan Niven would look after the band's interests in the rest of the world outside Australasia.

His subsequent inquiries revealed that MCA had shelved *Howling.* 'Not even released it. They refused to let me utilise it. Totally unprepared to be exposed as deaf incompetents. Wouldn't let me run with it. I had already done some remixes, at my cost, to bring more energy out of the performances. MCA? Musician Cemetery of America. Crooks. Look up Sal Pisello.'

Not unexpectedly, MCA decided to conclude its relationship with The Angels, providing the pathway for Niven to approach his long-time client, co-conspirator and collaborator, the irrepressible hard-rock band promotions whiz Mike Bone, CEO of Chrysalis records.

———

By the end of December 1987, the Howling Across Australia tour had seen The Angels play to over 320,000 people across Australia and New Zealand with gate takings of over $4 million ($10 million in 2021). The album had sold upwards of 150,000 copies in Australia. However, after slicing and dicing the Australasian touring income a dozen different ways, actual retained profits were probably less than 10 per cent of that.

December 1987 also provided a Christmas celebration for Mushroom Records with the release of the double concert album *The Angels Liveline*, with performances stretching back over nearly ten years. This long-anticipated album captured all that was unique and exciting about Australia's most popular live touring band. The 24 tracks had musical contributions from current and previous personnel line-ups. It was all there: the favourite songs, Doc's between-song raves, the chants, the audience responses and applause.

The larger part of the album was recorded at the Bankstown RSL Club in Sydney, with the balance of the tracks taken from earlier club and pub appearances and concerts. A live version of 'Am I Ever Gonna See Your Face Again' was issued as a single, as was a medley of 'Love Takes Care' and 'Be with You'.

In the early months of 1988 the band was enjoying a well-earned break from the arduous Howling tour, but the success of the album, which soon went to number three on the Australian album chart, prompted planning for another Australian tour scheduled for June and July that year. This would become the most ambitious show ever for the band. *Liveline. This is it Folks—Over the Top (Then, Now and Everything in Between)* was three hours long and had three chronological sets spanning a significant part of the band's history.

Due to the sophisticated theatrical nature of the show, performances would be restricted initially to playing capital city and regional theatres or town halls, with a planned future downsizing for the larger clubs and pubs that could provide the facilities and stage headroom demanded by theatre productions.

With his Flinders University drama-school background and training, Doc was in his element organising the planning and logistics for these shows, which were remarkable for the time. Sydney's Enmore Theatre had the band and crew in for collaborative stage- and set-design sessions followed by rehearsals for the first show.

The show commenced with a brief flashback to the early life of the band as the Keystone Angels, with Doc on bass guitar playing and singing a few songs off their first albums. The second act was a front-of-stage acoustic set while behind the scenes an elaborate multi-level scaffold, complete with a catwalk above the drummer, was erected for a high-voltage sound-and-light tsunami of the band's most popular songs for the final act. The show required closely choreographed split-second timing between the band and crew.

The Enmore shows were a sell-out success. Rave reviews led to additional performances being scheduled in the regional and inter-state touring program.

The first Melbourne show at the St Kilda Town Hall got off to a great start with the catchy vibes of openers The Chantoozies prepping the audience. The first two acts brought thunderous applause, but in the final act disaster struck.

Bob Spencer recalls: 'At the end of the "Money" song, Doc and I would engage in a "fight" which ended with me dragging a Marshall quad [speaker] box from one side, climbing onto it and, now taller than Doc, proceeding to push and kick him. That night Doc kicked the top edge of the box, it toppled and I went with it, breaking the headstock off my guitar, smashing my teeth through my lip and snapping my right wrist.'

The band came to an abrupt stop, shocked at what had happened. Bob Spencer, white as a sheet and in obvious pain and distress, was assisted offstage and an ambulance summoned. A mortified Doc hastily brought the concert to a close.

While Bob spent a night sedated in hospital, the band and crew returned to their hotel rooms. They were stunned by the incident, but also apprehensive about whether the tour could continue. With two sold-out shows at Melbourne's Palais Theatre only a day away and a further six weeks of concerts to go, the outlook was dire. A stand-in guitarist for the Palais shows was at least needed.

They rang around the Melbourne recording studios for leads on any musician who might be familiar with the band's repertoire. The name that surfaced was Jimi Hocking, a 24-year-old R&B hot-shot who already had a reputation as a 'gun' guitarist.

Jimi was emphatic. 'It's doable,' he confidently replied to an anxious Brent Eccles, asking if he had the chops to do a three-hour Angels retrospective. He was a fan, had the records, knew the old songs, he was a strong improviser and had a good ear. It was just the most recent stuff that might be a problem.

An audition at the band's hotel had them feeling optimistic. Hocking was good, very good. A full rehearsal was required the following day, then it was straight to the sound check and he was slinging his guitar to walk out in front of 3000 punters at the Palais. No pressure, mind you!

Everything considered, the Palais concerts went very well. Even after the first gig, an extremely relieved and pleased Rick Brewster said to Jimi, 'So what are you doing for the next few weeks then?' Overnight Jimi Hocking had found himself on a rock tour with one of the country's biggest and most popular bands. He acquitted himself magnificently, and further enhanced his reputation as one of the country's top instrumentalists.

The tour was another huge success, setting attendance records no other Australian band could come close to, including selling out the 8200-seat Perth Entertainment Centre no fewer than three times.

———

If John Woodruff had hoped that Doc might step up to a position of leadership in the band with John Brewster gone, it didn't happen. Doc had no interest in the role. Instead, Brent Eccles moved almost seamlessly into the vacuum, quickly becoming recognised as a capable organiser and fixer. He worked well with Rick, deferring on musical matters but willingly shouldering most of the day-to-day details associated with running the band.

Meanwhile Doc's personal life had moved on. The previous three years had seen the arrival of his second child with Dzintra—another boy, Kieran, in January 1986. But, sadly, this was not enough to tie him to hearth and home.

Now into his forties and surrounded by a second generation of much younger fans, Doc continued to live for the moment, clinging to what he felt was a rightful cosmic balance for the lost years of his youth but finding emotional responsibility challenging. Despite the fact that he was married with a family, he chose to equivocate over other attachments, refusing to label or define relationships. He characterised his infidelities as nothing more than casual dalliances, his euphemistic 'flirty dates'.

He got around with a satchel stuffed with books associated with a psychology course he was completing and his interest in philosophy. It also had tapes from the myriad self-help and motivational courses he was fond of attending, plus his diaries, songwriting notebooks, crystals and totems. He was certainly curious, but there was also a Peter Pan-like side to Doc in his spontaneous enjoyment of the small things in life.

This free-spirited and seemingly self-indulgent existence was suddenly disrupted when, at an after-show catch-up with friends at Benny's, a Kings Cross nightclub that catered to the music set, he met Kym Pymont. A Qantas flight attendant in her late twenties, attractive and intelligent Kym made an immediate impact.

They clearly enjoyed each other's company and soon, at least as far as the band was concerned, they were an item. Doc appeared to have changed for the better—the dark moods and introspection away from his performances had lifted and he seemed much happier and in a better place with Kym around.

Chapter 22

Salvation lost

Michael Gudinski and Frontier Tours announced a Guns N' Roses Australian tour for December 1988. By this time Guns N' Roses had become a bona-fide rock-and-roll juggernaut. With Alan Niven at their helm, they had pretty much toured most of the major North American and European cities in support of their debut album and single 'Sweet Child O' Mine', which was continuing to fly off the shelves of music stores everywhere.

One show was planned for Sydney, on Saturday 17 December, and demand was strong enough in Melbourne (which was then Australia's heavy-metal capital) for two dates (14 and 15 December). With Niven pulling the strings, a big tick from Gudinski and Guns N' Roses hero Izzy Stradlin's endorsement, The Angels were a shoo-in for the support slots.

This was also when Alan Niven finally got to meet John Woodruff and decisions were taken to finalise the next stages in their collaborative management agreement. Once Niven was back to the US he called Mike Bone, who headed Chrysalis Records and was an industry promotional legend for his unique and highly creative ability to get songs from new artists played on radio. Niven asked Bone if he wanted to sign Angel City.

According to Niven, Bone replied, 'I've got Doc. I've got you. Sure.' Niven recalls: 'It's the only time I have secured a recording contract from a single phone call. It may be a unique event in of itself.'

Chrysalis put up a recording fund of around US$200,000. The deal was that The Angels would go to Memphis and record at the illustrious Ardent Studios with Terry Manning. There are few recording facilities in the world that can compare with Ardent Studios. It has produced some of the best music in modern history by fostering relationships with leading producers. Terry Manning is among an elite cadre who have had long relationships with the studio.

'We gave the band time to write to their best and I was expecting a new set of songs,' Niven remembered. 'We booked them into Ardent, so as we could reach them and not have them on the other side of the 17-hour curtain. I admired their writing. I did not feel I had to micromanage this band.

'I was an idiot.'

————

Back in Australia the news of the Chrysalis signing and arrangements for recording sessions at Ardent Studios generated immediate excitement. Chrysalis Records had also arranged for The Angels to be the key attraction at an industry showcase bash at Whisky A Go Go in LA. Here they would have the opportunity to meet the other bands being managed by Alan Niven's Stravinsky Brothers.

On 2 June 1989, the band—along with wives, girlfriends, a soundman and a road manager—jetted off from Sydney bound for the US. Unfortunately, the planned big-budget recording session and generous timelines created expectations among the band members of a northern hemisphere summer of fun and frivolities away from the Australian winter rather than what was intended, the provision of adequate time for diligent songwriting and pre-production.

Alan Niven met the band at LA airport and, after checking into their hotel, The Angels joined Guns N' Roses for a few drinks. Angry Anderson, who was also in LA, arrived and the party got underway.

During the bonhomie of the evening Niven mentioned his displeasure that John Woodruff (who wasn't there) had already commissioned 20 per cent of half of the advance from Chrysalis. He thought this was premature: the advance was intended to fund the most important record of the band's career and his own company had deferred commissions to specifically ease any cash-flow issues. Woodruff had played no part in the approach to Chrysalis records or the contract negotiations.

———

Angel City had played the Whisky on every one of their US tours, going back to their memorable first gig in 1980. They were welcomed back to rattle the doors again on 6 June 1989 in what was hoped would be a turning point and relaunch of the band's long-held aspirations in the USA.

Chrysalis Records had the place packed solid with invited industry guests. The band was in fine form and blazed though their set, with Doc singing like a man possessed. LA rock mag *BAM* reported on the gig: 'The Angels are one of the truly great rock bands that pioneered the driving rock sound from Down Under.'

Looking on from the balcony VIP area were members of Guns N' Roses. At the end of the set, as the calls for encores increased, Doc called up to them, inviting the special guests to join the band onstage.

Time immediately stood still. Waiters stopped serving drinks, monster lines were consumed and patrons stopped dancing. History was being made. Road crew dragged in extra amps, mics and stands, then scurried around hooking up leads.

Alan Niven recalls: 'Axl joined Doc on stage, I think Slash and Duff also played. Not sure that Iz did, but I could be wrong. Pretty certain Steven didn't though. Angry jumped up too.'

To uproar, applause and astonishment from a normally hard-to-impress audience, the combined super-band then proceeded to rip into a medley of Angels' classics, including Guns N' Roses favourite 'Marseilles'.

The LA *Rock Review* summed up the night: 'When Doc invited most of Guns N' Roses down off the balcony to jam on "Marseilles" for the encore, it was no surprise to see that Axl knew all the words; it had been in his repertoire for years. The audience hadn't expected this, and a sold-out Whisky freaked out big time.'

———

The following day, Rick and Bob, along with Iz Stradlin, were Alan Niven's special guests to see Great White play at the New Orleans NBA Arena. The two Angels were both invited onstage to join the band on the cover version of 'Face the Day'. The two guitarists then flew to Memphis to rejoin their colleagues.

The band started work with high hopes that Terry Manning could help them produce the best album of their careers. They'd brought four songs that had been worked up at the Rhino studio in Sydney and a number of other partially completed song ideas left over from the Howling sessions. Chrysalis wanted the album to release in November 1989 for the Christmas market; from their mid-June perspective that looked completely doable.

Terry ran a tight ship at Ardent. The studio had significant involvement with gospel music and a reputation for strong work and behaviour ethics prevailed. Work started at 10 a.m., with morning tea, lunch, afternoon tea and a wrap at 6 p.m. Definitely no drugs or alcohol. For a band of night owls who not only survived but thrived on regular indulgences, bankers' hours and a dry ship were going to take some getting used to. Come knock-off time at 6 p.m. the lure of the musical delights of downtown Memphis were too strong.

Bob Spencer soon found his *nirvana*. He'd talked himself into jamming with an all-Black blues band one night. As he recalls: 'From then on, I spent many nights going out for a blow, or jamming with local musicians and striking up friendships. The natives were very friendly with the odd-looking little white bloke with the funny ponytail.'

Doc was in his element too. 'We'd crash any gig, any time. Even busk on the sidewalk. It was very easy for me being in Memphis—our knowledge of the old blues and jug band songs they played in those places. It felt like Beale Street had been waiting for us to complete those things.'

The distractions came thick and fast. Terry was an Elvis tragic. He knew all the songs and a tribute band, The Cow Demons, quickly came together. Terry used his connections to secure them a support gig at the annual Memphis fourth of July show on Mud Island. There were trips to look at Graceland, at Elvis's car collection and his aeroplane. Doc went on a conducted tour through Sam Phillips' Sun Studio. Even the Peabody Hotel's famous Duck Parade got a look.

Progress on recording at Ardent had been steady but pedestrian. When the four songs the band had brought with them were finished, attention was then focused on the other left-over song ideas in the Howling sessions folder. Then shocked surprise! Alan Niven—togged out in de rigueur all-black rock-band manager's gear and wraparound shades—flew in to check on progress.

Woodruff never did that! The band played the tapes of the completed songs through. Unfortunately, Niven was not impressed.

'When I went down to Memphis to hear the new tracks,' he recalled, 'I was distinctly underwhelmed. Again, I was delinquent. I saw them as peers, not fresh young rubes that I would have to mould, shape and guide.

'I expected to come and hear the kind of material that I personally found inspiring. I always relied on my own reactions, not those of the peer group or the environment. My simple conceit was that, if I liked something, lots of people would.

'I was expecting a new set of songs. Instead, it was all rather formless and lacking in insight and spirit. I was unhappy. I told them so.

'In a meeting, sitting again on the other side of a large table, I made my case that the material was subpar. The entire band disagreed. Years later, while visiting in Arizona, Rick Brewster would admit that I was right. Of course I was right. It was obvious.'

Niven had wanted the band to use the occasion to produce a US number-one album. He wanted cracker songs like 'Face the Day' or 'Marseilles'. He had expected the band—and especially Doc, who he saw as the band's poet, chief lyricist and most progressive creative—to use the time, the funds and resources he had provided to dig deep and produce it. He was extremely confident that he would know their number-one songs when he heard them.

He could take it from there. The band needed to trust him.

'I had already proven with "Face the Day" that the doors of radio could be burst open. I knew I had to deal with Woody and Mushroom having Australia. I didn't care. I could sell more records in California in six months than an Australian band could sell on their own continent in a career,' said Niven.

The band was stunned at Niven's response. He had been forthright but attempted to defuse the situation by suggesting a game of cricket! This only served to escalate the drama.

'It was burning hot, and we played out on the asphalt car park,' Rick Brewster recalled. 'While he was fielding, Niven took his shoes off and by the time we had finished his feet were blistered out of control. He was really disgruntled with the band, the producer, his feet . . . everything. He demanded a remix to the four songs we had done. He was a control freak—if things weren't done his way, he didn't like it. We said "no way"!'

Alan turned on his heel and returned to his hotel, only to find that he had been robbed. Furious and devastated by the loss of personal jewellery, he checked out and returned to his office in LA. The next day the band received his abrupt message: 'That's it, I've resigned.'

The mixes were not the only issue. Niven was also concerned about the internal dynamic of the band.

'Doc was nowhere to be found, he was absent from the studio,' he recalled. '"He's in his hotel room writing," claimed Rick.

'In hindsight he was probably in his room avoiding a showdown with Rick, who appeared to have decided that it was now his outfit to run and on anything to do with running the band or its future direction Doc was to be kept on the margins. In a nutshell Rick made a power grab and cocked the whole thing up.

'I like to believe in the brotherhood of a band and, as a manager, I encourage that, and try to avoid the circumstances of discord—fighting over shares of money etc . . . I love bands that share equally and who try to maintain the brotherhood . . . who try to live the myth. That's heroic. And I have learned firsthand what destroys bands—therefore my encouragement to share and employ a degree of equality.

'In GnR, the policy was that while one was a member of the band one would benefit from all moneys being shared—one for all and all for one. If you left the band and were not a writer, then the privilege ended. This method was used by lots of bands, Van Halen, for example, did the same. The Boomtown Rats famously lost the plot and fell apart because there was no composing royalty sharing and after the first publishing royalties arrived everyone wanted to be a writer. Sometimes it's in everyone's best interest to share.

'Both Rick and Doc flew out, individually and separately, to LA to try to get me to recommit, but I was deeply disappointed and up to my ass in other alligators. I admired Doc and the songs he performed. I had a faith there. I did not think I had to stare over anyone's shoulder from the back seat. I was stupid. On paper it was a great match. On the pitch they dropped the ball. It happens. Even Chelsea loses.

'The band would finally get its head out of its ass when they recorded *Skin & Bone*. *That* was the album I was hoping for. I knew it was in them.'

Unfortunately, by then Alan Niven was well out of the picture. The band remained at Ardent producing the record honouring their agreement with Chrysalis. But with just four new songs and the remainder being re-recorded and recut from previous albums, it was never going to be good enough. It quickly bombed. The band's US aspirations had foundered again.

They would return to Ardent in 1990 to produce the album that six months later became the Australian release *Beyond Salvation.* This was an entirely different and successful album generating local sales in excess of 70,000 and giving the band their first Australian number one. It also prompted another very successful Australasian tour.

———

Another casualty of the final days recording at Ardent had been Jim Hilbun.

Jim was by then a seven-year veteran with the band. He had laboured hard on the long tours of that period, and his composition 'Stand Up' had been the first single taken off the *Watch the Red* album, demonstrating his versatility as a songwriter, vocalist and sax and keyboards player.

Jim was a popular member of the band with quite a fan following in his own right; with Doc at one point about to leave the band, he had even been suggested as a replacement frontman. He had shared songwriting on just one track on the *Howling* album but had made a significant artistic contribution with that album's cover artwork in association with girlfriend Chrystine Carroll.

Jim was a laid-back band member with no pretensions about where he fitted in the greater scheme of things. He would work with what he was given. Frequently describing himself as the 'hired help', he had weathered the usual irritations of the band's artistic pecking order. While both Doc and John Brewster were at pains to be friendly from his first day with the band, Jim sensed the usual dismissive attitudes guitarists reserve for bass players. But he felt sidelined from songwriting collaborations and was only summoned to the studio, frequently at short notice, to provide his bass to the track. These requests would invariably be accompanied by comments that his presence wasn't really required—Rick or Bob could quite capably put down the bass track themselves.

With Jim electing to spend some time in his home state of California before returning to Australia, the decision from the band's management had been predictable.

Chapter 23

The parting of the ways

It's not hard to imagine the reaction of Chrysalis Records to the abject failure of the American version of *Beyond Salvation* in the US charts. After investing a not-insignificant US$200,000 with the reasonable expectation of some well-written, arranged and produced songs at the very least, there was no chance that Chrysalis would continue with the band. It politely advised that it would not be forthcoming with an advance for the next album. The band had been dropped.

Nevertheless, the band's relationship with Michael Gudinski and Mushroom was still good. The relative success of the Australian version of *Salvation*, a national number-one album, and the previous successful teaming to produce *Howling* meant they were going to be receptive towards funding another production. Mushroom's Frontier Touring Company had also supported the significant costs of special staging for the *Beyond Salvation* promotional tour in 1990. As a return on their investment, they had taken a profit share on the successful collaboration.

But as the decade progressed Australia experienced what Treasurer Paul Keating famously described as 'the recession we had to have' following the financial excesses of the 1980s. This inevitably led to plunging record sales, reduced gig attendances and a general sombre economic outlook. It also meant that Mushroom could only promise a modest budget to fund the next album. The cloth would need to be cut accordingly.

———

With an extended band break over Christmas 1989 there hadn't been much urgency in trying to find a bass player to replace Jim Hilbun. But over in Perth 21-year-old James Morley, a bassist with an Angels and AC/DC cover band, had scurried to the nearest phone when he heard that Jim Hilbun had left the band.

'Brent and Bob had jammed with us a couple of times at a club named Rockwells. I found out Jim had left so I got Brent's number and told him I wanted the gig. I flew over and auditioned. They just jammed and I played along with them. I slotted in perfectly and got the gig,' remembered Morley.

And his recollections of meeting Doc at that time? 'Doc was a very different, intriguing character; he was always deep in thought and careful with his words. A very worldly character, so for me, being young and impressionable, he was very intimidating yet at the same time welcomed me with open arms into the fold. He certainly was always a wordsmith, and to be a part of that process was something very special.'

———

The band had also come to recognise that John Woodruff's hands-off style of management, which had been useful to foster creativity in their early days, had inevitably lost the band critical focus and direction in a music industry that was constantly trending and evolving.

As part of the existing management contract, Woodruff received a 20 per cent commission on all the band's income, including publishing (songwriting) royalties. With more band members now involved in songwriting collaborations, his commissions had become greater than that received by the individual songwriters themselves.

And although the gross income from their highly successful local tours had been in the multimillions, after the deduction of management and booking agency commissions and costs Rick, Doc and Brent, as the band owners, received little more than wages in return for months of high-energy barnstorming. The increasingly difficult economic times made it important to both renegotiate Woodruff's commission from publishing income and to broach the subject of a more substantive contract review. Rick Brewster and Bob Spencer were delegated to sort it out. Doc was secretly relieved to let them get on with what would have been an embarrassing confrontation with his old friend.

'We went off to see Woody at his house overlooking the ocean at Coogee to tell him that we didn't want to pay publishing commissions anymore,' Rick Brewster said. 'He was clearly not happy but eventually said, "OK, if that's the way you feel about it, so be it."'

John Woodruff spoke to Doc later that same day to let him know that he had decided to drop the management of the band. A few days later he sent the band a brusque three-line note advising his resignation and put out a press statement explaining that he was relinquishing his management role with The Angels in order to focus on his new record label Imago and his recent signing of The Baby Animals. It was the end of a big chapter in the life of the band.

Brent Eccles immediately stepped up with an offer to manage The Angels for a 10 per cent commission. He'd already been involved in the day-to-day running of the band and had often been delegated to represent them in negotiations. He was capable and instrumental in driving much of the creative messaging associated with the big local tours. His offer would also improve the band's cash flow on a big tour by up to $5000 a week. It was accepted unanimously without hesitation.

Brent had also managed to hook a part-time evening DJ gig on Melbourne radio station 3XY. *Homegrown* featured demos by unsigned bands and artists and this had given him the idea of selecting a song each from three bands—The Hurricanes, The Desert Cats and John Woodruff's new signing The Baby Animals—to provide the flip side for 'Dogs Are Talking', The Angels' first single release from the *Beyond Salvation* album.

The songs would be promoted on the *Homegrown* show and would add to the leverage towards getting 'Dogs Are Talking' on the charts. The three bands would also be openers on a 'Dogs Are Talking' roadshow that would be the first of the tours to support the *Beyond Salvation* album.

This clever idea would help expose The Angels to the next generation of fans.

———

The highlight of the Dogs Are Talking tour was a massive show at Selina's at Coogee Bay Hotel. Designed to hold 2000, this was one of Sydney's top rock-music destinations but crowds of up to 3000 sweat-drenched patrons were frequently packed in wall to wall.

The three support bands were each given sufficient time to present comprehensive sets. Despite the impatient audience of hardcore fans persisting with their chants for 'Angels, Angels, Angels', the youth and vitality of the support bands set up the mood for the evening.

It was almost midnight when The Angels were finally welcomed to the stage with ecstatic applause. Doc, in his best physical shape for years, dominated the stage. Leaping and dancing, game face on, playing the crowd to perfection. It seemed as though the band had been injected with life.

The Angels were called back for encore after encore. Doc's crown was still firmly in place.

———

What the *Beyond Salvation* tours were to reinforce, however, was the differences between the old fans and the new fans. While the Australian release of *Beyond Salvation* introduced a great many younger fans to The Angels' music, for the older fans these new songs couldn't hold a candle to the old ones.

Spurred by Guns N' Roses' endorsement of The Angels' back catalogue, the younger metal fans were seeking authenticity. They appreciated the musical trifecta of loud distorted guitars, emphatic rhythms of dense bass-and-drum sound and vigorous vocals. For them, the band was sensational.

But to The Angels' hardcore fans, the new US-style glitzy metal makeover was a complete sell-out of their Australian pub-rock heritage. They were dismayed by much-loved songs from the 'classic' Angels albums being played way too fast or not at all, and by Doc's now incomprehensible and incoherent lyrics being drowned in the mix. This wasn't the same band they had grown up with.

————

A year or so earlier, the band had met Sydney-based English producer Steve James, who had worked with a who's who of British artists from Shirley Bassey to the Sex Pistols. The band admired his work and enjoyed his company. In early 1991 they negotiated for him to produce their next album, which would come to be named *Red Back Fever*. Steve's ethos was that artists didn't come to the studio to rehearse or practise; they came with pre-production completed and ready to record. Studio time and production was an expensive resource, and Steve had built a reputation of having the interests of the funding party at front of mind.

Coming down off a high from the local success of *Beyond Salvation* and its huge national promotional tour, the band owners had come to the sober realisation that after years of hard work they had really very little to show for it. And now the recession was forcing a new reality from which there were no exemptions.

As Rick Brewster said: '*Red Back Fever* had to be a low-budget recording. We were still suffering the effects of five months of living in Memphis and there was little money in the bank. But we needed to do a new album. We found a small 24-track studio called Trackdown in Camperdown. Between pub tours we started working with Steve on some new songs we had written since the Memphis sojourn.'

This arrangement helped confirm Mushroom's investment in the new album, but some of the band members were unhappy. In particular, for newcomers Bob Spencer and James Morley, after the enjoyable experience of recording at the world-class Ardent

Studios in Memphis, the decision to record in a small inner-suburban Sydney studio was something of a letdown.

'Bob and James were hired musos who hadn't had to share in the costs of recording *Salvation*. They were probably unaware of the true reality of the band's situation. We'd blown a fortune recording *Two Minute Warning* and we had done it all over again with *Salvation,* and we just couldn't do it a third time. We'd recorded *Howling* in Sydney and it had been a great album,' said Rick.

Apart from the disagreements over recording studios, there were also significant musical differences. Bob Spencer summed it up in this way: 'My vision for the band was to have funky riffs and grooves like Aerosmith. What I had in mind was moving forward in a way like Aerosmith had done. They were my yardstick. I looked at us and went, "Some of these guys want to go backwards, and I'm not a backwards sort of guy."'

Rick Brewster's perspective on how things stood musically is interesting: '*Beyond Salvation* [Australian] was an OK album. Great production let down by some B-grade songs and some shit lyrics. I really missed my brother's input. He and I had always been able to sort out the wheat from the chaff until a song started to glow. Nothing else would do.'

———

Doc by now was not in a good place. He shared just one songwriting credit on the *Red Back Fever* album. He found it hard to accept any of the responsibility for poor songwriting, preferring to blame the performance of their various record companies. As he summed it up: 'At the record company level in America, we just never got the type of support you really need. It was very frustrating and at times we came very close to breaking up because we were so disheartened by it all. That's what broke the back of The Angels—the attempts to crack the States.'

He was also heavily distracted and increasingly depressed in trying to deal with a perfect storm of personal issues. Self-medication on prescription drugs and alcohol didn't help. He decided to get away from it all, walking for days at a time with a small pack and his old army bivvy sheet into the trails and tracks of Lane Cove National Park and taking the train to access fire trails deep into the forests and fern dells of the Blue Mountains. He left the band to get on with writing and recording, surfacing periodically to put down the vocal tracks.

While recording *Howling,* John Woodruff had encouraged Doc to offer the band his folder of co-written songs and song ideas he had intended for his solo album project. Working up these already well-developed songs had the whole team's creative juices flowing and it had been a fruitful exercise. But now, apart from a song of Rick's and some ideas left over from the Memphis sessions, the cupboard was bare and collaborations—mostly between Bob, Rick and Brent—were rushed. The result was that two covers had to be included—Ian Hunter's 'Once Bitten, Twice Shy' and 'Natural Born Bugie' by Steve Marriott.

Despite the dramas and a certain lack of enthusiasm from the band, Steve James enjoyed recording them. He confidently worked around the band, getting the right sounds down on tape and even coaxing the right feel from Brent's sometimes elusive drumming.

But Doc's sporadic visits to the studio concerned Steve. He was surprised that an outwardly confident high-energy personality could mask weariness, loneliness and estrangement from the band, with the exception of Rick.

'Doc wasn't in a good headspace. He was depressed and cynical about the whole business—everything. He announced that he was leaving the band, and obviously that was a major problem. Brent managed to get him back now and then, and eventually I got some wonderful vocals down. I just got him to enjoy himself. I tried to get some feel out of it and use that wonderful depth he has got,' Steve said.

After recording was completed, Steve and his wife invited Doc and Kym to their house for dinner. Doc was very interested in a series of pictures on the wall of English comedian Sid James. When Steve told him that Sid was his father, Doc was dumbfounded.

'Tears started rolling down his face and he became visibly emotional,' Steve recalled. 'He told me that, as a kid growing up with his dad in the British Army, one of his weekly highlights was listening to *Hancock's Half Hour* on the BBC. He came over and gave me the most affectionate hug and just held on to me. It was like he was hugging something deep and meaningful from his youth. That my father held such an abiding memory for Doc was extremely moving for me.'

Chapter 24

Back to the future

With confirmation of his appointment as band manager, Brent Eccles threw himself enthusiastically into his new role and in early 1992 successfully pitched The Angels to support an Australian government campaign to combat alcohol-related violence. The band would spearhead a twelve-month initiative with a government-sponsored ten-week national tour. 'Tear Me Apart', from the *Red Back Fever* album, would be remixed and released as a single and the campaign's theme song.

There were plenty of raised eyebrows when the involvement of Australia's biggest pub-rock band in the campaign was announced but Doc, as band spokesman, was quick to articulate their position. 'We are not telling people not to drink; we've made a living for years playing in pubs. We drink. We are certainly not wowsers. This campaign is all about stopping alcohol-related violence, which I think everybody finds abhorrent.'

With a growing profile in federal government circles, the band

was also invited to participate in the Wizards of Oz concerts scheduled to be held at the Palace Theatre in Los Angeles. Again, this drew
some flak: the glittering high-profile event was ostensibly to showcase
young, unknown and unsigned bands and acts in front of US music
industry heavyweights and hopefully get them signed. That The
Angels did not have a record deal at the time seemed to outweigh the
fact that the band was neither young nor unknown stateside.

Others seemed not to mind. Mike Pollack reviewed the show
in *The Hollywood Reporter*: 'Angel City were the most original act
on the bill with a vocalist that can sing and a band that can play.'
Jim Filiault from *Kerrang!* wrote: 'The Angels are undoubtedly my
favourite band ever to emerge from Oz, I love their bare bones, no
frills bar rock. This band should be as large in the States as they are
back home.'

Not unsurprisingly, however, there wasn't a US record company
keen to sign them up. It was well known by industry people following the band that three of the majors had blown their investments
on their previous signings and the best-credentialled talent manager
in the US music business had soon let them go.

The final job before returning home was a catch-up with Terry
Manning to remix 'Tear Me Apart' ahead of its release as a single. In
Bob Spencer's view: 'Remix it? Terry turned the bloody thing upside
down. Fantastic!'

———

The Tear Me Apart tour commenced on 22 July 1992. The publicity
and tour dates ran in conjunction with a saturation TV advertorial
graphically illustrating alcohol-related violence against the 'Tear Me
Apart' soundtrack. None of this was lost on Albert Music, which

immediately released *Their Finest Hour*, a compilation album in CD format, which was a revolutionary new technology at this time. John Brewster supplied the liner notes, and it was soon outselling *Red Back Fever*, prompting radio stations to put the old Angels songs on their high-rotation playlists. The Angels were back on the airwaves and very much in the moment.

The tour was successful, but the brief return to the US had both Bob and James considering the next stages of their careers. They wanted to be more than contract musos on a wage. James particularly was attracted to LA for the next stage of his life and, on completion of the tour, he handed in his notice. Bob Spencer, still not happy about the band's musical direction or lack of it, also decided he would move on. He had spent six years with the band, an intense period of extensive touring and recording, and he too was ready to do other things.

———

The Adelaide concerts on the Tear Me Apart tour provided an opportunity for the first time in many years for the former Moonshine Jug and String Band to catch up again. Rick and John Brewster, together with Doc, met up with Spencer Tregloan and Pete Thorpe. The outcome was that they spent two days rehearsing for a couple of re-formation shows, the first at one of their old haunts, the Red Lion Hotel in North Adelaide. This was the first time Rick, John and Doc had played together since 1985.

To their complete surprise, they effortlessly resumed their old jug-band songs and harmonies. The arguments, anger and disagreements associated with John Brewster's exit from The Angels were forgotten.

'It was obvious how much Doc loved being in the jug band,' John Brewster said. 'The pressure was off him to go into character as The Angels frontman. In Moonshine he wasn't the main singer, we all took turns at it. So he just relaxed and played guitar, did harmonies, and when he did sing he was really melodic and a natural entertainer with a big grin on his face.'

It was a fun time for recollections, reconnections and enjoying quite a few joints and numerous bottles of red wine. The gigs ended up being so much of a buzz that an album of jug-band songs seemed both natural and almost inevitable. Why hadn't they done this back in the day? Two days at Alberts' Neutral Bay studio were booked in mid-January 1993 to produce Moonshine's album, which came to be named *Rent Party*.

———

With Bob and James gone from The Angels and no replacements found, fans and even the remaining band members started to think that the chances of The Angels re-forming again were becoming increasingly slim. Doc had advised Brent and Rick that he was intending to start a psychology degree and wouldn't be available for gigs in the foreseeable future. He also wanted to pursue acting roles in theatre and television, do voice-overs, club compering and DJ work. Both Brent and Rick were also doing other thing. So it came as something of a surprise to Brent to receive a call one morning from the New Zealand chapter of the Hells Angels to enquire if the band was interested in coming to Auckland to play their annual City of Cycles Ball. The conversation soon made it clear that the Hells Angels were very serious, so Brent advised that he would confer with the band.

To Brent and Rick's surprise, Doc immediately agreed. But the task of recruiting and rehearsing two replacement band members just for one gig seemed almost insurmountable . . . Unless . . . Doc had mentioned earlier to Brent how well the Moonshine gigs had gone with John Brewster.

Now it was Brent's turn to ask the obvious question. Should they get John back for the Hells Angels gig? 'We wouldn't have to teach him the songs,' he added. Stunned, they all stared at each other. 'Fine by me,' said Doc.

'It was the greatest [phone] call I've ever made,' Rick Brewster remembered. 'The Angels had ground to a halt. We'd been trying to come up with an album, trying to come up with songs, and not very successfully. Not doing any live work. In my enthusiasm, I think I told John we wanted him back permanently.'

'When Rick called me there was never any suggestion that I'd be joining the band to do just one gig,' John recalled. 'I didn't know what was in Brent's mind. All I knew was that I was rejoining the band that I'd started with Rick and Doc in 1974. I was excited to be reuniting with my brother. We'd exorcised those demons a few years before—but I was a bit apprehensive about Doc and Brent, to be honest.'

Then it was time to give Jim Hilbun a call. His departure from the band had not been handled very well, but Australia had got under his skin and he was back living in Sydney. He said he would like to swing by and talk about it. 'When I walked in, I found them working on all these new songs. I just fell back into it again. It was easy,' Jim said.

'The great thing for me was that these guys were still Angels,' Doc recalled. 'We didn't have to go through a long introductory process with Jim and John. We went over to New Zealand for three days and did the show. I really enjoyed it and we thought, "Well, this is all working. We all like it so let's keep going and see what happens.'"

Doc also had an eye to reality. He could see economic carnage all around. The pub-rock scene had been virtually decimated. New fire and noise limit regulations had encouraged pubs and clubs to install more poker machines rather than book live music. With youth unemployment high, record sales had plummeted. Digital recording systems were also fundamentally altering the recording industry worldwide and an inevitable shakeout of Australia's studios was soon to arrive.

The Angels knew that with John and Jim back in their line-up, they would instantly connect with their fans and offer them a real reason to come back to what was left of the pub and club scene. Brent Eccles was to prove himself as both band manager and master marketer. Together with wife Helen and agent Tony Grace they were to sell out a succession of tours under such esoteric banners as the Terra Australis Incognita Tour, the Barbed Wire Ball Tour and the Hard Evidence Tour.

The Terra Australis Incognita Tour kicked off at Selinas on 5 November 1993. It was a sell-out doors-closed show. With the reformed Rose Tattoo added to the line-up, John Brewster took The Angels' set list back to a heavier blues style for an evening that ended with 3000 voices chorusing '*We gotta get out of this place*'.

It was an incredible and atmospheric event. The astronomical door take was greater than any single concert to date. The band stood around mouths agape and congratulated each other when Brent shared the details after the show. Then all the gear was packed into semitrailers for the trip north for another sell-out show in Brisbane.

Australia might be still limping out of the recession of the previous three years, but The Angels were back in business. They were the biggest and most exciting live music show in the country once again, with radio playing their songs and supporting them every step of the way.

———

In March 1994, after a three-month break, the Terra Australis Incognita Tour resumed. The band flew to Western Australia for six shows, then back across the country to Cairns before coast hopping down to Maryborough to finish the tour.

After that Doc and the Brewsters maintained their frenetic pace with a promotional tour for Moonshine's *Rent Party* album, which included sharing the stage with their old jug-band friends The Captain Matchbox Whoopee Band.

Doc then indicated that he wanted to spend some time seriously pursuing acting roles in theatre and television. This, as all the other band members were well aware, had been a long-term personal ambition that he had set aside on a number of previous occasions for the greater good. Turning down the lead role of Javo in the film *Monkey Grip* had been one of the major regrets of his life.

The other members regrouped separately and, continuing the spirit of collaboration and renewed friendship, wrote and rehearsed some new songs. Somehow they managed to get hold of the keys to the recently vacated ABC Studios at Gore Hill, taking over the old control room as a workspace and rehearsal studio.

There was a good vibe about the place, and between racing pushbikes and games of badminton some serious work did occur. Eventually the band relocated to Cadillac Studios to produce the demos for eight new songs, two of which—'Turn It On' and 'Don't Need Mercy'—found their way onto their next release, *Evidence,* a compilation album that spanned the entire history of the band.

The album was only made possible by a deal wrangled by Michael Gudinski that enabled the cooperation of Mushroom records, Sony and Alberts Music. Doc took time off from stage show auditions and rehearsals to join the band at EMI's Studios 301 in the recording of the new songs with English producer Paul Northfield. Both the *Evidence* album and the single 'Don't Need Mercy' were then rush-released to coincide with their forthcoming Hard Evidence Tour.

Doc meanwhile had been auditioning for various stage productions and renewing contacts for various television dramas. He had been disappointed that the long-running *Rafferty's Rules* TV drama series about the workings of a local Sydney magistrate's court had concluded. He had enjoyed a cameo role in the second series, working with the producers to develop the character for Irishman John 'Jacko' Corrigan, where magistrate Rafferty became embroiled in a 'punk drug squatter's assault case'.

Using his previous practical court advocacy experience on behalf of his band mates, he had developed a script featuring a legal aid lawyer who might feature in a future series. There had also been his involvement with *Paris,* the rock musical co-written by Australian rock musician Jon English based on the myth of the Trojan War. Both projects had become victims of recession-driven cutbacks.

One of the productions Doc auditioned for was the lead role for a rock opera slotted to open in Sydney. *Bad Boy Johnny and the Prophets of Doom* had debuted in Melbourne in 1989 with the-then little-known actor Russell Crowe in the lead role. It was described as the story of Johnny, who rises from altar boy to the world's first rock-and-roll pope.

Doc was very excited to secure the lead role in the forthcoming Sydney production. He knew that without the broad-minded patrons that support similar productions in Melbourne the show would be controversial, but welcomed the opportunity to demonstrate his talent.

The production went into rehearsal and opened on 14 September 1994 at the Enmore Theatre. But despite a high-quality cast reviewers panned the show, and the curtain came down almost immediately.

Disappointed and disheartened, Doc returned to The Angels. A tour arranged for The Screaming Jets was reconfigured as The Barbed Wire Ball Tour with The Angels co-headlining. Australia's biggest pub and club venues were put on notice for impending mayhem and the band hit the road.

The year would finish on a high note!

————

The first months of 1995 produced two more songs from the Gore Hill and Cadillac sessions, 'Spinning My Wheels' and 'Blue Light'. Together with the re-released 'Don't Need Mercy' and 'Turn It On' (both from the *Evidence* album), they were released as an EP, *The Hard Evidence Tour*, to support a follow-on tour of the same name.

Unfortunately though, the long relationship with Mushroom was starting to sour. *The Evidence* 'greatest hits' compilation sold what the three contributing record companies would have considered a 'sub-par' 35,000 copies as punters upgraded the old favourites from their vinyl collections to CDs. The new songs consistently failed to connect with live audiences.

Mushroom was certainly aware that The Angels could still pack out huge venues with the well-promoted so-called 'original line-up', but the hard fact was that milking the old favourites at live shows did not generate CD sales for the new songs. Any discussion about funding a new album was not able to whip up much excitement. It seemed to be Mushroom's view that The Angels had received their time in the sun, and that the new sounds from new artists and acts represented better commercial prospects. Once again, the band was without a record company.

———

Bernard's marriage to Kym, in February 1993, had not got off to a good start. Replying to mischievous speculation from a member of the bridal party that his philandering days were finally over, his flippant reply—that there was nothing exclusive about his side of the arrangement—almost ended the wedding day straight away. Sadly, things were to go further south from there.

Bernard already had three children: with one of them he appeared to have escaped financial responsibility, but with the other two he was quickly reminded that they were approaching the age of expensive education obligations. He was well aware in his heart that rejecting Kym's wishes for their own family would be a definite deal breaker. Sadly, by 1995 their marriage was over.

The relentless rock-star lifestyle had also taken its toll on other marriages and relationships across the band. It was time for all of them to take a break . . . and something of a reality check. And so it was that The Angels dropped out for a while.

Bernard took the break-up with Kym badly. Depressed, he put himself in the hands of a 'Shrink to the Stars', who was himself soon to be struck off for drug addiction. Prescription mood stabilisers soon added to Bernard's troubles. His interest in psychotherapy and psychiatry—some of it in-depth study related to the degree course he was enrolled in—was also to prompt questionable introspection and self-medication.

And if the recession-induced shortfall in income from the band wasn't bad enough, the Australian Tax Office had Doc in its sights with a payment demand for tax on several years of previous earnings.

He was still pursuing an alternative career. An introduction to impresario and celebrity speaking circuit doyen Harry M. Miller was exciting, and Harry soon had Doc's motivational speaking career on its way. After a few lessons from Harry on how to sell the lessons from The Angels' hard-won success, a run of bookings up and down the east coast was quickly generated. Unfortunately, Doc arrived at his first speaking gig inebriated; his speech was a train wreck and Harry was left with a mess to clean up. Doc's speaking career was over.

By the middle of 1995, Rick, John, Jim and Brent had set themselves up in the Darling Harbour Rehearsal Studios, a grimy third-floor address in an old wool store that had been converted to a series of cheap and cheerful sound-proofed rehearsal rooms. Bands liked its funky vibe and car-sized goods lift that clanked up and down all day with bands, roadies, gear and equipment.

The plan was to start work on a new album. With no record company behind them, they would need to produce the record themselves. Brent rang Doc. What was doin'? Was he in or out? Did he want to start working again? Was he up for touring and recording again?

The call was timely. Doc needed to work. Getting such discipline back into his life was a path away from the abyss. After the wheels had come off *Bad Boy Johnny,* he had read scripts, been for auditions and tested for both a film and a play, but nothing had come from any of them. His solo album plans had also stalled. And after couch-hopping with friends and camping in the Lane Cove national park for a number of weeks he desperately needed a place to live.

Chapter 25

The last hurrah

The sessions that were to produce The Angels' studio album that came to be named *Skin & Bone* had commenced during 1995 in the spacious Darling Harbour Rehearsal Studios. It had already been a long time coming. It was the band's eleventh studio album and, sadly, would prove to be Doc's last.

At the outset there was some wrangling over who would have ultimate responsibility for producing the new album, given that the band had elected to do it themselves. Brent, as manager and co-owner of The Angels, was considerably circumspect regarding John Brewster's renewed influence within the band, but he agreed with Doc that Rick would produce the album.

First cab off the rank was 'Call That Living', an uncomplicated song strongly reminiscent of the band's very early *No Exit/Face to Face* days. Doc, John, Rick and Jim had all collaborated on writing this song while they were travelling between gigs in country Victoria the previous year. After a period in the ratings wilderness,

Triple M was relaunching itself back into the tradie-aligned hard-rock demographic. As part of this move, Doc was dragged into Triple M to refresh the station ID; his unique 'in character' voice, which could alternate between a desperate croak, maniacal cackle or soft breathless rasp, was just what was needed. The newly produced CD of 'Call That Living' was soon out of the pocket of his jacket and playing on air.

The fact that the song was not yet available and an exclusive Triple M scoop made it all the more desirable. The station execs loved it. If listeners wanted to hear the new Angels song, they knew where to park the radio dial! Triple M in Melbourne, Brisbane and Adelaide were quick to pick up the promo and pretty soon every one of the network's stations had punters on the phone clamouring to buy the new Angels CD.

Never one to let an opportunity to market a tour go by, Brent and Tony Grace soon had a national tour organised. With no new record deal confirmed, the concerts would be the only place where the new CD and a new range of merchandise could be bought. It was time to return to the Darling Harbour Rehearsal Studios to rehearse all the songs for the new shows.

It was around this time that Doc was encouraged to acknowledge his past behaviours. Susy Pointon had flown into Sydney from the US, en route to her new home in New Zealand, and Doc was going to meet his 14-year-old son Aidan for the first time. He made a special request to studio manager Ike Brunt: could Ike look out for a special visitor when he arrived and bring him upstairs.

When the bell rang, Ike opened the door to a tall, slender lad asking for Doc Neeson. As Ike recalls: 'We just said hello and went back up to the office. I looked into the studio and signalled to Doc, and he came out. Very nervous, he followed me to the office and looked at this young guy—and the young guy stared back at him. It was all very intense, and then they gave each other a hug. They didn't say much. I said, "OK, I'll leave you to it then," and started closing the door, but Doc grabbed me and said, "Oh, er, Ike, this is my son Aidan. Take care of him for me, will you? After the next set we will be taking a break and I'm taking him out to lunch."'

———

To fit with the back-to-the-future feel of the new single, an esoteric hook for the proposed tour was required. And what would be more appropriate than the moniker of a character who had been already immortalised with a popular song on the *No Exit* album. 'Mr Damage,' which John Brewster had explained at the time, 'was in part inspired by a popular headbanger at the infamous Comb and Cutter at Blacktown', who referred to himself with some little pride and to general amusement as 'Brain Damage'.

The Mr Damage tour kicked off on 8 August 1996. It was to be huge, covering the whole country. The western leg alone took the band from Alice Springs across to Broome, then down to Port Hedland, The Spinifex Hotel at Mount Tom Price, The Walkabout Hotel at Karratha, then Kalgoorlie. The semitrailer went ahead with the gear while the band drove and flew to meet up with it. In Perth, the truck was loaded onto a train while the band flew to Adelaide. Then back to the regular east coast itinerary that brought them up to Christmas.

Doc had been making a concentrated attempt to rebuild his personal life and kick his alcohol and prescription-drug dependencies. To support him, the band had committed to the tour being dry. John Brewster said: 'We'd decided there would be no alcohol whatsoever on the tour. So Doc didn't drink. And he was fantastic. It was like discovering the old Doc Neeson—the guy we did the jug band with and formed The Angels with, who was essentially a lovely guy. We went surfing. I almost pinched myself—I could not believe it was happening.'

———

When the band regrouped in February 1997, it was clear the new album wouldn't be completed any time soon. The Mr Damage tour had, however, been inspirational. Desert nights under the stars and the vast distances of an ancient land would be reflected in new songs.

But there were still mouths to feed and the money needed to keep coming in, so a new tour was conceived. As Tony Grace recalls: 'The Angels have always done interesting things and I give Brent Eccles a lot of the credit for this. He came up with the concept and John Brewster came up with the name, the Lounge Lizards. It was a semi-acoustic kind of vibe and they had guests, Ross Wilson and Angry Anderson.'

With Doc, this was the holy trinity of heavyweight Australian rock. As soon as the word got out—that Doc and The Angels, plus Ross and Angry, would be touring together—the phones ran hot with demands from venues for gigs.

The concept was for a show in the-then increasingly popular 'unplugged acoustic style'. Brent would use brushes instead of sticks with his drum set and Jim an acoustic 12-string instead of his electric bass. The guitars would be plugged straight into the house PAs. A different pace for sure, though as Angry Anderson said: 'By the time we'd finished rehearsals, we'd evolved into the loudest acoustic rock band in the world.'

The band would be clustered around a couch, where the artists who weren't singing could have a mic and provide back-up vocals. Other props included plants, palm trees, a clothes rack and a park bench, plus some incredible theatrical lighting. The result was brilliant.

Following the success of the tour the previous year, the Lounge Lizards' route began in outback Western Australia. Then it continued on to South Australia and up to Darwin, across to north Queensland and down the east coast to Sydney. Despite annoying hard-to-fix feedback squeals resulting from amplifying acoustic guitars that frustrated both the band and their techs, the tour played to capacity audiences up and down the country.

———

Back in Sydney, work on the new album continued at Darling Harbour. Remarkably, Doc was able to put down all the lead vocal and backing tracks over a two-week period. He had remained mostly on the wagon for the Lounge Lizards tour and the band was overjoyed at his best studio vocal performances in ages.

Meanwhile, Mushroom Records had engaged the band's former colleague from Alberts, hot-shot producer Mark Opitz, as A & R manager. Mushroom had also just released three Angels live-performance videos with encouraging sales. Sensing that Mushroom might reconsider their decision to drop the band, Brent suggested Mark might like to listen to a few of their new songs.

'We played him the tracks and, as he listened, I looked down at everybody's feet—and no one was tapping their toes,' John Brewster recalled. 'We'd learned from George Young that if you weren't tapping your toes then it wasn't happening! Mark was unimpressed and went back to Mushroom—and Mushroom passed.'

Rick and John, stunned at Mark's reaction, immediately reviewed the drum tracks to see if they could be improved. Digital recording provided many options that could not even be dreamed off when using tape, and a few hours' work yielded a considerably improved recording.

Not rattled by the rejection from Mushroom, Brent continued to cast the net around for another record company. David Williams and Andrew McGee owned Shock Records, Australia's largest independent CD distributor, and both of them were huge Angels fans. In August 1997 the deal was done and, while the album was being completed, Shock would release 'Caught in the Night' as a single.

Shock also brought in New York recording tech-superstar Kevin 'Cave Man' Shirley to do the final mix of *Skin & Bone* at Sydney's Studios 301. For an exhausted Rick Brewster the album was completed at last. 'After five years it was fucking done!'

———

November 1997 put The Angels on the road for yet another tour. This time a traditional rock-and-roll show, a second Barbed Wire Ball Tour with co-headliners The Screaming Jets and support band Horsehead. The tour was a success, finishing up in Brisbane at the RNA Showground, but something was definitely worrying and unusual with regard to Doc's performances during the tour. A number of reviewers described his performances as flat; both John and Jim had to step in to support his vocals when he appeared to forget his words or be out of tune; however, he did not appear to be inebriated.

In retrospect, it is extremely concerning that these issues were not checked out properly, but most punters didn't notice anything amiss. At the time the band considered that maybe they were just all over-tired; it had been a big year. Brent scheduled three weeks off in the run-up to Christmas, but most of this was taken up with writing liner notes for the new album and resolving the design for the album cover.

The Angels' *Skin & Bone* album was released on 2 March 1998 on the Shock label. Despite feelings of indifference among band members and lacklustre initial sales, the album received some excellent reviews and was nominated for an ARIA award as one of the year's best albums.

The next urgent need was to put a tour together again, and to go out and sell it!

And so we come round to where we started . . . The Angels induction into the ARIA Hall of Fame on Tuesday 20 October 1998. For Doc it was at last the moment of recognition and endorsement by his peers, something certainly as significant to him as any of the other awards, tributes and honours that symbolised public appreciation and acclaim that he was to receive in the years that followed.

But, sadly, all was not well in Doc's world. Already there were signs, a history of odd behaviours and uncharacteristic incidents that are too often dismissed as a result of so-called lifestyle. Unfortunately society then, as now, has considerable difficulty in responding appropriately to the mood, behavioural and cognitive symptoms that are often the first indications of disabling and possibly life threatening incipient conditions.

However, there were some amazing and exciting chapters of Doc's eventful life still to come.

Part II

THE MAN BEHIND THE MASK

Anne Souter

Chapter 26

A double-sided giant

It was 1988, ten years since I'd seen the 'Mad Irishman', Doc, perform with The Angels in Coolangatta that crazy New Year's Eve and I was about to meet him in person.

I was National Communications Executive of the Australian Freedom from Hunger Campaign. Part of my job was to write direct mail, TV, radio and press ads to raise funds for victims of natural disasters like flood and famine, and programs that rebuilt infrastructure and rehabilitated and reconciled people affected by war.

I was working on a campaign called Gardens of Life and needed someone like a bad-boy rocker as a counter to more conservative and conventional celebrities already on board to endorse the cause. My then boyfriend, artist and sculptor Pietro 'Peter' Calvitto, suggested we should enlist his friend, Doc Neeson, and he invited him over for dinner so I could meet him. Now I was going to actually meet that magnificent maniac I'd seen at The Patch all those years ago.

Doc was not at all what I had expected. Charming and softly spoken with a wonderful deep voice and extremely tall, he was very friendly and even seemed a little bit humble. He brought flowers and wine and was only too happy to help the campaign.

I remember on the day of the first video shoot offering Doc something to drink. It was about 10 a.m., so all I had meant was coffee or tea, but he had a different idea. Looking dead serious, he said, 'Yes, please! Some pink champagne would be nice.'

What? Well, that really threw me, but I realised this was not just anyone. This was Doc Neeson. I rushed to ring the office. 'I'm in trouble! I'm at the shoot with Doc Neeson and he wants champagne, so can you grab me a bottle of dry pink champagne from the bottle shop?'

Returning to Doc, I explained there'd be a slight delay with his champers because someone had to bring it up from the cellar under the office and it had to be chilled. He adjusted his sunglasses and studied my face very closely. This made me feel rather uncomfortable—a bit like I imagined an insect would feel if it were pinned under a microscope—but I had to keep up the act, so I smiled and he smiled back.

Within twenty minutes, the champagne arrived on a silver tray with two glasses. My assistant quietly walked in and discreetly laid the tray down on a table. 'Your champagne, Miss Anne,' she said with a bowed head, and left.

'That's champagne!' cried Doc, dumbfounded. 'I was only joking!'

'Oh?' I said in mock surprise. 'Really? Well, I'm having some.'

'What's going on here? You're not supposed to be drinking champagne! You're supposed to be making a doco to raise money to feed starving people!' He looked genuinely shocked, but laughed when I said, 'We always have champagne when we're working. Sorry, I assumed you were serious.'

He lowered his sunglasses and looked at me very intently. 'I think we're going to be very *close* friends,' he said.

My God, those eyes! There they were again. So deep, so intense, I could have drowned in them.

'Oh yes!' I assured him. 'Yes indeed.'

'Absolutely indeed,' he said, adding 'Miss Anne', and raised his sunnies again to cover his eyes.

Much to my delight, Doc brought his son Daniel along to a second video shoot to speak out with him. With his continuing support, the campaign raised over $400,000 that year through its annual appeal.

———

During the next few years with Peter, I came to know the man behind the mask of Doc Neeson—the very well-mannered and super-intelligent stealer of hearts. Bernard championed many worthy causes including the massive Turn Back the Tide rally at Bondi the following year, protesting against the sewage pollution at Sydney beaches.

Through Peter, I met Bernard's then girlfriend Kym and also Bernard's ex-wife Dzintra. One day Kym phoned to ask if Peter and I would like to see a Mötley Crüe concert with her and Bernard. Complimentary tickets and VIP passes. How could we resist?

We picked up Bernard and Kym and drove to the Sydney Entertainment Centre. From the minute we arrived we had to stop calling Bernard 'Bernard'. He was out in public now, so he was 'Doc'.

Inside the auditorium, we could see a giant fluorescent fist glowing red in the fog and pulsating to the beat. Girls in black leather miniskirts were standing on giant Perspex blocks, chained to them by their ankles—and that was just the beginning! Drummer Tommy Lee had a revolving drum kit on special 'roller coaster' equipment that allowed him to play upside down.

At interval we went backstage and found Doc standing in an alcove in the corridor looking lost.

'What's wrong?' I asked.

'How do I look?' he asked back, looking very worried.

'Great!' I reassured him.

'Really?'

'Yeah, really.'

'You look good,' said Peter.

'Thanks. I was just told I look like a bag of shit!'

'Who said that?'

'Never mind. Would you like to come and meet the guys?' he asked, knocking on a dressing room door.

At that moment, a striking black leather-clad Kym came striding down the corridor. But there was tension in the air.

'Hi, guys! Enjoying the show?' she asked, smiling broadly at Peter and me.

Tommy Lee answered Doc's knock. Behind him on a lounge at the back of the room was the actress Heather Locklear, looking like Sin itself in a low-cut red dress, red patent stilettoes and red lipstick, legs crossed with a tall champagne flute in hand.

In a gap in Doc's conversation with Tommy Lee, there was a rustle and creaking of old leather and dark figures came through the door. 'God! It's The Skids!' shouted Tommy. 'You're not supposed to be here! Hey *guys*! What are you doing? I thought you were still in LA. God love you!' This American heavy metal/glam-rock band, Skid Row, fronted by Sebastian Bach, was already massive in the States. 'They love us,' Tommy said, 'but they're like our heroes!'

Doc and Tommy had been talking privately when Doc's face lit up. He'd been asked to sing with the Crüe!

But only a few songs into the first set after interval, Peter and I found ourselves driving Doc and Kym home. Kym had a very bad headache, Doc said, and he needed to take her home.

Strangely, when we got back to Cremorne Point, where Doc and Kym lived, Kym asked if we would like to come in for a drink. It wasn't until over a decade later that I started to speculate that Doc may have had stage fright and that he'd asked Kym to fake a headache to cover for him.

How was it that such a self-possessed and famous entertainer as Doc, with such charisma, energy, stage presence and confidence, could sometimes be overcome by panic and want to hide?

———

In the years that followed, I came to know both Kym and Bernard's first wife, Dzintra, very well. They were both strong, highly intelligent and charming women; they both had long, dark hair, but otherwise they were nothing alike. A yoga teacher, Dzintra was calm and diplomatic and a sensational cook. A flight attendant, Kym was tempestuous, a great organiser and an avid reader; she liked to party, but also to have time at home alone.

Many years after Bernard and Dzintra divorced in 1991 he told me one night how sad he'd felt on the day of the divorce—sad that things hadn't worked out as he'd hoped and dreamed. 'That was eight years ago,' he said, 'but it's still sad.' When he picked a rose from our garden and put it in water next to a candle, which he lit,

I wondered if it was for Dzintra. He and Dzintra had kept up a great friendship since their divorce, which was very fortunate for their two boys, Daniel and Kieran. They continued to bring their sons up together, and Dzintra and I became friends.

Bernard proposed to Kym, who'd also become a friend, in skywriting. In February 1993 Peter, who was by then my second fiancé, and I attended the wedding of Bernard Patrick 'Doc' Neeson and Kym Therese 'Tess' Pymont at Cremorne Point Reserve on the Sydney harbourfront. Bernard was disappointed that the wedding car wasn't the exact model of Buick he had wanted, but his bride and the reception at a waterfront restaurant on D'Albora Marina at The Spit were beautiful. It seemed a perfect night and his two little sons were brought to the wedding reception by their all-forgiving mother, who picked them up later.

———

Peter had once complained to me that every woman who met Doc fell in love with him. 'Yeah,' he'd said, looking at me very seriously, 'so *you'd* better not!' But before long I'd fallen under Doc's spell. He had more charm than anyone I'd ever met. Peter was constantly trying to micro-manage me, so I broke off our engagement. And then, in 1996, Kym and Doc split up.

Dzintra ended up with Peter, who had long been friends with her and Doc, and I ended up sharing my house with Doc after his split with Kym. Happily, we all remained friends. We celebrated special occasions together and saw each other regularly. It was very special that we were able to share so much.

Chapter 27

Mr Damage moves in

In mid-June 1996, during the storm of their final marriage break-up, Kym suggested to Doc that he stay with me for a while since I had a spare room. I was thrilled. He arrived at my apartment in Cammeray with his guitar and a black backpack of books, notepads, CDs and a player. He liked my place because it had no street front and was hard to find. It had a secret courtyard and a trapdoor in the hall floor that concealed a wine cellar.

I loved the idea of having such a tall, charming Irishman around the place, so I welcomed him with open arms and a bottle of Jameson Irish Whiskey. He looked at the bottle very approvingly and said, 'I think I'm going to like it here!'

He was really distressed by his split with Kym and I was very worried he wasn't in any shape emotionally to tour, but he had a commitment to The Angels and I hoped the distraction of this tour would give him something else to think about.

On 11 July Doc flew off with the band to Alice Springs and

then Darwin. Three days later I rang him in Broome to wish him Happy Bastille Day and tell him about some plane wrecks in the sea off Broome, and a dinosaur footprint on a beach. He already knew all about this; he liked to research the places he travelled to.

He rang back later, remembering I would be judging a Youth Literature Awards competition. I'd told him I was nervous because I was the chief judge, and I'd never judged anything before in my life. 'Hey! I've performed with 100,000 drunks throwing things at me—chill out!' he said.

The Angels went on to Port Hedland, Mount Newman, Karratha and Perth. Doc arrived back at Cammeray at midnight on 28 July. I was waiting for him with champagne. He gave me a beautiful pair of freshwater pearl earrings from Broome.

But the next day things had changed. He didn't get up. There was a 'Do Not Disturb' sign on his door, which he later turned over to read 'Please Make Up My Room'. I was incredulous, and he then asked if I could take phone messages for him if they came when he was asleep. Later he asked me to deal with his emails as well.

That evening he decided that we should set some 'Rules of the House'. He asked that I never tell anyone where he was at any time. Was he something else as well as a rock star—criminal mastermind or spy, I wondered.

———

In August 1996 The Angels set off on their Mr Damage tour. When Doc returned, we were picked up in a limousine and taken to a Japanese restaurant in Neutral Bay and hidden away with singer Grace Knight. Doc and Grace were presented to Mikael Borglund,

the director of the TV series *Beyond 2000*, as a surprise for his
40th birthday. You never knew what would happen when Doc
was around.

It was also at this time that Doc was invited to perform at
a welcome home dinner for the Australian Olympic team after the
Atlanta games. He did something no other Australian performer has
ever done: he stepped up onto tables where the prime minister, the
New South Wales premier and the governor-general were seated—
and sang to them!

———

Doc had been avoiding people, but he and I would often chat around
my wonderful Jacobean round table over 'Chardonnay therapy' if
either of us had had a bad day. It was Christmas Eve 1996 and we
were sitting at that table when somebody began banging aggressively on the door. Doc had been telling me how sad he was about
the break-up of his second marriage. Kym had wanted a family, but
he already had one. He also had a large tax debt that he wanted to
clear first, and this had not gone down very well.

When I answered the door and told the rude knocker that Doc
wasn't in, a letter of demand for an enormous amount of money
and a notice of intention to start bankruptcy proceedings was thrust
into my hands. After staring uncomprehendingly at the papers, an
ashen-faced Doc asked me to pass the documents on to his accountant and then disappeared into his room. I could feel his pain.
I tried to comfort him. He just wanted to be alone. Shortly after,
Doc and Kym divorced.

Doc's accountant put a tax payment plan in place, but the tax
debt was an ongoing worry. It never went away.

Doc had a wonderful knack of being able to make light of his worries. He was a great storyteller. At the round table I heard some amazing stories and through them the memories and experiences that had shaped and inspired him, but also damaged and haunted him.

Doc the rock star was privately a man of phenomenal intelligence and curiosity—a poet, a romantic, a pacifist who wanted to know about everyone and how everything worked. Although outwardly strong-willed and confident, beneath the surface he was like a vulnerable and frightened child who was haunted by demons of the past. It was this inner child, as much as his romantic side, that appealed to so many women and made them want to look after him.

———

After Christmas I decided to put aside my work to help Doc put together stories for *Taxi Driver Confession Sessions*, a radio show he was creating to offer to Triple M. He also wanted to create a series inspired by some articles written by my journalist father called 'The Undertakers'. His idea was a 'radio rockumentary' called *Death Doco with Doc*.

I helped Doc with the research and lined up funeral parlour workers, my intensive-care nursing sister friend Lyn and even a grave digger for him to interview. Interviewing an embalmer's assistant, he asked if he could lie on the embalming table to see what it felt like. As one of his more questionable jokes, he pretended to stop breathing and to have died. This caused quite a stir at the funeral parlour. He recorded hours of interviews.

Sadly, Triple M decided not to go ahead with *Taxi Driver Confession Sessions*. *Death Doco with Doc* proved a little too dark and nothing came of that either.

———

I was enjoying myself enormously with Doc. We had many of the same obscure books, such as Philippe Jullian's *Dreamers of Decadence,* about symbolist painters of the 1890s, and we both collected and wrote dark, romantic poetry.

But one day I came home from work to find a stranger in the lounge room listening to soft, dreamy music with candles lit. This gorgeous blue-eyed redhead was waiting for Doc. They were doing a personal transformation course together, and although she seemed very nice (she left some lovely food in our fridge) I couldn't believe that someone I'd never met was in my flat alone, but I liked her, and we eventually became friends.

Then soon after Doc had a visit from a Melbourne girl. I took an instant dislike to her. She radiated great annoyance that I was in my own flat. And then he did something quite horrid. He flew to Melbourne to give a eulogy at the funeral for this girl's cat. My grandmother's funeral was on the same day in Sydney. Sometimes Doc could seem totally uncaring. He said he didn't like to break commitments once he'd made them, but he didn't like to make commitments in the first place either. That was his great paradox.

One day, to my great dismay, Melbourne Girl resurfaced. She had been carefully mapping out how their relationship could be resurrected and improved, but Doc didn't like this idea. That evening he took a call from her while sitting at the round table with me, and then stormed into his room shouting, 'I can do what I want!'

'Apparently it's her or you,' he burst out. 'Obviously it's you,' he added after a moment of silence. 'You never hassle me like that.'

'Oh! So, I'm the Chosen One now, am I? Congratulations on your good taste,' I replied. We toasted each other with some cold black peach tea before going into my room with champagne to discuss this matter in more detail.

Chapter 28

All hell breaks loose

Doc had confided to me that he sometimes felt very empty and alone and very down. This really concerned me. So I was really happy to see him reading a script for a leading role in a movie called *The Missing* and coming out with me to meet my friends whenever he could. He was also doing some voice-over work for Audi.

In 1997 'Caught in the Night' was released as a single and played frequently on Triple M (referred to as 'Angel Station' by fans because of the support it gave the band). Doc was also working on a special project for the station—the *Docomentaries* album show—and he narrated the TV show *Conspiracy* (although he didn't get a credit for that!).

When the artist Sno Brewer decided to paint Doc for the Archibald Prize, I hoped this would be a great morale booster. It was a wonderful painting. It looked as if Doc had been beamed down out of the sky. Singing into a microphone with his signature red tie wrapped around it, he was in dark jeans and a loose white shirt illuminated by the moonlight. And there were those eyes—those wild, haunted eyes. The ones that everyone fell in love with.

In 1998 Sno Brewer did the artwork for The Angels' new album *Skin & Bone*. Doc had been looking forward to the national tour to support its release, but he became dizzy at a gig in Sawtell and fell, suffering concussion. He kept losing his balance and some rehearsals had to be cancelled. Taken to hospital, his vertigo was eventually diagnosed as Ménière's syndrome. This, he discovered, was triggered by stress. He didn't tell the band, insisting the condition could be controlled by a prescription drug.

His condition had seriously delayed rehearsals, so much so that he was learning lyrics in a doctor's waiting room the day before the first gig at Northpoint Tavern. Doc was a perfectionist and had an immense fear of failing to deliver great gigs. But as well as Ménière's syndrome, he was also battling Attention Deficit Hyperactivity Disorder (ADHD), which made it hard for him to focus on any one thing for long.

Doc was under huge pressure to perform really well. After virtually no rehearsals, he was very stressed and the dexamphetamine prescribed to help with his ADHD had given him high blood pressure, which required another drug. He had been berated by the wife of a band member for blowing out rehearsals and told he had to get it together 'for the sake of the band'. She didn't know about Doc's health issues and her comments cut him to the bone. He sent her flowers the next day because she had made him feel guilty about 'jeopardising the tour'.

———

The *Skin & Bone* tour continued, and in April Doc hosted Great Moments in Rock on Triple M, which was a huge high for him.

On 20 October we went to the 12th Annual ARIA Music Awards at the Capitol Theatre in Sydney, where The Angels were inducted into the ARIA Hall of Fame.

The following month Doc undertook a Core Transformation course at the Roundhouse at the University of New South Wales, and then The Angels played alongside Jimmy Barnes and INXS to a crowd of 75,000 people at a concert at the MCG to celebrate Mushroom Records' 25th anniversary. The media reported that they stole the show. And then it was off to Adelaide, to headline the concert after the inaugural Adelaide 500 in front of a crowd estimated to be 40,000 strong.

——

After Doc's divorce from Kym had been finalised, I sold the Cammeray apartment. We'd decided to buy a bigger place together. Doc was on tour so there was no time for him to help with the move. It was a nightmare. He had more things in storage than would fit into a large house and we were moving to another flat.

Then a mystery girl began calling and leaving cryptic messages on our answerphone. Who the hell was 'Me'? A twenty-page astro-logical report on Doc's compatibility with Melbourne Girl suddenly appeared on our kitchen table.

Doc was confused and unhappy despite the *Skin & Bone* album having gone gold. He went into seclusion. He listened to music, telling me that some music has a vibration that you can tap into to heal yourself. I didn't find out which type of music this was as he had the 'Do Not Disturb' sign on the door outside his room. He also had a Shetra Spiritual Alarm Clock that loudly sang mantras.

One day I overheard a snatch of a phone conversation Doc was having with a clairvoyant; he was seeking guidance on whether the Melbourne Girl or I could be the right woman for him. And there were others. He didn't know what to do, but it was no use asking any of us, because I'm sure we each wished the others would be swallowed up in a sinkhole.

Doc was way more interesting than anyone else I had ever known. He was charming, talented and intriguing. He was a qualified Reiki practitioner who fixed aches and pains with power he said he was bringing down from the universe via energy from his hands. After training in neurolinguistic programming, he also knew how to hypnotise. I had fallen in love with Peter Pan, but he was a Peter Pan who had studied psychology as well as hypnosis and mind control.

One night, I decided to ask him how many girlfriends he actually had.

'I have special girls in a fair few cities,' he replied earnestly.

'I see. I should have warned myself about you before I met you.'

'Oh, don't be like that. All my girls are very special. You'd like them all.'

I suddenly realised I would have to either live with the reality of Doc's Special Girl or not live with him. I didn't like either of those options, but I also realised that he probably saw something he loved in each of us. He loathed convention and was obviously polyamorous.

Once I had realised this, I could handle it—especially since in 1998 it was me he wanted to spend Valentine's Day with. I'd been invited on board the Greenpeace flag ship *Rainbow Warrior* after it had docked in Sydney, so I took him with me.

We had a fantastic dinner out that night, but he didn't eat much.

He had to take one of his other girls out for dinner, he told me! When he came home to me afterwards, the other girl went ballistic which really upset him, so I tried to console him. 'Thank God for you,' he told me, but I felt quite disturbed.

Once, when I got to know one of Doc's other girls and we decided we really liked each other, we gave one another a commiseration present. But with this one, it was a case of hell hath no fury.

To learn how to better deal with this kind of drama, Doc enrolled in a self-awareness course that involved smashing tables.

Chapter 29

Fortress against the world

In 1999 after Doc and I took a trip to the Blue Mountains, we decided not to go home. We'd come to hate the city, so we stayed at Jenolan Caves overnight.

We went for a walk to a huge cavern known as the Devil's Coach House late that night. Impressed with the acoustics, Doc broke out into song, singing 'Amazing Grace' to me and some cave bats flying out towards the moon. It was magic!

The next day, at lunch in the magnificent art-deco grand dining room of Caves House, we ordered a bottle of wine that had been stored in the cold dark of a 340-million-year-old cave. Then, after watching a platypus swim in the Blue Lake and hunting water dragons along the banks of the Fish River, we went house-hunting.

Doc did not take kindly to being controlled. That's why he wanted to move as far away as possible from The Angels' manager, Brent Eccles. It wasn't that he didn't like Brent, it was just he would be harder to contact, something he found very appealing. A move from the flat we'd bought in Artarmon to the Blue Mountains seemed like a very good idea.

The mountains were also attractive because my friend Colin Offord, a brilliant singer-songwriter and inventor and builder of weird hybrid instruments, who Doc greatly admired, lived there. Among Colin's friends was an amazing dancer, Aku Kadogo. Doc had once told me he thought she was 'one of the most exciting dancers in the world'. I agreed but wondered how Colin would feel about Doc capturing one of his entourage, and how I would feel. But Doc soon forgot about Aku . . . until more than a decade later, when he started to write a song inspired by her called 'She Came Out of Africa'.

In July 1999 we moved into our own 'castle' at Faulconbridge. We lived in a bushfire zone, but the big blue skies, occasional falling stars and fresh air more than made up for this. My nickname for Doc of 'Bear' was now 'Bear of Faulconbridge'. He changed my nickname from 'Fairy' to 'Fairy of Faulconbridge', and we each had a special 'throne' chair.

Our new home was like a fortress, set high above a very quiet street. The only sounds were birdcalls during the day and crickets and frogs at night. The street backed on to national park, with nothing but bush at the end of it. There were large decks at the front and back and in the backyard was a swimming pool, beyond which were rocky outcrops beneath tall gums and wattles.

It was our fortress against the world not only because it had good security, but once we were inside we couldn't be reached unless we wanted to be. And not everyone was allowed to visit— only people we really liked and trusted. This included Brendan and Fiona, a husband-and-wife handyman team who could do all the things we either couldn't or didn't want to do. They never let us down and were hard-working and fearless, with a warped sense of humour. They were perfect, so we soon became friends.

One day, after deciding we should all go out for dinner together, Doc suggested that Brendan dress as a real badass rocker visiting from LA. He became 'Speed Skunk', and Fiona pretended to be Sid Vicious' dead girlfriend Nancy Spungen. She dyed her hair platinum blonde and Brendan's hair jet-black with a wide bleached streak. He fashioned horrifying body piercings for himself.

But Skunk's attitude became so bad that Doc, wearing a genuine police jacket given to him by a fan, served Skunk with a warrant and arrested him on his birthday for the offence of being 'too young'.

Doc also counted two local policemen, both very into music, among his new friends. Emboldened by this, he once used a paddy wagon as a taxi after arriving by train very early in the morning from a rehearsal in Sydney to find no cabs. He had his guitar and an amp, so the four kilometre walk home from the station did not appeal. There was only one thing for it. He rocked up to Springwood Police Station and asked for a lift.

When the officer behind the counter laughed and said 'No way', Doc reminded him 'The police force is a public service. You guys are here to help people, right? Well, I need some transport. You can't expect me to walk home with all this gear! Isn't there someone on highway patrol who could give me a lift?'

The officer caved in. 'I'll just make a call, Doc.'

Soon after a paddy wagon pulled up and Doc was told to get in the back. 'Sorry, Doc,' the officer said. 'I'll have to lock you in because we're not allowed to take passengers, and people travelling in the back have to be secured.' Doc arrived home in police custody, smirking to himself.

Doc and I had so much fun at our Faulconbridge castle. We'd lounge in our pool on transparent Li-los with built-in drink holders sipping vodka on the rocks, floating head to head discussing the crimes we considered some of our friends had committed and how to deal with them. Doc hated how I liked to wear a hooded wetsuit because he always preferred to be naked. He was extremely unimpressed by what he disdainfully referred to as my 'enlightened Muslim get-up'.

One day, bored with the pool, Doc decided to conduct an archaeological dig in the front garden, but he didn't want to do the digging. He stayed inside reading a book on Second World War air force squadrons. When I uncovered some lava tubes he dumped his book and watched as I ripped out some ferns and unexpectedly revealed a rock overhang with a tiny waterfall. I'd found a small cave in the front garden!

'I thought you would have sussed that,' said Doc, popping a bit of chocolate into his mouth. 'I've known there was something interesting here for ages.'

'Why didn't you tell me?'

'Y'didn't ask.'

At about this time we became highly disturbed at the prospect of what was called the 'Y2K millennium bug'. Major computer problems causing all kinds of chaos, including fuel and water shortages, were expected at the beginning of the new millennium because of the way computers had originally been programmed. A cave at the bottom of the garden where we could find refuge would be useful.

Fearing a home invasion at this time of crisis, Doc decided I should learn how to shoot. He would show me what to do. We went to an indoor shooting centre and did a crash course with a local security company and got firearms licences. Doc was very good at hitting the target, but after I scared the hell out of a bank teller by accidentally producing the wrong licence as ID, we decided not to get guns.

In August, after Doc pre-recorded a program called *Rock the Millenium* for Triple M, we had a housewarming party complete with a security guard to stop invaders. Doc had picked up the idea of security from the American band Cheap Trick, who'd once come for a barbeque to the house in Cremorne where he and Kym had lived. They'd brought a number of security guards with them. But Faulconbridge was a very safe neighbourhood so there was nothing for our guard to do. Doc instructed him to escort smokers to the garden, unless they were smoking dope. Then they could stay inside.

However, there was plenty for our friends to do. Doc had bought a ten-man tent to accommodate anyone who wanted to stay over and couldn't find a bed in the house. The trouble was he didn't want to have to put up the tent, so his brother Terry and friends were recruited to assemble it.

We had breakfast the next day with a couple of stayers. Doc would only eat a proper breakfast: muesli he had made himself, or bacon (fat-free yet crispy, but not too dry) and poached eggs (yolk side down) on lightly buttered (with unsalted butter) wholemeal toast, served with black tea.

And Doc didn't drink just any tea. It had to be weak, black Earl Grey with ginger and honey and a nip of Scotch, although sometimes he would drink dandelion tea with calendula, nettle, red clover and dandelion burdock.

Doc's cat, Ned, was similarly particular. He liked ham. But not just any ham—it had to be gluten-free, thinly sliced, premium English.

———

We had some great dinner parties at Faulconbridge. Sometimes Doc and I would invite our neighbours in for drinks or a meal. Lachlan and Serena were our favourites. Together with them, or with Speed Skunk and Nancy, we'd improvise percussion instruments. Seed pods could be maracas, cutlery could be tapped on glasses, and glasses could be filled with water to make a glass harp. Doc would also make singers out of people who said they couldn't sing.

Doc always brightened up when guests arrived. The neighbours loved him. 'I'm sorry to interrupt your dinner, neighbours,' Doc would announce through my megaphone from the top deck at the front of our castle, 'but I just want to tell you how cunning Annie is. And, just quietly, how fat she is right now, after eating my chocolates.'

I'd snatch back my megaphone and announce to our neighbours that my heist was only in revenge for his most recent 'crime', which I would describe in graphic detail.

Our two black cats and a reptilian friend, Napoleon—a baby blue-tongued lizard I'd rescued from Doc's cat Ned—often watched this show from secret hiding places.

Napoleon had an injured leg when I found him, so Doc had made a home for him out of a top-hat box he'd punched through with ventilation holes, even cutting out a window to the sky. He'd become quite attached to this poor little creature by the time I called WIRES (the New South Wales-based Wildlife Information Rescue and Education Service) and didn't want to give him up even though it was illegal to keep blue-tongues as pets.

'Who would know?' Doc asked. 'Anyway, I'll set him free when he's better.'

Doc gave the carer a reptilian stare, and asked, 'So why can't I keep him?'

'Doc?' the carer asked cautiously.

'Yes.'

'Doc Neeson? Oh my God, I'm a big fan of yours. So you want to keep this lizard?'

'Yes,' said Doc, looking the man straight in the eye.

'OK, Doc, no problem. Just keep doing what you're doing,' and then the carer got Doc's autograph.

Soon Doc transferred Napoleon to a terrarium; he caught small insects and fed them to him with tiny pieces of meat and water. After he let Napoleon go, he began to tame an extremely loud and greedy one-eyed possum he called Cinderella Thunderfoot. Sometimes Doc would chat with her, but whatever he said was private. Thunderfoot belonged to him.

———

I'd accepted a job in an ad agency at Castle Hill, a place very hard to get to by public transport so Doc often drove me to work. However, one day I shot off without him.

I hadn't told anyone I lived with Doc and didn't want to mention it when The Angels' 'No Secrets' came on the art studio radio in case no one believed me. But halfway through the song the phone rang. An artist Angels' fan picked up. 'Yeah, she's here. Who's calling?'

The artist raised his eyebrows. 'Doc Neeson? Yeah, right, so who's really calling?'

'I'll take that,' I said.

'So, this is Doc Neeson is it? It's some joker who thinks he's Doc Neeson.'

I grabbed the phone.

'You slipped out on me, Fairy! Shouldn't have done that, because now I'm here anyway and you didn't get a lift,' came the voice at the other end.

'What? Where are you?'

'Just behind you,' he said. I turned around, and there he was!

'*No way!*' my colleague exclaimed. 'How did you do that? You're on the radio, man. Are you *real*?'

'No, I'm an illusion,' said Doc. 'I'm taking my Fairy out to lunch because she missed her ride.'

The colleague's jaw was on the floor as I was swept off to lunch.

––––––

In July 1999 Doc was in Darwin with The Angels for Darwin River Rocks. The first gig was described in the *Northern Territory News* as 'one hell of a party', but on 12 July Doc rang. The tyres of the plane he'd been on the day before had disintegrated as the aircraft took off. His band mates and Mental As Anything were also on board.

They had circled for two hours to burn off fuel before turning back and attempting to land at Darwin. Doc told *Northern Territory News*, 'I thought we would die, like Buddy Holly.' He'd even written a goodbye note to his sons. He was very keen to get home, but I wasn't sure whether it would be Thunderfoot or me he'd want to talk to first.

Chapter 30

Showdown in East Timor

Following closely what had been happening in East Timor, Doc had become a great admirer of José Ramos-Horta, who was the country's new president. Australian troops were stationed in Dili as part of INTERFET, the international peacekeeping force. Doc was keen to do something for them, and in September 1999 (just before The Angels' successful Liveline tour) came up with the idea of a concert to entertain them. He knew that many of the troops would be homesick, just as he had been when he was in the army. But which other artists would he ask to join him?

He rang Kylie Minogue and John Farnham, and soon he had gathered Gina Jeffreys, James Blundell, The Living End and HG & Roy as well.

He'd sent out a press release, started to arrange sponsorships and was plotting out the logistics when suddenly John Farnham's manager, Glenn Wheatley, was sending Doc plans! He received a tour book called 'Tour of Duty Survival Kit' from

Glenn's company Talentworks that had a 'Thank you' from it and 'the producers'.

Almost overnight Doc's idea had been hijacked. It was now Glenn's Tour of Duty Christmas Concert for the INTERFET troops, and Doc was receiving orders to attend rehearsal, to have an army physical, to get vaccinations. Glenn was very, very good at logistics and promoting himself and his artist, but this was *Doc's* baby and he had not invited Glenn to take over.

While Doc was grateful for John Farnham's participation and recognised his great talent, he was disappointed that somehow the purpose of the concert now seemed secondary to the promotion of John. Glenn did seem to be doing a great job, however, so Doc decided to just step aside.

But on 1 December 1999 our lives were to change in a most horrible way. Coming back from rehearsal, Doc's car was rear-ended by a truck while standing stationary at a toll booth. When he arrived home that night he seemed OK and the car didn't look too bad, but it was quickly written off by the insurance company. Doc had actually been injured very badly, even though he didn't yet know. He had a hairline fracture of the collarbone and other injuries would soon surface.

Doctors advised Doc not to do the Dili concert, but Liveline was over and everything had been arranged. He'd never been stopped by physical discomfort before. Stubborn as always, he numbed his pain as best he could and performed despite multiplying back and neck problems.

After his return, he would sometimes tell a reporter 'I got a bit of whiplash' when he had in fact sustained permanent nerve and spinal damage. I saw the real picture, and it wasn't pretty. I was around when no one else was.

———

Watching the Dili concert at home on TV, I heard a newsreader announce, 'The first casualty of the concert was Doc Neeson.' My heart stopped. There on my screen were images of Doc in a makeshift ambulance in extreme heat. He was suffering from dehydration and heat exhaustion.

He made a quick recovery and went out to remote areas separate from the main concert to do some small shows for troops who had been unable to make it into Dili. This included at the enclave where five Australian journalists had been murdered in 1975.

Underneath his calm exterior, Doc was very angry with Glenn. The night before the concert, at a reception for the artists, Major General Peter Cosgrove (the Australian military commander in charge of the operation) had offered an informal 'thank you' to the major sponsors and organisers. Glenn's name was mentioned prominently, as the initiator and artist coordinator. Doc's wasn't.

Doc confessed later that he had felt 'quite vengeful' at the reception, so the following morning made an appointment to see Major General Cosgrove. 'I told him the true position regarding who actually initiated the concert and recruited the talent,' Doc said. 'I told him it was me—and he asked his aide to check on the internet and he found the news about what I'd done, published in a number of major papers. John and Glenn were holidaying in China then and they were just two of my recruits when I announced the concert. I thought the Major General should know that the project was *mine!*'

Major General Cosgrove made a speech before the concert on 21 December. After thanking Glenn and the many others who'd been involved, he said there was one person everyone especially owed their thanks to . . . 'And it is—Doc Neeson!' Cameras zoomed to Doc's smiling face. Onstage, and out of the corner of his eye,

Doc could see Glenn. He was having mixed feelings at this moment, but he was delighted to hear Cosgrove's words. Doc had been 'one of us—a "chalkie",' Cosgrove told the troops.

The soundtrack to this 'moment of truth', as Doc called it, was the roar of a 10,000-strong crowd. 'After battling Glenn at every turn,' Doc told me, 'this was a great victory for me. Now I feel proud.'

I watched the concert on TV. It had an Australian TV viewing audience of 3.4 million—the largest live viewing audience of that year. Roy Slaven introduced Doc as 'The Tyro of Timor—The Mad Medico of Music—The Dangerous, The Deadly, The One, The Only . . . Doc Neeson!'

Doc brought back an unedited tape of the concert that we watched together. After Doc performed 'Be with You', Kylie, dressed as Santa, twisted around The Angels' song 'Am I Ever Gonna See Your Face Again' by getting the audience to sing the chorus. While she stood looking as innocent and sweet as could be, with a hand on her hip, she shouted at the audience, 'No way, get fucked, fuck off!' Doc checked out her cleavage, and she smacked him away. Kylie and Doc really played up. To his great delight, he received a very naughty Christmas card from Kylie with a photograph of her laughing in her underwear.

When checking Doc's credentials and service record, Major General Cosgrove discovered that he was overdue for a Service Medal and arranged for it to be awarded to him. And he wrote about the concert and Doc in his autobiography, which was published years later.

Back home, Doc took his spinal surgeon's advice and stopped performing with The Angels. He was forced to undergo extremely painful nerve conductivity and other tests by the insurance company representing the owners of the truck that had slammed into his car. This and his realisation that his injuries were far more serious than he had thought sent him spiralling into deeper and deeper depression.

Chapter 31

Doc Neeson's
Rock 'n' Roll Circus

One of the worst things for Doc about the car accident in 1999 was that some people in his band doubted that he had the compounding health problems he did have following his injuries. This lack of faith in Doc's integrity was what triggered some very deep resentment on his part. He could have shown the doubters his X-rays, MRIs and medical reports and certificates, but he didn't think he should have to.

He also had to put up with hostility from fans who believed doubters in the band. A few years later he received a phone call from a key administrator of The Angels (Australia) Facebook fan page, Ash Farmer, who alerted him that fans were being told Doc had abandoned The Angels and faked his car accident! This sent Doc off the rails.

Doc knew that his accident had happened at a very inconvenient time for the band and that everyone had mortgages to pay and children to support, but so did he. He guessed this was the last straw and was probably right because after he drove a courtesy car to an Angels rehearsal after the accident, one band member had angrily told people the accident car didn't have a scratch on it.

Doc was seriously hurt by the lack of sympathy he received from fellow band mates. His injuries, which seemed minor at first, soon started to create major problems for him, but he usually brushed them aside, not wanting to appear in any way incapacitated.

The period 2000 to 2003 was a time of great struggle for Doc. Band members had become estranged. In an interview at this time with Paige Kilponen of *Sunday Life,* Doc said that his car accident had brought about 'the end of The Angels', but he hadn't resigned. He was finding it very hard to walk, but he didn't want to stand down as the band's lead singer. He intended to return when he recovered but in the meantime, he insisted, there could be no Angels without him. So an arrangement was made where John, Rick, Chris and Buzz agreed to keep going but not play under the name The Angels. Instead, they'd perform as The Original Angels Band, with John Brewster as lead singer.

———

Early in January 2000, when Rick Brewster's wife Sue dropped in unexpectedly to see how Doc was faring, I wondered how I'd get him out of bed. He'd been in a lot of pain and very despondent, so I'd invited his boys Daniel and Kieran, their mother Dzintra and Peter Calvitto up for lunch, hoping to cheer him up. He was still in bed when they arrived but dragged himself up, only to have to lie down again soon afterwards.

It was claimed in Bob Yates' book *The Angels* that we were 'having a party' with Dzintra and her husband that day, when in fact I was almost in tears watching Doc try to put on a brave face knowing how much pain he was in. And Dzintra's 'husband' was no one's husband. He was my former fiancé, now Dzintra's companion, and Doc's best friend—which goes to show how little Rick knew of Doc's private life.

———

Doc was finding it increasingly difficult to come to terms with the fact that he would no longer be able to do his signature high-power performances, and 2002 was a particularly hard year. The painkillers he'd been prescribed had kept him in a joyless state of exhaustion and depression.

However, despite this, he continued to write lists of things he could do to try to improve his life. But sometimes it all just got too much, and he would communicate in cartoons.

We used to swap cartoons and leave notes for each other about anything and everything, but one day I arrived home to find a frightening note in Doc's handwriting pinned to the kitchen door with a knife. I was too scared to stay in the house, so went back outside and phoned him. When there was no answer, I cautiously went inside to find him sitting at the kitchen table. When I tried to talk to him, he became very angry with me. I decided to leave and was two blocks away from the house when I heard him shouting my name. He was beside himself. Abandonment! He couldn't stand it. So I turned back.

'I didn't mean to scare you. Sorry. I'm just so angry,' he said, burying his head in his hands.

———

Then a friend Doc had met through disaster relief fundraisers, entrepreneur Mark Filby, came to him with an idea. Before he knew it, Doc was 'Ringmaster' at 'Doc Neeson's' Rock 'n' Roll Circus' on the Central Coast. There were fire-eaters and body painters, acrobats, podium dancers, sideshows, a bizarre acts competition—and music!

Doc liked the idea of being ringmaster and would drag himself out of bed to perform. He was optimistic: even if it didn't pay yet it certainly would soon, he said. He had faith in Mark. He calculated that the more he performed, the more he would be owed. He had to keep going or Mark would never be able to break even, and he would never be paid.

In 2003 Doc was hospitalised many times and regularly attended the Royal North Shore Hospital Pain Clinic. Because of the intense shoulder pain, and bad back and mobility issues, he had no time for frustrated phone calls from the Brewsters. He would drink vast quantities of whiskey and then have to cancel meetings with Steve White, who he'd appointed his manager after the departure of Brent Eccles. Steve had a very impressive track record, having promoted bands such as The Police, AC/DC, the Church, Ted Mulry Gang, The Cure and Cheap Trick. He had also managed, or was soon to manage, Angry Anderson, Rose Tattoo, Leo Sayer and Lee Kernaghan.

Wracked with pain, Doc was becoming very angry with the world. He spent most of his time furiously writing song lyrics and thoughts in notepads. After months of virtually no income, he told me he felt as if he was dying inside.

Then one night after the circus he discovered that the accommodation he'd been promised hadn't been booked. He was stranded on the Central Coast car-less. There was no alternative other than to catch a few trains home. On his way to the station, walking through a car park near the venue, he came across a man fighting with a woman. He intervened and was slashed with a flick-knife.

He arrived home with his arm in a makeshift sling he'd made from one of his stage shirts. Blood was seeping through.

I insisted that things could not go on as they were. In future there would have to be a written contract covering conditions and payments for both his and the performances of others, otherwise 'The circus shouldn't go ahead.'

Doc wouldn't hear of this. The circus must go on. No matter what.

———

The circus eventually closed, but Mark remained. He was always coming up with new ideas and Doc was an Ideas Man. Mark now wanted to involve Doc in businesses that centred around gambling. Doc did love the occasional spin on the pokies, but all these business ideas required a lot of money and hard work. Already plagued by never-ending debt, the last thing Doc needed was the ongoing expenses that always seemed to go hand in hand with Mark's ideas. But he believed in Mark, so ended up doing even more for him and never saw anything come back in return.

Chapter 32

Management nightmare

The War of The Angels lasted for eight years and, after a short-lived period of peace brokered in 2008, combat resumed. I was witness to it all as Doc had nominated me as his point of contact.

His requests for meetings to resolve band disputes were repeatedly ignored and he was under constant attack. If you keep kicking someone when they're down, sometimes they can't get up. When Doc no longer defended himself, it was because he'd become tired of being attacked. This was a source of great aggravation to those whose accusations he ignored.

When The Original Angels Band put out a DVD and performed gigs under the name The Angels, fans naturally thought that Doc was back with the Brewsters. One of the gigs, within walking distance of our Faulconbridge home, even had an ad in the local newspaper using Doc's photograph! At home at that time and wiped out by worsening back pain no painkilling drug could eradicate, the day after the gig Doc was bailed up on his way to his doctor by an angry fan who had travelled from interstate to see 'The Return of Doc' to the stage. He'd been told by one of the organisers at the gig that Doc 'couldn't make it'.

Similarly, fans who went to an Angels gig at a Sydney hotel were told simply that Doc 'couldn't make it'. To check this out, one of Doc's friends rang the venue to ask if Doc Neeson was back performing in The Angels. He was told 'Yes'. Fans were angry. As far as they were concerned, they had wasted their money as it was Doc they had come to see.

Doc was very dark on management. Someone was always doing something he didn't like and he considered he could do better if he had the time. That one of his managers did not get back to him when his main admin, Deb Martin, made the disturbing discovery that an unknown person was selling a demo disc of his unpublished Red Phoenix work *Swords of Paris* on eBay, and then ignored his repeated pleas to do something, was unforgivable. He developed a deep mistrust of all management and their motives after this.

On 29 October 2002 Doc performed at The Basement in the Farm Hand Benefit Concert to help raise desperately needed funds for Aussie farmers affected by the worst drought New South Wales had ever seen up to that time. But apart from that he was largely unable to work outside the occasional voice-over jobs, which rarely paid more than they would an unknown voice-over artist with no 'name'.

———

A lot of people wanted to help Doc. One of these was the motivational guru Brad Cooper. Doc had always loved transformational seminars so Brad's 1999 seminar series 'The Winning Edge' was something he could not resist. It promised 'A morning that will change your life and an afternoon that will shape your future'; it would be 'real, direct, honest and hard-hitting'. Doc enrolled, and Brad's intoxicating talks soon drew him into Bradworld.

Doc and Brad became friends, and Brad confided in Doc about a difficult court battle he was fighting that would eventually result in Brad being sent to prison for five years for his part in the collapse of HIH Insurance.

Despite this, it wasn't long before Brad had arranged meetings for Doc and gave him useful advice. Doc was looking for a less taxing career. Maybe he could be a motivational speaker like Brad? He had some really exciting off-the-wall ideas, including starting a training camp for out-of-control kids—Sergeant Neeson's Hell Camp for Brats.

Brad offered Doc a beachfront house on beautiful Balmoral Beach to chill out in while he thought things through. It was a great place to write and enjoy a refreshing dip in the sea. Brad's world fascinated Doc, partly because it was dangerous and partly because it was so extravagant. Doc soon found himself spending more and more time with Brad.

Brad's lifestyle was partially funded by introducing high-powered businesspeople to each other for a mutually beneficial outcome. Brad offered Doc gigs at private parties, or at least the chance to showcase his music, but Doc was in constant pain and largely unable to take advantage of this.

One day in 2002, Brad invited us for dinner at The Bather's Pavilion, one of Sydney's best restaurants. He directed us up onto the roof, where he had arranged a special table standing alone under a full moon looking out to sea. A large glass jug of iced vodka and fresh lime arrived with a bottle of French champagne followed by food to die for, all compliments of Brad.

Not long after this, Brad was arrested and Doc, who believed Brad to be innocent, tried to support him as best he could, but Brad was in a rage and exploded. Doc didn't like aggression and swore he would never see Brad again.

———

In early 2003 Doc and I spent a week at a yoga centre at Mangrove Mountain so he could learn techniques to help the chronic and debilitating back problems that had seen him in hospital for a month. This did little to lift his depression and reduce his anxiety. Distressing emails had been going between Rick Brewster (on behalf of himself, his brother John, Buzz Bidstrup, Chris Bailey, Bob Spencer and James Morley, who were then The Original Angels Band) and Brent Eccles and Doc.

When no resolution could be reached, Doc wrote a scathing letter. He informed Rick that he was extremely underwhelmed by his 'very antagonistic letter', obviously written by a lawyer, in what Doc termed 'verbose gobbledegook'. He told Rick that he would respond when he had fully absorbed its 'totally indigestible contents'.

Shortly after this Doc and Brent—as joint directors of The Angels holding company Tutankhamun Pty Limited—decided to hire a lawyer. The lawyer wrote to Rick, John, Chris and Buzz, who were claiming to own the name 'The Angels', to formally object to their intention to licence the name for use by their band, The Original Angels Band—which did not include Doc, Brent or Jim.

I was Doc's main support at this time. I was working full-time in the city every day and many hours every night for Doc, who hated computers with a vengeance.

By May, Doc's condition had sufficiently improved so that a few people were now interested in becoming his manager and taking over the work I had been doing. Doc liked all of these people and didn't want to offend anyone, so he eventually found himself with a number of 'managers'. One stormed off when he found out he was not Doc's only manager and declared Doc to be unmanageable. Eventually another two had to be paid off to stand down.

Doc didn't really want to know about any of this. More important business called. He and our friend Stephen Coburn were writing a national anthem for the Australian micronation known as the Principality of Wy, with its ruler Prince Paul. Prince Paul respected Doc and had bestowed upon him the title of Duke of Rock, which Doc regarded as a great honour.

On 14 August, Doc was invited to a charity gig to see The Rockets, a band he'd never heard of, at the Civic Hotel in Sydney. They invited him to get up on stage for a set of Angels classics. The guitarist had a style he really liked, with a natural rhythm and powerful feel.

That guitarist, David Lowy, was an Angels fan and he quickly asked Doc if he would sing with The Rockets again. But Doc turned the tables on David by asking him instead to join his own new band, Doc Neeson's Angels, which would eventually evolve into Red Phoenix.

Chapter 33

The rise and fall of Red Phoenix

Doc loved planes and the concept of flight. He sometimes wondered if flying machines might have stopped humans from evolving wings, and he had always loved the idea of the legendary phoenix rising from the flames to be reborn and airborne again.

For all the time I knew him, Doc had wanted to fly a microlight, but to my knowledge he never did. Such was his obsession with flight that he sometimes dressed as a World War I pilot. He insisted on wearing a genuine black leather flying helmet, including goggles, and black leather jacket on the rare occasions we had a VIP breakfast guest such as Doc's then best friend Bob Bowes—especially imported from Adelaide.

Doc believed in reincarnation and thought he'd been a fighter pilot. He and my ex-fiancé, Peter Calvitto, both believed they'd not only been fighter pilots in World War I but that they'd known each other in the past. Each claimed a memory of having been shot down. Doc remembered flying alongside Peter, with a wing on fire, and saluting him as his plane exploded and went down. Peter had the same memory.

When Doc first met David Lowy, they discovered a mutual fascination with planes. David owned a Lear Jet and some Spitfires—in fact a whole aviation museum at Temora in New South Wales. David was the son of Frank Lowy, of the Westfield empire. He was also an aerobatics champion, and it was this that really excited Doc.

Doc was delighted when David joined the band and insisted on personally flying them to remote gigs. He wasn't just a great guitarist, he was also a very experienced pilot with his own planes!

While Doc wanted to fly, David wanted to be an 'Angel', so it seemed like a match made in heaven. Doc noted in his diary that his new band must have been the first band in the world to get a Lear Jet before they had a hit record.

Soon David and Doc decided to go into a joint business venture. While Doc would contribute creativity and music industry knowledge and contacts, David would be the financial backer, underwriting the venture as well as playing in the band. But we had to make one huge sacrifice for this to happen. David demanded that Doc move to Sydney so he wouldn't be late for meetings. So we sold our Faulconbridge fortress in July 2004 and rented a townhouse at Lane Cove.

By now the outlook for Doc had greatly improved. He was performing in Doc Neeson's Angels and, together with David, had Jim Hilbun of The Angels and two former members of Dragon, Alan Mansfield and Peter Northcote, with a new manager Steve White on board. This really was a new beginning.

Doc knew that the other Angels were now either very disappointed or very angry with him, but nonetheless his solo band Doc Neeson's Angels would roar ahead without them, sometimes in a Lear Jet.

In 2005, Doc Neeson's Angels flew from Australia to The Bahamas to record an album at Compass Point Studios in Nassau with the legendary Memphis producer Terry Manning. This time the band line-up included Jim Hilbun, the brilliant bass player and saxophonist of The Angels who could also sing; David Lowy and Peter Northcote on guitars; and Fab Omodei on drums. They were now managed by former Angels' drummer and manager Brent Eccles.

I was then on my way home from Germany but stopped off in Nassau for Doc's birthday. Like St Patrick's Day, Doc's birthday was a day you couldn't miss or you'd never be forgiven.

He picked me up from the airport and drove me to Compass Point Studios. Alongside us some guys were smoking on the back of a flat-bed truck, the smell of dope smoke wafting through the open front windows of our car. The driver was also smoking.

Doc was driving too close. He wanted to talk to them! I couldn't see this ending well.

'Having a good day, gentlemen?' he asked.

'Yo man!' answered one.

'Don't worry,' said Doc, turning to me. 'There're no other cars on the road.'

'Rock on, dudes!' he said, as he gave them a thumbs-up.

'See! It's gonna be fun here, Fairy!' said Doc.

When we arrived at Compass Point Terry Manning's wife Sherry showed me a guitar-shaped strawberry cake she was planning to serve the band for afternoon tea for Doc's birthday.

In the studio Doc was marvelling at the mic he'd been using. It had once been used by Elvis Presley! This was at the very top of the range in the studio, which included original German Neuman MD Telefunken and Australian Rode mics that Terry particularly loved.

Late that night we went to a waterside restaurant overlooking a quiet private harbour with fairy lights and row boats moored just below our table. But it was a strange night: Doc was really on edge. I felt uneasy. After long hours in the studio, he had strained his voice so badly that his vocal chords had become inflamed and he was unable to get the anti-inflammatory drug he needed. He was worried he'd stuffed up the recording.

The next day we drove to a very exclusive part of town—a closed community where Sir Sean 'James Bond' Connery and his wife Micheline lived. Doc managed to talk his way through the barrier by saying we were visiting Micheline. Doc just wanted to see the houses. They were palatial, and in striking contrast to the shanties and tiny pastel-coloured box-like houses near Compass Point.

Walking along the main beach Doc pulled a little piece of sand-blasted glass shaped roughly like a heart out of his pocket. He'd found it in the sand and thought it had my name on it.

Our day had been wonderful, but that evening Doc became very agitated and started shouting at me. Was he drunk? I didn't think so. This was weird.

Two mounted police in white uniforms appeared out of nowhere. They asked what was going on. 'Everything's fine, sir!' Doc replied.

Whatever the problem was, it left with them. What was going on with Doc? He didn't want to talk about it.

Doc was in a foul mood the following day. He hated how every single dish had chili in it and how most of the local women were enormously fat. And he was facing some re-recording.

But three days later, something amazing happened. Terry Manning asked Sir Sean Connery to read part of a Winston Churchill wartime speech for Doc's song 'Wavelength'—and he agreed!

Sir Sean had even sat in on a think tank to find a new name for the band. He suggested 'Resurrection', but Doc was still cranky and said he hated it.

On Doc's return home, he gave me a CD of this song written on by Sir Sean. I couldn't believe it—a personal message to me from 007!

———

When Doc arrived back in Sydney in mid-February, he was hoarse. The next day he went into hospital for a major thyroid operation.

It was during this time that I saw the minutes of a meeting held at Compass Point between David Lowy, Doc and Brent Eccles. Now I understood what had been eating Doc.

The minutes confirmed that Doc had acknowledged that his physical and mental health issues had prevented him from fulfilling all of his obligations to what had become known as 'The D&D Joint Venture'. His vocal sessions at Compass Point would be extended to allow completion of all the tracks, and when this was done he would undergo thyroid surgery and attend a clinic to resolve his 'issues'. Doc had given David Lowy the power to make the decision, on behalf of the D&D Joint Venture, as to whether or not the joint venture would go forward with Doc as the lead singer—or with an alternative singer!

The intermittent battles with the Brewsters continued as well. I was worried. Doc's way of dealing with this was to drink.

———

In March 2005 Doc flew to the remote Cottonwood de Tucson rehabilitation centre in Arizona's Sonoran Desert. David Lowy had arranged this to ensure that Doc would make a good recovery and nail it as frontman with their new band, which still didn't have a name.

Two weeks after arriving, Doc was hospitalised with high blood pressure. Some of his usual prescription medications weren't available in America. He'd also been abruptly taken off other drugs altogether, which was extremely dangerous.

Doc faxed David Lowy from Cottonwood, in response to a fax David had sent him. A well-known figure in the music industry had identified that one of the problems the new band faced was that it was 'old'.

Doc's response was that he'd rather hear what this figure thought would work than just a list of problems. He was also concerned that there seemed to be no move to use the brand 'Doc Neeson'. At worst, his name would raise interest and open a few doors. He asked if David would open a shopping centre without using the Westfield brand, answering his own question with: 'Only if you wanted to start at the bottom again. Why hide a strength?' Perhaps this music industry figure was the wrong person to deal with. If Doc's new band could find the right audience, he was sure they'd be blown away.

Doc came back from Cottonwood still a tortured soul, but his band now had a new name. 'Doc Neeson's Angels' had become 'Red Phoenix'—partly inspired by a place near Compass Point called Phoenix Hill.

Both Jim Hilbun and Doc's friend Michael Jaques worked to design the new band's logo. Jim's design was chosen. Jim had also decided that all band members should change their surnames to Phoenix. Doc was 'Red Phoenix', David was 'Head', Jim 'Jed', Fab 'Fed' and Peter 'Ped'. Now they were 'Phoenii'—in the same way that members of Mitch Hutchinson's band, Interstellar, which would feature Doc in the future, would be addressed as 'Interstellar Voyagers' and members of The Angels had been called 'Gentlemen'.

―――

Red Phoenix's songs were more than great. They were catchy, haunting, romantic, raunchy—nothing like The Angels songs Doc had been writing lyrics for for so long. Everything should have been going really well, but there was no money for a proper film clip, or marketing and promotion, because the cost of the extended recording sessions in the Bahamas and Doc's rehab in Arizona had blown the budget.

Doc was not happy to find the promotional clip for 'Lonely with You' out of lip sync. He also didn't like what had happened to his song 'Running Like a Cat'. A jazz part had been added and, although he was delighted with Terry Manning's arrangements in general, he felt that this was quite incongruous. He had written to David from America about this, suggesting that they record and insert a short new section to set up the jazz mood as a 'dream sequence', in which the song's character dreams of a happier place than the one he's in that has him 'running like a cat'—a bit like the dream sequence in the middle section of The Beatles' 'A Day in the Life'.

Listening to 'Running Like a Cat' in our kitchen, he wrote the word 'DISCOMBOBULATION' in very large letters on a pad and fixed his eyes on his cat, Ned.

Doc quite liked jazz, and especially this piece, which had been Jim Hilbun's inspiration, but he had wanted his song to evoke vulnerability and defiance, not coolness. He stabbed his pen into the pad. 'Too squishy. Needs more throb,' he wrote.

But he let it sit. There were now other things on his mind, like how we could no longer afford to keep renting our townhouse in Lane Cove. We needed to buy a new place soon, but all we could find was another rental property. It was cheaper and larger. Doc loved it and there was no talking him out of it.

In June 2005 we moved to a huge two-storey house in Chatswood West; as in Faulconbridge, it felt like a fortress. It was in a cul-de-sac and had a music room for Doc under the house and a secret concrete bunker room that was good for recording. A huge multi-level garden backed on to the bush, and it attracted a strange bird that seemed to be a cross between a tawny frogmouth owl and a laughing kookaburra. Doc ultimately managed to tame it.

At this time Ron E. Sparks at 2WSFM became interested in supporting Doc and Red Phoenix. He wanted to be given as many anecdotes about the band as possible, but Doc felt like he was swimming against the tide. He couldn't stand the publicist and he found her work 'disappointingly ordinary'. He became very uncooperative.

Doc had put a lot of effort into making Red Phoenix stand out, paying great attention to how his vocals were presented and right now this was his main focus. The vocals on 'Hell's Doors' needed to be in a new 'clipped and spat' style. Some of his lyrics were haunting while others were designed to shock.

He wrote far more songs than were needed and was very despondent when some of them weren't used. It was such a shame they went to waste.

———

Things started to improve with the release of the first Red Phoenix EP, *Lonely with You,* on 4 July 2005, and a new chapter in Doc's life began. He started to write a 'To Do' List, which read:

Red Phoenix:

Naked girls, body-painted

Topless chauffeur

YES!

Lonely with You had four songs: 'Lonely with You' and 'Living a Lie' (written by Doc and David), 'Tough Love' (Doc and Jim) and 'Hole in My Head' (Doc).

Soon after this, *Wavelength* was released (another Red Phoenix EP with video). On the EP were 'Wavelength' (written by Doc and his friends Russell Grigg and the late Gerry Caulfield, featuring Doc and Sir Sean Connery), 'Big Star Now' (written by Doc and Jim Hilbun), 'Modular Man' (by Doc with David Lowy, Jim Hilbun and Peter Northcote) and Doc and David's song 'Lonely with You'.

The self-titled *Red Phoenix* album was released on David Lowy's own Cuban8Music label. It featured sixteen original songs, at least some of which could have been hits with proper promotion.

Doc explained to Peter Holmes of the *Sunday Telegraph* that Red Phoenix wasn't 'some Angels resurrection band'. It was a whole new entity, and the first album, recorded in the Bahamas and in Sydney, was an independent album funded by the joint venture. The story was published on 3 July 2005 and headed 'A Phoenix rises from sea of pain'. Doc had talked about how his 1999 car accident had nearly stopped everything from happening. He said he had twice contemplated killing himself due to the unbearable pain he had been in before years of medical treatment and procedures finally started to pay off.

I had certainly known about his depression and his pain, but I was horrified. He had seriously contemplated suicide twice? It had been heartbreaking to see him trying to walk. For the best part of two years, he had found it excruciatingly painful. But finally, after extensive physio, swimming, yoga and movement coaching, he had managed to dig himself out of the deep, dark hole he had been in.

———

Everything had been surging ahead and there were glowing reviews of the gigs, but on 15 October 2005 Aaron Chugg, who was then tour manager, sent a gig update to the band. Due to several factors, the number of confirmed shows at the end of the year had been dramatically reduced to just one . . . in Western Australia.

Doc had already had to cancel all the Queensland dates after the promoters couldn't give him a realistic deal. They'd only offered a straight door deal after they'd apparently suffered financial losses from The Original Angels Band touring that state not long before.

In Aaron's opinion, Red Phoenix meant a lot more now than The Angels, but as critical feedback on the Red Phoenix record was growing he hadn't wanted to lose their positive momentum with inferior live shows that would use up valuable budget. He'd thought the budget could be better used in the year to come, but then the Perth gigs were blown out.

Also that month, a jury found Brad Cooper guilty of thirteen charges, including bribery and making false statements. Doc couldn't believe it. Either Brad had pulled the wool over his eyes or Brad had been framed. Doc had been so sure Brad was innocent, but the jury had been unanimous in finding him guilty. Now Doc didn't know who to believe anymore. He no longer felt he could trust his own intuition, and this put him in a very bad state of mind.

On 23 December 2005 Doc sent David Lowy a Christmas card that read: 'Money's tight, times are hard, here's your fucking Christmas card!' Not a real good move, but Doc couldn't stop laughing.

There were many changes within management, and publicists came and went. Red Phoenix gigs were few and far between. Doc was angry most of the time, and underneath he was seething. Why was confirmation of the Red Phoenix gigs being left until the last minute? This caused marketing and the production of artwork to be so rushed that there was no time to make any changes.

———

One day when we were sitting on the back deck of our house in Chatswood West watching the frogmouth kookaburra that had been given the name 'Devo', Doc decided to go to his studio to unpack some new equipment. I went downstairs when he didn't answer my call and found him on the floor. He said his back had locked up. He was pale and clammy, so I wanted to call a doctor. No, he'd be alright, he said. He'd lie down. When he got up, he wanted to be left alone.

I found him wandering around the house, completely disoriented and unintelligible. This was very alarming. I had no idea what was going on.

Brent Eccles arrived, and he too was alarmed. We concluded that Doc was drunk. Brent was very upset, warning that Doc could lose David's support.

Things took a turn for the worse. I took Doc to hospital against his wishes. He'd had a stroke. He didn't want anyone to know, so no one was told. The joint venture between David and Doc was terminated in mid-2006, and Red Phoenix disbanded.

Chapter 34

Targeted by the Taliban

In July 2006, Doc and I found ourselves having a drink on the back deck of our new flat in Westmead wondering what the neighbours were like. Never in a million years would we have imagined that one of them, Mitch Hutchinson, would inspire Doc to re-form Doc Neeson's Angels, and that together they would do hundreds of gigs together and have one of the most mind-blowing adventures of their lives.

Back in 2005, as Red Phoenix was taking off and Doc and Brent Eccles were trying to manage a difficult situation with the Brewsters, Doc had received a very disillusioned email from Brent.

Brent had resigned as Doc's manager in 2003 and was by then living in New Zealand, although he had continued to support Doc. His email had said that some of his best music memories related to The Angels, but more recently his worst. For five years he had stood for what he believed was right for the members of the band and their company. He had been involved in endless legal meetings and spent many, many hours writing letters, researching, reading contracts and acting as an umpire. He did not want to fight anymore.

Brent had offered to advise Doc if he wanted to continue to fight, but what lay ahead was a minefield. Doc had already spent many thousands of dollars on legal advice. If he continued to fight, he knew he could soon be bankrupt.

Brent continued to stand by Doc through 2006, a year of very bad blood. One director had withheld a reply to an important email for five weeks, probably provoked by Doc's tendency to make people he was angry with wait. The other Angels were angry that Doc had performed as Doc Neeson's Angels (DNA) with David Lowy in 2004 and then Red Phoenix (with one other Angel) in 2005, and now in 2006 he would enrage them even more by re-forming DNA with some new players.

DNA had a changing line-up that had included or would include Jim Hilbun or Mick Skelton, Alan Mansfield, Dave Leslie, David Lowy or Mitch Hutchinson (who started off as a rhythm guitarist and ended up music director as well). DNA would take in members of Mitch's own band Stellar, including Mark Fenwick, Dave Roberts and Justin Bianci, who with Doc and Mitch would also perform as the Doc Neeson Band and as a more unusual outfit called Doc Neeson Electro-Acoustic when using the name 'Angels' was causing too much grief.

The following year, 2007, Doc broke free from all this acrimony. He'd had a massive year in a very positive way. He again re-formed Doc Neeson's Angels again with himself on vocals, Dave Leslie (formerly of Baby Animals) on lead guitar, Mick Skelton (formerly of Thirsty Merc) on drums, Sara Graye (formerly of the all-girl band Nitocris) on bass and Mitch Hutchinson on rhythm guitar.

———

At this time, the Army Entertainment Corps approached Doc to entertain Australian troops in the Middle East. The danger of performing in a volatile war zone was irresistible to him. He loved living on the edge. However, before they left Australia—flying out of Darwin in an RAAF Hercules to perform for 400 coalition troops in Kuwait, and then 2500 Australian troops in Afghanistan and Iraq—there were a few preliminaries to be attended to. In October 2007, Doc became an Australian citizen. Astonishingly, at the ceremony in Parramatta 'Am I Ever Gonna See Your Face Again' was played straight after 'Advance Australia Fair', because the registrar considered it a national anthem too.

Doc's GP had advised him against going on this trip, and the travel doctor the army sent Doc to had also advised, a week before his departure, that Doc could not be considered 'medically stable' and in a position to safely undertake a two-to-three-week trip to the Middle East. So Doc went to another doctor. This doctor, who had become a friend, gave him a letter that read: 'Bernard Neeson has several serious illnesses and is fit to undertake a two-to-three-week trip to the Middle East.'

I hated the thought of him going to a war zone, especially after learning of the grave risks the band had been told they'd be facing. My concern was compounded when Doc started to write a new will, accompanied by the lyrics of a new song he had written to raise funds for organ donation called 'Live On'.

We had quite a row over this trip, but I accepted that it was his choice and not mine. He wrote a beautiful note explaining why he felt he had to go, in which he assured me that he would be home safely in one piece and not looking like Swiss cheese.

Doc Neeson's Angels left Australia on 16 October and each band member was given the honorary title of 'Major'. Major Mitch, a very accomplished guitarist in Doc's band, his right-hand man and a highly regarded school teacher, shared his diary of the trip with me. After leaving Darwin the band flew to the Seychelles and then to the United Arab Emirates and Kuwait.

On day three, Mitch wrote:

Hercules today from Kuwait to Kandahar not a pleasant travel experience. Afghanistan from the air looks like Mars probably does: no trees, no roads, no water, no anything except rocks, sand and dust. The army band works really hard! Unpacked the Herc, set up—including building a stage—sound check and concert started in under two hours!

The troops really liked the show. Each act had a few glitches but what can be expected after sleep deprivation and jet lag? The non-Aussie troops really got into 'Face Again'— licence to swear is a universal thrill. Doc really revved the troops up. They loved it! This was the only gig I've ever done with the crackling of machine guns in the background.

Then it was back into a Hercules for the flight to Tarin Kowt. 'Never have I seen such an inhospitable, remote place,' lamented Mitch. 'Yet it is strangely beautiful. The mountains rise from nowhere to great heights in the shortest distances.'

Doc told me that flying into Tarin Kowt, the band's plane was tailed by a heat-seeking missile, causing band members to fear for their lives. He said that when the plane landed and executive band manager Dave started to hassle drummer Mick Skelton for the set list, Mick responded angrily with the threat of a fist fight to sort him out!

Neither Mitch nor Doc wrote anything about this experience in their diaries, but Doc told me that he had seen the missile flying alongside the plane. The pilot had had to take evasive action, sending the plane into a deliberate and terrifying nose-dive.

The gig in Tarin Kowt was massive and, according to Mitch, 'probably the biggest of the whole tour'. The soldiers went crazy. 'The soldiers here have only just lost a comrade to an IED [improvised explosive device], so it was great for them to have the show to provide some small relief from their sorrow and also the dreadful job they have to do.'

———

Wearing Kevlar body armour, the band travelled in ASLAV tanks. They were guarded by armed soldiers specially assigned to 'take the bullet', as one of them explained. Doc rather liked that. He also liked being a major for the duration of the tour.

There were small gigs in Kandahar, and then the main event, attended not just by Australian troops but also a much larger crowd of British and American troops. It was a great success. Less than a week before Doc Neeson's Angels arrived, a mortar had hit the spot where the stage stood. This was very unsettling, but the band was fully committed to this tour and there was no turning back. When he set his mind on something, there was no way to stop Doc.

On the day of the main gig Doc lost his footing on some steps. He didn't make a big drama of it and Joseph Catanzaro from *The Bulletin*, who'd been shadowing him, later wrote that the 'grimace of pain' on his face when he tripped was due to the severe spinal damage he'd sustained in his 1999 car accident. But that was only part of the reason; Doc had also been suffering from painful foot ulcers—something he may not have shared with the doctor who had cleared him to undertake this trip.

We'd had a heated discussion about the ulcers before he left after I saw the look on his face when he was trying on the heavy-duty army-approved shoes required for the tour. 'I'm going no matter what you say! This is what I'll be wearing,' he said.

On day five of the tour, Mitch wrote:

Flew to Kabul International Airport. In the capital, we were greeted by snipers on the roofs of buildings littered with bullet holes and shrapnel scars. Then came a briefing. This time it was really serious, culminating with, 'Civilians, if all the uniformed members are dead after an attack, you will need to use this radio. Here's how . . .'

And, 'All uniformed members are to have weapons loaded inside the vehicles in case of an attack.' Another gem was, 'We can't give you specifics, but there is a clear and present threat en route to Kabul base.'

In Kabul, Doc Neeson's Angels played to a massive crowd at the International Security Assistance Force Base. Troops from 37 countries packed out a baseball field at the base to watch the show. Mitch noted in his diary:

Kandahar was the first gig I've done with machine gun battles in the distance; Tarin Kowt was the first gig with rocket assaults after a day spent 'brassing the hell out of the Taliban'; and Kabul is the first gig I've been driven to under guard of three armoured soldiers inside a bullet-proof Landcruiser. 'Intense' fails to even begin to describe this. I have an emotional dam inside about to burst. I wonder what tomorrow will bring?

The army newspaper *ARMY* gave Doc's tour a great write-up.

Joseph Catanzaro wrote of the roaring crowd at the first gig at Tarin Kowt in his story 'No Sleep till Baghdad': 'The clatter of small-arms fire from outside the perimeter [was] drowned out by an explosion of guitars, drums and bass.' Doc had appeared before the troops, he reported, decked out in black with trademark red ribbons at each wrist and his backing band was 'spot on'. And rhythm guitarist Mitch Hutchinson and drummer Mick Skelton attacked 'their instruments with ferocity'. He called bass player Sara Graye and lead guitarist Dave Leslie 'electric'.

By the time Doc Neeson's Angels began their encore with 'Am I Ever Gonna See Your Face Again', Catanzaro reported that the troops were on their feet. 'The profanity-laced refrain from the Diggers was loud enough to wake the Taliban, alive or dead.' Doc told Catanzaro, 'It was like a cloud was lifted from [the troops]. Like they got back some sense that life can be fun.'

The drive through Kabul on day six was a bizarre mix of dodgems, war games, *Mad Max* and *Dukes of Hazzard,* according to Mitch. There were hordes of people and any one of them could have been carrying a bomb or calling ahead to alert Taliban waiting to detonate an IED.

———

On day eight the band returned to Kuwait. Mitch proclaimed their concert at Camp Ali Al Salem that evening 'superb'. Doc Neeson's Angels were joined by Gary Bradbury, Alexis Fishman and Mike Goldman for three songs and Doc went crowd-surfing, just like they were back in Australia!

At the air force base, they boarded a Hercules called Mambo 33, which arrived flying a pirate flag just like the one Doc used to fly on his car at home only larger. 'The crew were delighted to be flying our band again,' wrote Mitch, 'and they said it was a real shot in the arm for them to be part of the tour.'

Arriving at Baghdad International Airport in full ballistic armour, helmets and goggles, the band was rushed through tunnels to a bunker to wait for a bus to the Australian Contingent's Force Level Logistics Asset.

Before getting on the bus, Doc called me from Baghdad International Airport to tell me that they would soon be travelling along Route Irish, the most dangerous road in the world. Linking the airport to the Green Zone, a heavily fortified area in the middle of Baghdad where the band was staying and playing, Route Irish was controlled by the army at both ends but not in between, where the al-Qaeda was active. The band would be travelling in armoured vehicles so 'don't worry', said Doc. He assured me he'd call me as soon as they got to the end of the road. When I finally heard from Doc two days later, he explained that the band had narrowly cheated death when the driver of their vehicle just managed to escape the explosion of an IED. He couldn't tell me where he was for 'security reasons'. (He would've liked that.)

Mitch recounted: 'The bus we travelled on before we drove along Route Irish was a weird mini-bus with armoured vehicles the army referred to as "the Cavalry" in front of us and behind us. We visited the palaces, lake and gardens that Saddam built. It was all very upsetting really. When we arrived at SECDET XII, the blokes were really pleased to see us. We went to their bar "The Light Horse" and drank near-beer and smoked tobacco mixed with molasses and strawberries through what looked like a massive bong. The cavalry guys really showed great Aussie hospitality!

'The thing that strikes you most', he wrote, 'is each soldier's willingness to talk to new faces in what is essentially a prison. So many stories of loneliness and separation. Our second show was our best—energy pouring from the stage to reinvigorate troops worn down from stress and monotony.'

On day ten the band toured the International Zone, returning to the gigantic Crossed Swords landmark for a closer look. The speed bumps at each end of the parade ground were made from Iranian helmets. When the band arrived at Camp Victory, they were informed that eight rockets had landed inside earlier in the day.

The band also visited the Al Faw Palace (former residence of Saddam Hussein, now under the control of international forces). The news of two more rockets hitting the base did nothing to reassure them that everything was going to be OK. But they did start to unwind and made themselves at home in their frightening but fascinating new surroundings.

On Dave Leslie's birthday, Doc and the band had a party in what had been one of Saddam Hussein's lounge rooms. They sat on luxurious antique lounge chairs with gilded legs and ate Dave's cake.

The big gig in Baghdad was a huge success after having been cancelled and rescheduled due to intelligence regarding an imminent rocket attack. All the non-military personnel were rushed back to their accommodation and were not allowed back without full Enhanced Combat Body Armour and an escort of uniformed soldiers.

The band then travelled to Camp Taji, a huge combat base in northern Iraq where 26,000 Americans and 50 Australians were stationed. They flew there in the dead of night packed like sardines into a giant blacked-out Chinook helicopter normally used for troop movement. It was capable of flying faster than an attack helicopter.

Before the band left Iraq, Major General Mark Evans, Commander of Australian Forces in the Middle East, presented Doc with the National Service Medal and the Australian Defence Medal.

———

On his return home, Doc presented me with a framed photo of Tarin Kowt with its towering barren mountains. It had been given to him in recognition of him having helped raise the morale of the troops through the Forces Entertainment Program. He told me Doc Neeson's Angels had been the first western rock band ever to perform in Afghanistan. If this was true, blonde bombshell bass player Sara Graye was probably the first western woman ever to play rock there!

The trip affected everyone in different ways. Not long after, tour manager Aaron Harvie left the music industry to do something he had a real passion for. He became a contestant on the TV program *MasterChef*, making it into the top seven.

Doc was deeply affected by his experiences in the Middle East. While cheering Aaron on one night, he suddenly became very quiet and withdrawn. He looked very pale, and his skin felt clammy. He said he was OK but felt a bit light-headed. When he stood up, he collapsed.

The following day I noticed the words 'Post Traumatic Stress' on a specialist referral on our kitchen table. I told him he had to take things really easy from now on. I would take care of everything. He grabbed hold of me and hid underneath my hair, as if he would never come out from under there or let go.

Chapter 35

Unholy reunion

In July 2007 Doc Neeson's Angels began recording *Acoustic Sessions* in Sydney with a line-up of Doc on vocals with shake, rattle 'n' roll, Buddhist bell and acoustic guitar; Jim Hilbun on basses, guitars, keyboards, saxophones, harmonica and melodica, whirly tube and vocals; Dave Leslie on acoustic, baritone and three-fingered guitars and vocals; David Lowy on acoustic guitar; and Tim Powles on drums and percussion, 'most things shaken and hit', right-hand piano and vocals. On organ and Wurlitzer was Garth Porter, formerly of Sherbet. And just to make it extra special, together with The Eagle Street Singers, Sophie Glasson was on cello, Dr Jay and Indi Star on violins. This album was Doc's reinterpretation of some of the original electric recordings of The Angels—and what an album it was! One step further than Baroque 'n' roll.

That same year Doc Neeson's Angels were one of the super acts in the *Countdown Spectacular* tour, a series of tribute concerts that followed the success of the original Countdown Spectacular tour of the year before. What a blast it was for Doc to be sharing the bill with fellow legendary musos like Glenn Shorrock, Beeb Birtles, Rick Springfield and Martha Davis of The Motels. It was just like a big progressive party for Doc—from Newcastle to Perth via Brisbane, Sydney, Hobart, Melbourne and Adelaide.

Doc Neeson's Angels lit up this piece of rock history by blitzing all eleven shows on this tour. Its line-up was Jim Hilbun, David Lowy, Dave Leslie, Paul Wheeler (Icehouse) and Doc. When Doc signed the contract for the tour, he added a completely over-the-top rider. Instead of stipulating the usual list of preferred drinks and incidentals, his rider read: 'Two tame white tigers, a Roman bathhouse, unlimited Dom Perignon champagne with crystal flutes, and three air hostesses in transparent uniforms.' I was very happy to see him in fine form again.

This was also the year Doc sued his former band mates, the Brewster Brothers, in the Supreme Court in Sydney. He accused them of breaching the agreement made with him in 2003 after they performed with Chris Bailey and Buzz Bidstrup as 'The Angels' without him as frontman. Doc won, and The Angels were in limbo. The name could only be used if the five original members played together.

Later, Angels' manager Dave Edwards suggested that the band 'just get back together', but many thought it was wishful thinking that the 'Great War of The Angels' could be over, just like that. It turned out that Dave was right. Mediation was a success, despite Doc and Buzz's dismay at turning up to see the Brewster Brothers, Chris Bailey and their barrister looking like they were prepared for a fight.

———

In April 2008 Doc reunited with Rick and John Brewster, Buzz Bidstrup and Chris Bailey to re-form The Angels to celebrate the 30th anniversary of *Dark Room*. The fans were over the moon, and the reunited Angels toured nationally. Albert Music also released a 30th anniversary edition of the legendary *Face to Face* album, along with previously unreleased material and a DVD of a live concert in Melbourne, *This Is It Folks!* The re-formed band was now known as The Angels Reunited.

But something in Dave Edwards had changed. He seemed a lot tougher. For Doc this was a whole different ball game. He felt he was not being respected and eventually lost faith in management. It was wise that the band members had kept their options open. Doc was also performing in Doc Neeson's Angels and as Doc Neeson in solo gigs, and Rick and John still performed as The Brewster Brothers. Chris and Buzz had also kept their own interests going. Doc still wrote songs, including with Mitch Hutchinson.

But no matter what was happening in his life, good or bad, Doc never neglected his charity and community work. He'd performed at a Droughtbusters fundraiser, and together with Mitch's band Remember This, fronted by feisty Suzy Leigh, at the third Miracle Babies Annual Ball in May of 2008 to raise funds for humidicribs for premature babies. Suzy often wore a red tie, just like Doc. Doc soon became an ambassador for this cause and also lent his support to children's cancer research.

On 28 August Doc and the Brewster Brothers were inducted into the Australian Songwriters Association Hall of Fame in recognition of their songwriting contribution to Australian music. Doc told me this had been a dream come true! I was surprised they hadn't been recognised before. After all, as Angel City, when they toured the USA nineteen years earlier, they had all been given Honorary

Citizenship of the City of Memphis, Tennessee in recognition of their songwriting and music. And Doc had long been an ambassador for the Arts in South Australia.

The Angels Reunited's 30th Anniversary tour was a great success, with a stand-out gig at Selina's in November where The Angels and Rose Tattoo shared the bill. But, although touring was going well, tensions remained.

At first any arguments were minor or in jest, such as when Chris Bailey had a problem with the tour poster because his image wasn't on it. He wanted a picture of himself on the poster 'naked—with a horse', he said in an email that made Doc roar with laughter. But then the real arguments began.

One day a band member commented to Chris in an email that the band could still function without him or Buzz. Doc tried to reassure Chris that this comment had probably been tongue-in-cheek, but Chris wasn't buying it.

To try and lighten things up, Doc put up a post on Facebook about 'A Most Serious Incident Concerning Breasts', in which he publicly informed Chris that it had come to his notice that Chris had 'invaded' his 'sacred territory' with a pen by autographing a breast of one of Doc's fans. 'I can't stress strongly enough that breasts are, always have been, and always will be my domain,' said Doc. 'At no time did I ever invite you, Chris, or any of the other Angels, to sign my women.'

Chris proudly admitted his guilt, but couldn't make any promises with regards to his future band-related activities. At this Doc wrote a new post titled 'Sacred Numbers', which began, 'Due to a couple of my fans complaining that I dwell too much on the fascinating subject of breasts, now ALL my fans will have to miss out on fun for a very long time. So next I will be discussing MATHS . . .'

Some of the cracks that were forming under the reunited band's brittle surface were missed in a 2008 documentary Called *No Way Get F*#ked, F*#k Off!* shown on SBS and filmed as The Angels Reunited were getting ready for a tour.

In late November Doc was alarmed to hear that John was likely to be in hospital for three weeks following a quintuple heart by-pass operation. As he'd also probably need three months recuperation, the plan was that he'd be replaced by his son Sam in three cities on The Night Attack tour and by David Lowy for one show in Melbourne. Most of the band was very unhappy that Rick had made this arrangement with management and David Lowy without consulting them. Doc had grave doubts that Sam would be up to stepping into his father's shoes, but he later begrudgingly conceded that Sam was 'adequate'.

In 2009 The Angels toured nationally to sell-out crowds, with Tom Brewster filling in for Buzz Bidstrup when he was not available. Neither Doc nor Buzz were happy because again this had been done without any consultation with the others.

Then the band dynamics began to take a dangerous turn when Doc took a small role in a supernatural comedy TV drama series called *Spirited*. It seemed that one day he might take up acting rather than gigging after all, and this went down like a lead balloon.

———

Doc and I decided to get away for Easter. We drove through the Blue Mountains into the Megalong Valley, where we came across an old church. Finding the door open, we went in. The church was dusty. There were dead flowers on the altar and dirty crockery in the vestry. The guest book hadn't been signed for a long time. It was as if the church had been abandoned.

The following day we went back with cleaning gear—and candles and incense, on Doc's insistence. I also took yellow roses and lavender for the altar. To my horror, Doc insisted that we sing 'Hallelujah' together. I was terrified of singing, but he wouldn't take 'No' for an answer. I was gob-smacked when he told me he thought I had a lovely voice, and that when I sang with him he felt really happy. What a wonderful compliment!

———

Back in Sydney, it was becoming clear that the tour wouldn't be financially viable. Rick and John sought advice on raising the very poor percentages coming to The Angels from the Alberts deal. They were told their chances were slim. When John Woodruff had had to buy the band out of the fifth year of their original contract, he signed off on the band staying on an extremely low percentage indefinitely.

Doc reluctantly agreed to chair a band meeting, but he wasn't happy. He hadn't received the comprehensive agenda he'd been promised so he emailed the band that he didn't want to chair a 'rabble meeting of fractious issues'. Get it together!

Unknown to the others, at this time Doc was also trying to hold Doc Neeson's Angels together. His agent Harley Medcalf told him he should just let the band go because the management of The Angels Reunited was going to fight until the bitter end.

In the end Harley bowed out, but he gave Doc parting advice to accept David Lowy's suggestion to remix the Red Phoenix album, to perform the best of these songs live and to rebrand the band simply as 'Doc Neeson' but not until after The Angels' tour in October/November. However, Doc Neeson's Angels' gigs had already been booked and it seemed wherever Doc turned that people were trying to stop him from fulfilling these commitments.

Doc appeared to be dealing with all this reasonably well, but in private he was really going to pieces. He was trying to drink away his problems, and on more than one occasion he smashed up our flat and I had to call an ambulance because he'd injured himself. This was incredibly distressing.

Finally, it all became too much and we decided to live apart, with me going back to the Blue Mountains and Doc staying in Sydney. This turned out to be a very bad idea because we missed each other so much we would be drunk or in tears on the phone most nights. Every week we would spend six to twelve hours travelling to and from each other's places to spend a few days together. By then our relationship was purely platonic, but we still regarded each other as best friends.

Chapter 36

Never-ending war

On 12 August 2009, in what had been a very tough and demoralising year, Doc was named by the *Irish Echo* as one of the Top 100 Irish Australians, along with Ned Kelly. A great honour that came not a minute too soon.

After the filming of a new doco about The Angels, *MAX Masters*, in September 2009 things took a turn for the worse. The band fights escalated probably in part due to some very successful gigs by Doc Neeson's Angels. By 2010 the guys were not getting on at all.

At first Doc kept his options open, but he started to feel that the only way he could channel his creativity properly, without being challenged, was as a solo artist writing songs with people he felt comfortable working with. He was sick of the continuing verbal battles within The Angels, but he still wanted to do special Angels gigs . . . from time to time.

Doc got on well with Buzz and Chris and was tired of having to defend them against others who constantly found fault with them.

Being back in The Angels felt to Doc as if he was in kindergarten without a teacher. He wanted his solo work to take precedence.

David Lowy had assigned David Edwards as The Angels' band manager. Doc wasn't happy with this, so he decided to get a personal manager—Sam Righi of Big Deal. This enraged Dave. Doc was struggling to stay positive, but it was hard being challenged by negative emails from members of the now warring again Angels.

———

Nevertheless, in April 2010 Doc's dream of turning an Angels gig into an orchestral concert came to fruition when The Angels Reunited performed *The Symphony of Angels* at the Adelaide Festival Theatre with the Adelaide Art Orchestra. This was something he'd been wanting to do for quite a while, ever since Little River Band had performed a rock symphony with the Adelaide Symphony Orchestra at the 1978 Adelaide Festival. Now at last The Angels would be doing something similar, maybe even better!

Unfortunately, the orchestra was so loud at rehearsals that Doc had to really scream. He became quite distressed, because he couldn't find a doctor in Adelaide to inject an anti-inflammatory drug into his vocal chords as was often done in Sydney.

The rehearsals were also marred by sniping within the band. Doc's voice-strain issue was worrying and frustrating for everyone. When he was late to rehearsals because he wasn't able to get his injections, tempers frayed. Doc had also been very worried about having to relearn so many lyrics from Angels' songs he'd not played for a long time, especially 'Dawn is Breaking'. Doc wanted to rest his voice but there'd been no time, just as there'd been insufficient time to rehearse.

The show—performed in front of a massive rumbling, foot-stamping crowd roaring 'ANGELS! ANGELS! ANGELS!'—was sensational. It was a night that would undoubtedly go down in Australian rock history as one of the greatest Angels gigs ever. Some die-hard Angels fans had even flown in from overseas.

The opening overture, somewhat reminiscent of *Phantom of the Opera*, had been written more than a hundred years earlier by Brewster Jones, a famous conductor/composer who happened to have been the Brewsters' grandfather. This provided a magnificent start to what came next—a set list straight from rock heaven.

Out of the blood-red shadows came the all-powerful Angels with the force of a dark wind from hell. And, while they thundered, the orchestra wove a spell into the storm until the whole thing took flight. Beautiful young violinists, after wafting in like gentle spirits, suddenly unleashed a fury that turned them into wrathful demons, burning bright among powerful horns and other orchestral splendour. The Angels' classics and old favourites such as 'Outcast' had been miraculously transformed.

To standing ovations, the second half of the show offered an acoustic set with Doc accompanying himself on his rare 1930s Dobro guitar made entirely of metal. The romantic piano songs, 'Love Takes Care' and 'Be with You', were followed by the shock of 'Wasted Sleepless Nights', with organ accompaniment. Doc sang and spoke the threatening words of early Angels favourites including 'Dawn is Breaking' and stood with outstretched arms in blinding white light. He jumped into the front stalls, which had become a mosh-pit, moving slowly through the crowd, who were screaming for more.

———

Back in Sydney things turned really sour, with the Brewsters constantly arguing with Buzz Bidstrup. Doc had once sided with them against Buzz, agreeing that Buzz tended to foresee problems instead of positives. But now Doc realised that because of his good business sense all Buzz was doing was paying close attention to detail.

So now it was Doc and Buzz versus the Brewsters, with Chris Bailey, who they all loved, 'sitting on the fence' as Doc put it— which was a horrible place to be.

Doc spent months writing diplomatic and placatory emails, with no satisfactory resolutions, and this started taking a serious toll on him. With the Brewsters no longer willing to work with Buzz for reasons largely not understood by Doc, things were very unpleasant for everyone.

As early as February of this same year, Doc had been experimenting with new material from a few high-profile musos, as well as some unknowns. He still hadn't found the right new sound, but things were moving along. He saw it as an organic process—just like in the early days of The Angels.

Dave Edwards had suggested a Brewster–Neeson–Brewster run, but Doc felt he should now focus on solo. That's what he was being told by a lot of people like Sam Righi. The more he did with The Angels, the less time there would be for solo work.

After the symphony in April 2010, the Brewsters' lawyer informed Doc via his lawyer that he had breached the Reunification Deed by refusing to play or record and pitching himself for shows against the band. It was claimed that according to these deeds Doc had effectively resigned. Doc denied this.

After the symphony in August Freehills, the Brewsters' new lawyers, claimed Doc had left the band. It was not acknowledged that there were issues Doc wanted resolved and that the Brewsters did not seem interested in resolving them.

On 24 August, Chris Bailey emailed the band suggesting that they grab any gigs offered to them, in particular some of the venues mentioned by Dave Edwards as 'possibilities', but there were no actual dates proposed—not that Doc was aware of anyway. Dave would not look into any new gigs until everyone agreed that they wanted to proceed. Well, Doc would not agree to proceed with anything if he didn't know exactly what and when it was.

Chris thought that the upcoming band meeting scheduled for September to discuss future plans would be the most important meeting of the band's life, but it seemed that everyone other than Chris was preventing it from going ahead.

When Doc told the Brewsters he was concentrating on his solo venture, with a view to a possible transition from The Angels, they were furious. He was again told that he was contravening the Reunification Deed. Doc was so angry he didn't sleep for days.

'Edwards has blown out all The Angels gigs for January,' he told me, 'including two Brisbane symphony shows, just because I was late getting back to everyone about some proposed gigs I'd said I was interested in doing.'

Doc had been waiting to see what gigs Sam Righi had for him. When Sam confirmed Doc's solo gigs before The Angels gigs had been confirmed, Doc felt obliged to do them. But Sam made it very clear to Doc that whenever there were clashes between his commitment to The Angels and his solo gigs, there would be confusion. It was an untenable situation.

Doc didn't feel respected. He told me he believed that no one except Buzz was prepared to listen to him. Frustrated and angry, he decided the only solution was to hang out for a couple of days with

Pirate, an ex of mine who he'd become very close to. Pirate, better known as Murray Barnes, was a former captain of the Socceroos. He made damn good dry martinis.

———

It wasn't long until the The Angels' management company, Spitfire Music, started representing the Brewsters' solo venture—The Brewster Brothers. Doc in the meantime had had to change the name of his solo band from Doc Neeson's Angels to Doc Neeson Solo because there was a huge furore over him using the name Angels. There was another incarnation too that attracted no criticism. The Doc Neeson Band was a version of Doc Neeson's Angels. Doc loved these guys because they respected him and each other.

Doc's first solo electro-acoustic gig with them was on 12 November 2010 at Notes in Sydney's Newtown. To his delight, Jim Hilbun and former AC/DC bass player Mark Evans joined them, together with Australian tennis star and Wimbledon champion Pat Cash. He played 'Am I Ever Gonna See Your Face Again' with Doc and the band during the encore. Afterwards, Doc told the Doc Neeson Band that 'A champion band beats a band of champions!'

Then Doc was informed that he could not use an illustration of his own face in his solo band's logo because this image belonged to The Angels. 'So I'm not allowed to be me now! Terrific!' he shouted, throwing a book of William Blake poetry to the floor. 'No bird soars too high if he soars with his own wings,' I read when I picked it up.

Doc chose not to argue his right to use the image. He was exhausted by the arguments. Instead, he apologised and had the artwork changed. He'd opted for placatory diplomacy rather than defiant self-defence.

'They're trying to crush me!' he shouted into the sky one night. 'The fuck they'll crush me—I'm a DIAMOND!'

———

Then the official Angels Facebook page created by 'Emptyhead', which happened to be the name of a company run by a relative of Dave Edwards, became Rick Brewster's Angels website. That all The Angels fans had now become Rick Brewster fans didn't seem fair.

On 20 September 2010 Dave Edwards wrote an email criticising Doc for taking on an agent to book solo shows. There had been no obligation for him or any other band members to go through The Angels' agency for their solo work. There was no contract to this effect; he had the right to work with any agent he chose. This was confirmed by David Lowy. The band knew the score—he was planning a solo career and would not be available after October. Doc did not consider this to be a resignation. To the best of my knowledge, not at any time did Doc formally resign from The Angels nor did he resign as a director of The Angels' holding company, despite pressure to do so.

———

The war between Camp Neeson and Camp Brewster had become so savage that fans had started making death threats to one another. Others were trying to eat away at Doc's achievements or bury them. His personal Wikipedia page was regularly edited by people wishing to tarnish his reputation. His achievements were replaced with his self-confessed human failings, but as a director of The Angels Doc believed it was his responsibility to protect the integrity of the Angels brand, which would be damaged if his own name was smeared. This was a case for his main admin, 'Detective Deb'. No lie about Doc ever escaped her eye. Together, she and Doc fought an endless battle to set the record straight.

Doc was later referred to as a 'rock warrior'. He certainly appeared like a gladiator in this fight. Jim Hilbun had once told a journalist that being in The Angels was 'like being in the Colosseum, except without the blood . . . Well, no, that's not true, I saw lots of blood.'

Chapter 37

Demons closing in

The Angels Reunited had been killing it in early 2010. They'd been really well received and were playing to sold-out houses. But the arguments continued, particularly regarding touring schedules.

Doc and Buzz expected to have a say in where and when they were to play. Management had agreed to circulate details and budgets for the gigs so that band members could sign off on all shows before they were confirmed, but this was not happening. Any delay or silence on Doc's part was interpreted as a 'Yes'. Buzz and Doc complained about this in writing.

The Brewsters seemed reluctant to disagree with management on anything. Things became so heated that they soon refused to even sit in the same room as Buzz. They wanted to have a directors' meeting without him. Because Buzz was a co-director Doc initially refused, but eventually he agreed so he could get to the bottom of things.

Disgusted after the meeting had resolved nothing, Doc retreated to my place in the mountains. He was happy then—so glad to be away from all the fighting.

———

There was talk of using other singers during the reunification period. This was like a razor on a wound to Doc. He angrily turned to me and asked: 'Do fans pay The Stones good money to have their favourite hits sung by Bill Wyman when they've always heard Mick Jagger sing their hits? NO, but send some lamb to the slaughter . . .'

All of this made Doc even more determined to continue performing independently of The Angels with his own band and to write and record new songs with others, including Buzz. He was still lead singer of The Angels (although he now said he was having an indefinite break) and still a director of the relatively new Angels' holding company, Angels Next Chapter (ANC). But, as the Brewsters had done with their Brewster Brothers act, he was preparing to go into the studio to record a new solo album.

The brothers and management were not happy. It was then that Dave Gleeson sprang up as the new 'Doc', performing in 'The Angels'!

The Fukushima earthquake and tsunami in 2011 affected Doc deeply. After seeing a newspaper headline, 'Island of Lost Souls', he started working on a powerful song about the disaster but couldn't finish it. John Brewster had sent an email. Doc had quit the band, it said, and The Angels weren't Doc's to do with as he liked. He said that he and Rick had written most of the songs. (Doc regarded himself as the main lyricist, but the two Brewsters did make up two-thirds of the Brewster–Neeson–Brewster songwriting team.)

Doc, by his actions, had abandoned them, he said. Dave Gleeson would sing with them as a 'guest', and there would most likely be others.

On 22 August 2011 Rick, who had once been Doc's friend, sent an eight-page letter listing everything he and John held Doc responsible for, and informing Doc that he was no longer an Angel.

On 2 December that year we found ourselves staring at a post that had just gone up on The Angels Official and The Angels Australia Facebook pages. It read: 'Following the departure of original Angels frontman Doc Neeson in 2008, Dave [Gleeson] formerly of The Screaming Jets, plans to give his now permanent stint with his new band a red hot go when The Angels rock out Penrith Panthers EVAN Theatre next Friday, December 9.' This was insane, because 2008 was the year Doc got back with the others to form The Angels Reunited. It had not been the year of any departure.

Doc continued to believe that there could be no Angels without him. His fans had told him that he WAS The Angels. He was the heart of the band and without its heart the band could not survive, but now there were two lead singers. No wonder the fans were confused.

I lodged formal complaints, demanding the official Angels and Angels Australia pages be corrected. A small retraction was finally made on the official Angels website. A journalist had been responsible for the article, and it did not reflect the opinions of management or its publicist, it said. Yet it remained the lead post, presumably under management's control, for days after my repeated requests to remove it.

Doc's achievements with The Angels—together with those of its original five members—were used to springboard Dave Gleeson into the position that Doc had held for so long. Doc had nothing against Dave, but to him this was not The Angels anymore. It was a new band he called The Screaming Angels—a hybrid of The Angels and The Jets.

In any case in 2011 Doc performed on the Mötley Crüe tour as 'Doc Neeson Solo—The Voice of The Angels' with Mitch on rhythm guitar and bass when Jim Hilbun, who normally played bass, was on sax. On drums was Mick Skelton of Red Phoenix, and on lead guitar Danny Spence. He brought out a limited-edition EP featuring the new songs 'Dr John' (Neeson–Pippan), 'Water' (Neeson–Grigg–Caulfield) and 'Inside Your Dreams' (Neeson–Grigg–Koppes). 'Dr John' was written about one of Doc's own doctors, who loved it so much he wanted to play it in his waiting room.

Even though it might have looked otherwise, Doc did want The Angels to continue, just with fewer gigs of a higher quality alongside the solo interests of all five original Angels. He was proud to be the band's lead singer, but it couldn't go on the way it was. He wanted respect and consideration and believed these were the two main points of contention. After talking to early Angels' manager Alan Niven in Arizona and discovering that he had just won a long-running court case against the Brewsters, Doc started talking to his solo manager, Sam Righi, about relocating to LA.

On 27 October 2012, the Doc Neeson Band performed its last gig—joined by Mal Eastwick—at the Bayview Tavern.

———

Doc began plotting while powering away on his solo album plans when, without warning, he suddenly formed another new incarnation of The Angels, called The Angels 100%, with himself as lead singer. It would be without the Brewsters or Chris Bailey, although privately Doc and Chris had always been on cordial-to-very-good terms.

Doc hoped to tour the new band nationally, and then try again to crack the States. This time everything would be different. The Angels 100% featured Doc, Buzz Bidstrup on drums, former Angels Jim Hilbun on bass and sax and James Morley and Bob Spencer on guitars. This band was set to take off like a jet fighter.

Tragically, Peter Calvitto died that year, and then Doc fell ill on Christmas Eve and was taken to hospital. He was diagnosed with a high-grade brain tumour on 4 January 2013—his birthday. The nature of the fight had changed. Now it would be a fight for Doc's life.

Chapter 38

Shattered dreams

By 2012 The Angels without Doc was obviously a fixture. It really rankled Doc that Dave Gleeson was now playfully being referred to as 'Doc Gleeson' by some fans.

One fanatical Doc fan had created a poster featuring Doc punching the air; it screamed 'It's Neeson not Gleeson!' Other fans followed suit and adopted this as their Facebook profile image. There was even talk of creating a special event called 'D-Day', when all Doc fans would change their profile pictures to this poster. That day never came.

While The Angels 100% was made up of five original and legendary members of The Angels, only two of the originals—John and Rick Brewster—were in the new line-up billed as The Angels. Doc had been offered a large payout to stand down by an undisclosed party but had refused, so he had simply been replaced.

Under Dave Edwards, Spitfire (now known as Difrnt Music) took over the management of The Angels 100%. Publicist Cat

Swinton stepped in as a buffer between Doc and Dave, who didn't often see eye to eye.

Doc was very unhappy that for quite some time he'd no longer been able to speak directly with David Lowy on band matters. David was incredibly busy in the family Westfield business, but Doc regarded David as a friend as well as a business partner and band member. He had agreed to defer to David in all business matters, just as David had agreed to defer to Doc in creative matters, but once David had put the band management under Dave Edwards' control things had changed, and there was nothing Doc could do about it.

His morale seemed to be declining, but there was still some fight left in him. One Friday when he had just missed the bank and wanted more than the ATM limit for the weekend, he called his bank manager personally. Told it was impossible for the bank to reopen, Doc wouldn't have a bar of it. Following Doc's orders, the bank manager took $2000 cash from Doc's account and delivered it to him at home.

The new line-up of The Angels was happily cruising along without Doc, or Dave Gleeson on occasions. But one morning Doc caught sight of lean blonde leather-clad Leanne Kingwell fronting the band. He was not happy. 'Doc', the character he had created and his alter-ego, was now a woman. And she was singing 'Be with You', a song he thought only he should sing. He immediately put pressure on Cat Swinton to find work for The Angels 100%.

An offer for a really good gig was soon on the table. The trouble was it was for a mining company. Doc, together with Leo Sayer, was a patron of Aussies Against Fracking, the anti-coal seam gas mining movement. Although The Angels had done gigs for mining companies in the past, a gig for one now was completely against his principles.

Doc battled against doing this gig. He was deeply distressed but this time he had no energy to fight; he was on chemotherapy. Slightly consoled by the fact that this gig was apparently to mark the closure of a mining operation, he reluctantly agreed to do it to save his band. Tragically, this gig was the only one ever performed by The Angels 100% as a headlining act. Others were planned for early 2014, but he rejected them because the proposed sponsor was a mining company.

Leo Sayer has positive memories of his and Doc's collaboration on the vitally important cause of stopping fracking. Leo recalls:

> Although he was very ill, Doc joined me to make 'No Fracking Way', our song of warning about the detrimental and devastating effects of the CSG industry in Northern Queensland. He was so committed to this cause, and we agreed to stand together against fracking after long conversations about our love for the far country and the threatened environment of the bush and its people. People up there looked on him and his band as their champions, so it was doubly sad for me and for them that we lost him so soon after that recording. I felt I'd only just got to know the real Neeson and I had found a soul mate. While he was with us, he did a hell of a lotta good, and for that he deserves to be remembered by all of us. I certainly won't forget him.

———

On 15 April 2013, Australian rock royalty turned out in force for a massive concert at Sydney's Enmore Theatre to raise funds for Doc's medical and living expenses. Most of Australia's top performers including Angry Anderson with Rose Tattoo, Suze deMarchi with

Baby Animals, Jimmy Barnes, Diesel, Jon Stevens, Dragon, the late Jon English, Mark Gable, Peter Garrett, Rob Hirst, Jim Moginie, Don Walker, Mi-Sex, Noiseworks, Diva Demolition and even David 'The Hoff' Hasselhoff and Richard Fortus of Guns N' Roses, who had flown in from America, took to the stage together with the Red Phoenix band. The five original Angels—Doc, Buzz Bidstrup, Jim Hilbun, Bob Spencer and James Morley also performed as The Angels 100%. This very last band of Doc's had been scheduled to perform on the 2014 Rock the Boat tour to Noumea. The fans were excited, and he was determined to do it despite his ill-health. However, in August all of his upcoming engagements were cancelled on the orders of his doctors. Doc's health was failing.

Soon supportive fan mail started to pour in. An American fan, Paul Andrews, told Doc to keep up the fight. He'd just played a couple of *Dark Room* songs to a friend in New York City. His friend was blown away. He wanted to know when the band would be touring again. 'You've still got new fans to make in old markets, Doc,' Paul wrote. This really lifted Doc's spirits.

An Australian fan from Adelaide posted a death threat to Doc's cancer: 'NO WAY, BASTARD! GET FUCKED! FUCK OFF! Takes more to conquer him! Get out of The Doc's head, asshole! Thousands of us will see you dead before you take him down!'

———

The Rock the Boat cruise went ahead without Doc who was fighting like hell to beat this terrible disease that was slowly destroying his beautiful mind.

Doc loved life in all its forms and was interested in everything, in how it was made and how it worked. He had studied the brain, even trying to reprogram his own. He strongly believed that with the power of the mind you could overcome just about anything. He tried in so many different ways to improve the function of his own.

Doc had once used an intensive brain reprogramming technique called Holosync on himself. He would put his 'DANGER: HIGH VOLTAGE—KEEP OUT!' sign on his bedroom door and lie in there in the dark with his headphones on, listening to the course CDs on a loop, even as he slept. He had learned 'I rule my mind, which I alone must rule.'

Surely there was no crueller affliction than brain cancer for someone like Doc. People all over the world were praying for him.

———

Despite his illness, Doc was still making plans. He was hoping to write new songs with Buzz Bidstrup and Jim Hilbun, and record them at Alberts. He wanted to do a duet with Marianne Faithful and hoped to collaborate with David Bowie.

There were many similarities between Doc and Bowie. They shared a fantastic sense of humour and a love of privacy. While Doc was often known to make himself scarce, and sometimes disappeared for days, Bowie had once disappeared for seven years! They were both extremely charming, but also loved to shock. And both were cynical about fame and what it meant.

Both were passionate about acting and both wanted to write a rock musical. Bowie had already written *Cracked Actors* in LA in 1985, and Doc had been in two rock musicals, playing the lead role of wicked priest Father McLean in *Bad Boy Johnny* and *Achilles in Paris*.

———

Doc still had so many things he wanted to do with his life. He wanted to go to Berlin, where Bowie lived.

'I want to do something that will freak out my doctors,' he told me.

'Let's go to Berlin,' I said.

'What will we do in Berlin?' he asked.

'We could go to the Pergamon Museum and stand under the Gate of Ishtar which once led into ancient Babylon. We could try raspberry beer and have dinner at a restaurant on a crane above the city,' I said.

'I'm liking this. What else?' he asked.

'We could get married in the red Hall of Mirrors in Clärchens Ballhaus, where Albert Einstein used to drink.'

'*Yes!*' he said. 'I want to do *all* that, and I'd be honoured to be your husband.'

Doc's positivity was infectious. 'I want to go to Iceland too,' he added. So I put together an itinerary that was more realistic, replacing Iceland with some potentially life-saving treatments at the Hallwang Clinic in southern Germany. But it all came to nothing when we were hit with the reality of the cost.

———

Stuck in Australia for seventeen months before his death in 2014, Doc fought with all the strength and determination he could muster. As well as mainstream treatments, we explored many alternative treatments and possible cures in Victoria as well as New South Wales.

In March 2014 he recorded his last song at Alberts in Sydney. It was a cover of the Vanda and Young song 'Walking in the Rain' that they had recorded in the 70s.

Mike Amato, one of America's top tour managers, made a surprise visit to see Doc in hospital. Mike had managed Mötley Crüe, AC/DC, Skid Row, Marilyn Manson, Kid Rock and Linkin Park, among others, and Doc had always liked him. He spent the whole day with Doc, bringing with him a wicked little book, *1001 Bizarre Rock 'n' Roll Stories: Tales of excess and debauchery.*

Former Angels' managers John Woodruff and Brent Eccles, who had flown in from New Zealand, took Doc and Jim Hilbun to lunch at a restaurant by the water. It was a beautiful sunny day, and they ordered Doc's favourites—bruschetta, calamari, tiramisu and Chardonnay. And, of course, a martini.

They reminisced about the old days touring in the USA and laughed about a tree they called the Jimi Hendrix Tree, under which they'd stashed drugs to avoid them being confiscated at the Canadian border. They even toyed with the idea of going back to see if the tree and the old storage tin were still there.

Doc told them there was still so much he wanted to do. He didn't see why he couldn't perform in a barber's chair again, as he had once done when he'd broken his knee. This lunch was Doc's last one out. It ended with him singing an idea for a new song.

———

One of the last things Doc wrote was a draft letter to the Brewsters. He thanked them for their best wishes for the next step of his journey and wished them luck in theirs, but he never sent it.

On the same notepad were fragments of new songs, strange sums using shekels (an ancient unit of weight and coinage in Biblical times) and disjointed, worried notes he'd written to himself about how to respond to legal letters.

It may have been far better for Doc if he had been allowed to leave the band when he had wanted to. He wouldn't have had to live through the constant warring, which was so destructive to everyone's health. But then the world would have missed out on some truly great music.

Chapter 39

The unstoppable frontman

Doc Neeson was considered to be one of the most theatrical of all Australian frontmen. He liked to dress as a gentleman in a dinner suit or tuxedo and shifted between multiple personalities on stage. One moment he would be the enchanting romantic, the next a raving lunatic, but no matter how he appeared or behaved there was one thing that remained constant: he was unstoppable.

During the 26 years of our friendship and partnership, I bore witness to Doc's dynamic and determined nature and his fearlessness and resilience. When he wanted to do or have something, he set his mind on it. If it was forbidden, he questioned the rules and often did it anyway.

More than anything else, over most of his life Doc had proven himself to be a survivor. As an Angel touring France on the band's first European tour, full of good wine, good humour and the French equivalent of Dutch courage, he used his PMG telegraph-pole climbing skills very late at night to scale the Eiffel Tower.

Halfway up he was stopped by two gendarmes with machine guns trained on him. Doc found that experience exhilarating.

Then, after a near plane crash, two divorces, a knife attack and numerous car crashes in Australia, he survived a heat-seeking missile attack and a car-bomb explosion during Red Phoenix's tour of the Middle East. He battled through tragic personal losses, a stroke and other life-threatening medical conditions, as well as the unrelenting stress and grief of the never-ending band wars.

Doc took all the risks—he leapt off speaker-box towers, crowd-surfed and did super-high star-jumps and other extraordinary manoeuvres. If an accident was waiting to happen, he was the one heading towards it. Frontman on the frontline. He was uninsurable. The very nature of his performance put him at risk at every gig.

Like Jim Morrison of The Doors, Doc could stir up a crowd so much that a riot would break out. His daredevil antics were legendary. His stage act was often nothing short of spectacular. He had at least twenty stage falls and other accidents, including seven significant head injuries over the course of more than forty-five years as an entertainer.

Doc's first head injury happened at school in Northern Ireland in the 1950s, when a teacher dragged him over to a piano in the corner of the classroom and repeatedly banged his head hard on the keyboard after he deliberately dropped a 'costly' sewing needle down a crack in the floor to see if he could get it out.

After being conscripted into the Australian Army, Doc sustained head injuries jumping out of helicopters with heavy equipment. In April and July of 1985, he sustained two more significant head injuries in Texas and LA. Disturbing symptoms emerged and Post Traumatic Concussion Syndrome was diagnosed.

Then he found himself hypersensitive to light and sound and suffered blackouts and collapses that required hospitalisation. Totally worn out by a ten-week tour of Australia with The Angels, he was hit by blinding headaches, myalgia and throat problems.

He was overwhelmed and frustrated by his ill-health and became very depressed. One medical report stated that he'd become paranoid about the other band members thinking he was malingering.

On 7 November 1986 Doc collapsed while performing at an RSL club. After being treated at hospital, he was advised that he'd not properly recovered from his head injury in the USA. A neurologist ordered audio-diagnostic tests that detected hearing damage caused by long-term exposure to high-volume sound.

On 22 December of that same year Doc was knocked unconscious when he hit the top of his head on a crossbeam above the stage at Selina's at the Coogee Bay Hotel in Sydney. Following this injury he suffered headaches, blurred vision, vertigo and panic attacks. In mid-March 1987, he had yet another accident. At Newcastle Workers Club he injured his neck, and there was no time to recover. The touring schedules were punishing.

Three months later there was the serious incident at the Herdsman Hotel in Perth, when Doc was dragged into the audience and a tug-of-war broke out between fans and band crew. He shattered his knee and needed a cast on his leg and crutches. He didn't think that was a good look and decided to perform in a barber's chair instead.

After so many head injuries, Doc was still suffering neurological problems when he collapsed on stage and lost consciousness on 1 February 1988. With a heavy schedule ahead, there was no time to take a break. The death of his mother in March left him grief-stricken and traumatised—but he pressed on, nonetheless.

Three months later, Doc was still nowhere near recovered from his previous injuries when, leaping around the stage to thrill the audience, he slammed into a steel beam that was too low for his height, knocking himself out cold. At another gig, he climbed almost five metres to the top of the PA speaker boxes and, as a finale, leaped off the speakers and came slamming down onto the stage with such force that he went straight through the wooden floor. Unfazed, he finished the last song with only his head visible above the hole. The band and audience collapsed in fits of laughter.

Then he was struck in the face by a half-full beer can at the Bellair Hotel in Newcastle in August 1991. There were trips on low risers, and vertigo. Doc didn't like conflict and he would dive into a crowd to break up a fight. Many people thought he was reckless, but Doc had an innate sense of justice. For much of his adult life he believed he was indestructible and invincible.

Doc suffered Ménière's syndrome for many years when he was stressed. It could hit without warning and sometimes he was thought to be drunk and very clumsy. Nothing could take away the anger and humiliation when he was wrongly accused of being drunk and he would often respond by getting *very* drunk.

A medical report written in 1988 stated that Doc didn't smoke, drank very little and took no illicit drugs. However, as time went on, he became very fond of white wine and whiskey, but he was very choosy. He had definite preferences and, if he couldn't get what he really liked, he would prefer to drink mineral water. And not just any mineral water—it had to be chilled sparkling Perrier or Voss still water from Norway.

Sometimes Doc really did overdo it, but in 2010, after being convicted of drink driving, he and I quietly worked together to design a new anti-drink driving campaign. Our proposed TV ad started off with Doc staring intently into the camera saying, 'Don't be a fuckwit and think drunk driving is OK—unless you think it's cool to risk winding up in a cemetery.'

Even though he could sometimes be self-destructive, Doc knew it was not OK to drink and drive. He had been involved in many other anti-drug and anti-alcohol initiatives prior to this, including the Tear Me Apart campaign with The Angels as part of the National Drug Offensive.

———

Doc never gave up if something seemed too hard, or even impossible. He'd be damned if he was going to let anything get the better of him. If something was broken he'd try to find a way to fix it, including electrics given his training as an electrician. His perseverance was amazing. He once performed at Selina's after being electrocuted on stage at St George Leagues Club by a live microphone earlier on the same night!

In 2005 he was blasted by deafening feedback in his in-ear monitoring system at the Mercury Lounge at the Crown Casino in Melbourne. This was excruciatingly painful. When he returned to Sydney, a clinical audiologist reported dry blood in both his ears and confirmed severe high-frequency sensorineural hearing loss in the right ear and mild high-frequency sensorineural hearing loss in the left. That hearing loss was highly likely to be permanent. But Doc didn't tell anyone: he ploughed on like a dreadnought.

He often took on too much and would become fatigued. He did just about everything management requested of him, including most of the interviews despite not really liking being told what to do. This may have been why he was fond of trespassing. The more serious the warning signs, the more tempting it was.

One day he decided to check out the abandoned Renaissance Centre in Katoomba. Once an arts and crafts centre, this massive building now lay empty and vandalised. Behind the security fence were some gorgeous dark red roses. Determined to get these, Doc found a gap and we squeezed through and crept inside. Doc flashed the torch he always carried and, seeing the wonderful architecture, took a phrase from The Angels' 'Dawn Is Breaking'. 'A masterpiece in ruin!' he said, smiling at me.

Doc's energy, defiance, spirit of adventure and sense of humour never left him, even as he lay seriously ill in Royal North Shore Hospital during the Christmas of 2012. He wore a string of flashing lights around his neck so the nurses would be able to find him in the dark. He could not be stopped.

On his first night back home, he recorded his hospital thoughts in a notepad. '17/1 first night home' he wrote, followed by a big black scribble with pen holes stabbed into it. Then a short skit, 'Hospital Daze', starring Dr Back, Dr Neck (who was 'swivelling to take an eyeful' of Nurse Leg) and an anaesthetist called Dr Sleep, who was 'assisting Dr Head to do a cranial reduction'.

In 2013, when he was admitted to Lady Davidson Hospital, he created a miniature heliport in his room for toy helicopters and a drone. (He would become too confused to operate them and they then sat motionless in his room.)

He laughed at the prospect of dying soon. There was still so much left that he wanted to do.

Chapter 40

The power of the crowd

Doc had always admired Albert Einstein, incorporating his equation $E=mc^2$ into his own signature. This was his way of acknowledging Einstein and saying at the same time that he and the fans were one. He believed tremendous energy was created by the music of The Angels and the power of the mass (the fans).

Inspired by Nikola Tesla, the unsung inventor of electricity, Doc also believed in manifestation: that anything could become reality. It was Coe Uttinger who had first encouraged him to believe in himself and to trust the universe to bring him all he desired.

_____

Doc became the master of the crowd. Crowds reached out to him, and he would reach down and touch their hands. He liked to tease and bend them to his will. Worshipped like an idol, he gave them his all, but he could be terrifying as well. 'Menacing' is a word that was often used to describe him, especially by Angels drummer Buzz Bidstrup.

But there was often a very gentle side to Doc at gigs. Women in the audience thought he was singing only to them, and often they were right. He would single someone out and concentrate on that person, bringing intensity to a song that would go through the crowd like an electric current.

He had total control over his audience, some of it coming from his study of hypnotism and psychology. In 1986 he studied John Kehoe's Six Laws of the Mind, writing a paper that included an analysis of his own interaction with energy flows. The following year he completed a certificate course in Mind Science and in 1991 he undertook a program in Ericksonian Hypnosis with the Australian Institute of Neuro-Linguistic Programming Inc.

———

When Doc sang love songs he could melt women's hearts, young and old. Some of his older fans had been coming to see him for over twenty years and would scream out his name, hoping he'd turn their way.

Sometimes his female fans wrote to him and sent photographs, believing they had a real connection and confiding so much on paper. And sometimes they were right. Doc usually read every personal letter or email he received, so he did get to find out a lot about many of his fans. From time to time he would respond personally and he really felt for those having problems. He would try to help them if he could.

One fan, Olivia-Mai, regularly wrote to Doc pouring out her secret fears, hopes and dreams. She once sent him a beautiful guitar inlaid with mother of pearl that her late partner Rudi had made. Doc thought it was far too valuable for her to part with, so he personally returned it. She also sent Doc a song she had written for him. She'd called him a mirage and an enigma, which made him smile.

I knew that being the only woman in his life was about as likely as being able to capture a whirlwind or the sun. I knew he could never give 100 per cent to any woman. He was a wild man who liked to be free. Doc was nobody's man. Charming and romantic, he could break hearts without even realising.

Many men wanted to be Doc or tap into his energy. They loved the power and freedom they felt at his shows.

Whenever Doc heard of fans seriously ill in hospital, he'd try to visit. If a fan had tried to suicide or was at risk, he agonised over ways to help. Quite a few men in prison wrote to him to thank him for taking the time to talk to them and hear their stories. Because of what Doc had said to them, they would become people others would be proud of. That's why fans loved Doc so much—he cared about them.

Doc stashed away in old boxes the many letters of gratitude. He felt very proud of his fans, but he was particularly proud of Ricky Small. A paraplegic following an horrific mining accident, Ricky would rage in a wheelchair at Doc's gigs. Doc felt he owed his fans a great debt.

Chapter 41

Out of the darkness

Death is not extinguishing the light,
it is only putting out the lamp
because the dawn has come.

Rabindranath Tagore

Doc spent a lot of time in his room alone with the door closed. He wasn't sleeping, as many friends and family thought, but was listening to tapes: on building self-image, on co-dependency recovery, core transformation, transformational and vibrational healing and primordial sound meditation. Doc thought his voice could be used for healing, so he was interested in mantras.

He liked to use every spare minute to write and to learn something new. Whenever he travelled, he packed a bag full of books, notepads, tapes, CDs and a player.

At home he often worked until the early hours, writing and learning lyrics or making notes about the obstacles he was facing and how he would overcome them. He also drafted letters, read or wrote poetry, and worked on other creative projects with me. Even when he appeared to be asleep, he was often listening to music or motivational tapes.

Until the moment Doc lost his fight with cancer on 4 June 2014, he had seemed indestructible. His voice, so deep and filled with passion and charm, had finally been silenced. I felt like my heart had been ripped out, but he left behind a legacy of music that will be enjoyed forever and carried through so many people's lives.

So many great Australian bands are where they are today thanks to Doc's mentoring, including Baby Animals. Midnight Oil's Peter Garrett learned his signature hand movements that 'explore space' from Doc. The virtually unknown Adelaide girl band Legless grew into a 'monster' called Diva Demolition after Doc discovered them.

And in a Sydney sound-recording studio, a microphone and mic stand left by Doc are still there as if waiting for his return. In the words of one fan, 'Doc lives on.'

Jimmy Barnes and his family posted their own rendition of 'Am I Ever Gonna See Your Face Again' on YouTube just after Doc's death, and in Las Vegas on 5 June Axl Rose and Guns N' Roses performed 'Marseilles' as a tribute.

On 15 June Mark Gable from The Choirboys and the Rob Pippan Band performed at the Northern Sound System in Adelaide to celebrate Doc's contribution to the music industry. Four days later Doc was posthumously inducted into the South Australian Hall of Fame during a celebration of his life.

In the Blue Mountains, a hundred-piece ukulele orchestra called The Blue Mugs was formed. Led by our former neighbour Serena Joyner, who became a great musician and singer with Doc's encouragement, from time to time it would pay tribute to Doc by including the songs of The Angels in its repertoire sometimes with

Buzz Bidstrup on drums and his wife Kaye (KB) on ukelele. When Serena started her own band, Smashed Avocadoes, her drummer was none other than Buzz.

Some former solo band mates, led by Mitch Hutchinson, also pay tribute to Doc by performing his songs on his birthday.

There are plans afoot for a street in Elizabeth in Adelaide to be renamed after Doc, and a special memorial plaque has been installed in the Hall of Fame at the Northern Sound System near Elizabeth, only a few hundred metres from the site of the Hydaway Club.

I'm finally finishing two special projects I was working on with Doc—a book of dark poetry called *The Flowers of Armageddon* and a story for young adults called *The Storm and Hell Cat Saga*. I also hope to raise a Celtic cross in his name in Parramatta.

I dream that Doc's space odyssey album *The Other World* may soon see the light of day. Doc had been working on this with his friends Russell Grigg, Jane Cox and the late Gerry Caulfield. He played the voice of a hologram, a brilliant genetic scientist who has created his own world on the other side of the sun.

Since his father's death, Doc's son Kieran has joined Sydney's annual Seven Bridges Walk to raise money for cancer research. In Copenhagen and London, Kieran's brothers Daniel and Aidan are following in their father's footsteps.

The songs of Doc and The Angels are now immortalised on the soundtracks of many films and TV dramas, including *Holy Smoke, Red Dog, Underbelly, Backyard Ashes, Catching Milat* and *Hawke: The Larrikin and The Leader*.

American and Canadian super-bands—including Guns N' Roses, Pearl Jam and Nirvana—continue to cite Doc as an influence. Alice Cooper still remembers Angel City, and Keith Richards once said on radio that The Angels were his favourite band. On a mountain in Arizona, world-beating record producer and friend Alan Niven has built a shrine to Doc.

'Doc's Army', a closed group of Doc fans led by friend and former chauffeur 'Commander G', is gathering in cyberspace to ensure that Doc's memory is never sullied. Their anthem is Irish singer Eilera's song 'Marching Towards the Dawn', and each has taken an oath to defend their hero to the last.

'Somewhere my spirit will speak out. I will haunt you,' Doc wrote on a notepad in 2014. These words should not surprise anybody. As General Peter Cosgrove said, 'He was a rascal, but a very good rascal.'

Epilogue

The last word

Alan Niven*
former manager of The Angels from Angel City

Doc was no enigma to me. He was always Irish, sometimes intoxicated and forever inspiringly poetic. His spirit was of Celtic lineage and legend. The arcane Druid secrets of Merlin, the ancient power of Ireland's High Kings and *The Book of Kells* were somewhere deep within his DNA. He was a back-beat shaman. The blood in his veins was of the same colour as his collar: true blue. He would man a barricade. Storm the Bastille. He would watch your back—not stab it.

I was privileged to call Doc a friend. We literally physically fought over the meaning of songs. We dealt with some of the same demons, some of which were actual and never left us. We both aspired to artistic statesmanship, to the expression of the higher common factor while avoiding the lowest musical denominators. 'Face the Day' caused me to up my game as a composer. We both understood the troubadour tradition of binding society together by performing songs in which all could recognise one another. If I could have written 'Imagine', Doc would have upped me and written 'All You Need Is Love'.

Where did the 'Doc' come from? Bernard Patrick Neeson borrowed it from the Old West. From Doc Holliday, who most infamously resided in Arizona. Before the gunfight in Tombstone, he and the Earp Brothers lived in Prescott, Arizona. Retreating from one unliveable city after another, I have lived in Prescott since the early 1990s.

We Prescottonians know a thing or two about Doc Holliday. He was a gambler, a drinker, a drug user, a bit of a lad all around. Perhaps born in another era he might well have thought to seek notoriety and fortune by fronting a band. Maybe he might have called it the Cocked Pistols.

The kindred spirit shared by the two Docs is easy to identify. They were both unconventional, living in the social margins where rebels become artists and musicians. Or dissolute gamblers. With outlaw attitude. They both defied unthinking social compliance. It was within them both to not only speak truth to power, to challenge evil, but to demand either answers or actions.

The best in rock-and-roll become voices for the disenfranchised—spiritual sheriffs. The best rock-and-roll suspends alienation and brings people together—by their own consent. Doc Neeson was one of the best. He carried a mineral stone with him. In it was carved the letter E. 'It's to remind me to pursue excellence and not accept compromises,' he told me.

In a just world Doc would have had the opportunity to connect with greater audiences. The Angels were often referred to, in the business, as the thinking man's AC/DC, but where AC/DC were smart was in escaping from Australia via the UK. For some reason, The Angels' management thought to grab for the brass US ring first and compounded this strategic error by signing to MCA, commonly referred to as the Musician Cemetery of America. Short-cuts in foreign territories often end in a swamp.

If Doc Neeson had lived in Tombstone in 1881 he would have made the long walk down to the OK Corral. He would have been the first to go over the top.

*Alan Niven is one of the world's top record producers and band managers, and has also been a major force in music publishing. After starting off at Virgin Records, he became president of Stravinski Brothers Productions Inc. and co-founded Tru-b-Dor and Enigma Records. He produced and managed acts like Guns N' Roses, Great White, Clarence Clemons and The Angels in the USA, where he signed Mötley Crüe. Under the pen-name Etha Graham, Alan (aka 'The Reverend' after penning a magnificent manifesto for the betterment of mankind) co-composed four albums for The Angels' Brewster Brothers. Alan was the recipient of gold or platinum records on eleven titles and has contributed, one way or another, to global sales exceeding 250,000,000 albums. Among the titles were Guns N' Roses' *Appetite for Destruction,* the bestselling debut rock-and-roll record of all time, and *Beyond Salvation,* the first album by The Angels to reach number one in Australia. He was instrumental in putting together the Artists Support Japan permanent online benefit concert for victims of the 2011 tsunami. He currently co-hosts an American Rock Talk radio show with renowned rock journalist Mitch Lafon, and contributes music reviews and other pieces to magazines such as *Classic Rock* in the UK.

Acknowledgements

From Jon Bradshaw

Doc was interviewed literally thousands of times during his life. There are in fact hundreds of thousands of words on the internet about him, spun and embroidered into the rich tapestry of opinions, facts and fantasies, distortion and sensation that make up Australian music's populist gospels back to the Big Bang of Rock.

Journalists probed and prodded to find what lay behind the often cryptic and obscure lyrics of his songs and dark stage manifestations. He often grew irritated at questions that illustrated a complete lack of knowledge about either him or his art. On occasion, as something of a consequence, his stories owed more to entertainment than veracity. He enjoyed being a mystery, an enigma.

Of course, apart from my personal recollections, a memoir like this takes much research and talking and corresponding with many people. I need to especially thank Buzz Bidstrup for the opportunity of interviewing him on several occasions; also to Anne Souter for connecting me to a number of very helpful people including Alan Niven and Susy Pointon and for their interest and contribution to the project

I do need to acknowledge the content of numerous on-line and other recorded conversations with Doc and various members of The Angels and their management over the years, interviews including with the ABC, *Rolling Stone*, *Juke* and *RAM* magazines.

Bob Yates's benchmark book *The Angels* (Random House Australia, 2017) provided quotes from John and Rick Brewster and others that I considered more accurate in a verbatim sense than similar quotes reported elsewhere.

I am particularly appreciative of help from my friends from the early days in Adelaide. Among them Brenton Spry, Alan Hale and family, Rod Schubert, Peter Collaton and Frank and Alan Tarney.

As my first book I have been a sponge for any input that might enhance whatever talent I might have brought to the exercise. To score the counsel of literary doyen Richard Walsh, Allen & Unwin's consulting publisher, was master class stuff! Thank you sincerely, Richard, for your much valued advice and counsel.

Finally, thank you to my co-writer Anne Souter. It has been a difficult journey, not the least combining two very different perspectives of the complex multi-faceted personality that was Doc. He said on a number of occasions that he hoped that any biography reflected the totality of his character. I'd like to think we have given it a decent shot.

From Anne Souter

When Doc asked me to write his biography in 2012 I said 'No'. I thought it would be far better written by one of Australia's top rock writers, but every time I invited one over to discuss this I got nowhere. Doc was determined that I would write his story because he told me I knew him better than anyone else, but still I declined. I thought it was going to be too big a job for me and that someone with far more music industry knowledge should do it, but eventually I began to work with Cat Swinton to collect more of Doc's amazing stories.

Cat was a pillar of strength in Doc's final days, organising the massive Rock For Doc concert in 2013. Doc was deeply touched by the selfless support and love shown to him by Cat and Support Act, the charity he had long supported but never dreamt might one day come to his aid, and so many of Australia's finest entertainers. It buoyed him up when he was at one of the lowest points in his life.

In 2015 Doc's old friend Jon Bradshaw approached me for help with his own memoir, which covered growing up in Adelaide with Bernard, their shared interests as band mates and early entrepreneurial ventures. We soon decided to join forces, which resulted in this very revealing Doc encyclopaedia.

I'd like to thank Doc himself for giving me the wealth of research material that Jon and I were able to utilise in this book, and for sharing his life and love with me.

Special thanks also to my wonderful friend Alan Niven for giving invaluable information and insights to Jon.

A huge thank you to my father, Gavin Souter AO, for helping me through terrible times, and nominating Doc for the Order of Australia for his services to the music industry and Australian community.

Also to Deb Martin for her meticulous research and unfailing support of Doc by running his fan sites on a voluntary basis, and to Deb and Max Hill for great photographic work and friendship. And the many other renowned photographers including

Bob King, Phillip Morris, Grant Matthews, Rob Tuckwell, Anna Bartle (Rockchique), Kevin Moss, Pete James and Brian Woodwick (Woodeye), who generously donated their awesome work. True legends all.

Many more thanks to my sister Gretel Blackburn, Doc's sister and brother Maureen McNeece and Kevin Neeson, Mitch Hutchinson, Buzz Bidstrup, Jim Hilbun, Gerard 'Leo' Sayer, Mick Gibson, Heather Ross, Mel Davies, Jen Barclay, Elizabeth Mortison (Wilder), Ricky Small, Robert Werner, Lisa Norris, Annie Wright, Jackie and Mikael Borglund, the late Peter Jess, Lulu Malm, Erin Fry, Michael Jaques, Dzintra Neeson, Kym Moore, Judy Mermaid, Tina (Power) Straker, Ivana Bonansea, Erika Birmingham, Theo Kats Antoni, Tim Mitchell, Gavin Robertson, Judy Josling, the mystery man who donated a luxury bed to Doc at the end of his life, the late Anthony O'Grady and last but not least David Lowy and Brent Eccles for their very great and much appreciated support, and Allen & Unwin's 'bomb-throwing' Rebecca Kaiser for transforming the manuscript into something extra special.